SORCERER AND WITCH IN MELANESIA

SORCERER AND WITCH IN MELANESIA

edited by

Michele Stephen

RUTGERS UNIVERSITY PRESS
New Brunswick, New Jersey

First published in the United States in cloth by
Rutgers University Press, 1987.

First published in Australia by
Melbourne University Press, 1987.

Printed and bound in Australia

Library of Congress Cataloging-in-Publication Data

Stephen, Michele.
  Sorcerer and witch in Melanesia.

  Bibliography: p.
  Includes index.
  1. Ethnology—Papua New Guinea. 2. Witchcraft—Papua
New Guinea. 3. Medicine, Primitive—Papua New Guinea.
4. Papua New Guinea—Social life and customs. I. Title.
GN671.N5S78 1987   133.4'3'09953   86-26072
ISBN 0-8135-1227-7

CONTENTS

ILLUSTRATIONS

ACKNOWLEDGEMENTS

This collection of essays had its origin in a conference held in 1982 by the Research Centre for South-West Pacific Studies, La Trobe University. The conference—'Sorcery, Healing and Magic in Melanesia'—dealt with too many diverse themes to be taken up in a single volume. This collection necessarily has a much more limited scope; nevertheless, it has grown out of the challenge and stimulus provided by the conference discussions. I wish to thank all who participated in the meeting and thus have contributed significantly to the ideas presented here. I also thank for their help in the conference organization: Ondine Spitzer, Margot Hyslop, Ross Bowden, David Dorward, Bob Newman and Paul Sillitoe. The Research Centre for South-West Pacific Studies funded the conference and has generously subsidized the publication of this book. I am most grateful to the Centre and to the present Chairman, Ross Bowden, for this support. For their comments on an earlier version of the manuscript, and for their continued help and encouragement, I am indebted to Dawn Ryan, Peter Lawrence and Gilbert Herdt. John Pittman made valuable comments on parts of an earlier manuscript. Suggestions by Donald Tuzin and Gilbert Herdt have contributed importantly to the overall organization of the collection. Finally, I thank all who have assisted in the production of the book. John Stephen drew the maps and helped with the preparation of the diagram and plates. Margot Hyslop provided bibliographic information. Shirley Gordon and the office staff, Department of History, La Trobe University, have given support in innumerable ways. A special acknowledgement is due to Merelyn Dowling, who has typed with infinite care and patience the manuscript's many versions.

INTRODUCTION

Beliefs in sorcerers and witches—human beings attributed with magical or mystical powers to harm others—have long been the subject of anthropological interest. Ranging from the reporting of exotic customs by eighteenth and nineteenth century travellers to the micro-sociological analysis and psychological theories of modern scholars, interpretations of witchcraft have varied over time, reflecting the shifts in emphasis and approach that have marked the development of anthropology as a discipline. Studies of witchcraft and sorcery in Papua New Guinea have been influenced largely by British social anthropology, particularly in the postwar years. Thus, for forty years, theory shaped on the anvil of African experience has provided the context for discussion of the Melanesian data.[1]

Reviewing the general state of witchcraft studies in 1970 and noting the predominance of African studies, Mary Douglas commented, 'It is interesting to reflect on what would have happened in British anthropology if work in New Guinea had developed as quickly as in Africa' (1970:xxiii). Had New Guinea provided the lead, she suggests, anthropological understanding of witchcraft might have progressed very differently—so, of course, might our understanding of the Melanesian data. While the obfuscating influence of African descent models applied to New Guinea Highlands social structures has been debated for over twenty years—a debate resulting in Melanesianists becoming more aware of their theoretical assumptions and even leading Africanists to a reappraisal of descent models (Barnes 1962; Langness 1973; Lawrence 1971; Karp

1

1978)—the influence of African theories on studies of sorcery and witchcraft has passed almost unnoticed.[2] This is partly a measure of the small interest Melanesianists have shown in these topics until recently.

Furthermore, it has long been recognized that the New Guinea data by no means comfortably fitted Africanists' theories about the social functioning of witchcraft. More than twenty years ago, Marwick (1970, first published 1964) outlined basic differences between Africa and Oceania, urging that more systematic attention to specific instances of sorcery accusations would at least produce data comparable with the African material, and that only then could the apparent differences be fully understood. He observed that in Oceania accusations of sorcery or witchcraft appeared to take place not within the local group as in Africa, but between members of different communities. Sorcery rather than witchcraft seemed to predominate. Legitimate as well as illicit uses of sorcery were reported for Oceania, whereas Africanists reserved the terms 'sorcery' and 'witchcraft' for socially condemned practices. Melanesianists have not been unmindful of these differences. Patterson (1974–75) and more recently Lindenbaum (1979) and Zelenietz and Lindenbaum (1981) have made significant contributions to formulating a specifically Melanesian configuration. Nevertheless, as the essays presented here reveal, discussion over the last several years has been limited—and continues to be limited—by assumptions, definitions and theoretical orientations largely borrowed from African studies.

This collection of essays highlights important aspects of sorcery and witchcraft in Papua New Guinea that have so far been overlooked or obscured by existing theoretical approaches. Each author presents new ethnographic data and interpretations that challenge explicitly, or implicitly, existing assumptions and generalizations.

The need to rethink basic issues was underlined by a conference on 'Sorcery, Healing and Magic in Melanesia', held in 1982 by the Research Centre for South-West Pacific Studies, La Trobe University. The conference ranged over a broad spectrum of topics and addressed many interesting issues, but its single most important result was to demonstrate the extent to which our understanding of Melanesian sorcery and witchcraft remained clouded by definitions and theoretical models that simply did not fit the complexity of the available data. Such, in brief, is the problem taken up in this collection of essays. Six of the chapters began as papers delivered at the 1982 conference, and have since been substantially revised for the purposes of this book. Bowden's chapter on Kwoma sorcery and the final chapter were specially written for the collection. The authors include several leading authorities on Papua New Guinea; all are experienced scholars who have done extensive fieldwork in the region.

The book is arranged to provide a representative view of the complexity of the ethnographic data for Papua New Guinea; and to allow several different interpretative approaches to be presented; while at the same time paying close attention to more general problems of definition, comparison and interpretation. Seven substantive chapters, describing different Papua New Guinea societies (including Highlands and coastal regions), are divided into four sections, each dealing with a particular aspect of the topic. The final chapter provides an overview of the ethnographic evidence for Papua New Guinea and its problems of interpretation. It pursues in greater depth the issues I merely raise in this brief introduction. Some readers, particularly those unfamiliar with Melanesia, may prefer to begin with the overview chapter and then turn to the substantive chapters; for those acquainted with the issues involved, the existing format allows a more satisfactory presentation of evidence and argument.

The first part of the book draws attention to the importance of sorcery as a dimension of Melanesian religion. Peter Lawrence points out in the opening chapter (the keynote address to the conference) that this aspect is almost entirely overlooked by current theoretical approaches. As others have commented (Douglas 1970:xiv; Crick 1976:110), it seems ironic that Evans-Pritchard's enormously influential *Witchcraft, Oracles and Magic among the Azande*—essentially a study in the sociology of knowledge—should have inspired a host of postwar African studies of witchcraft that turned investigation entirely away from

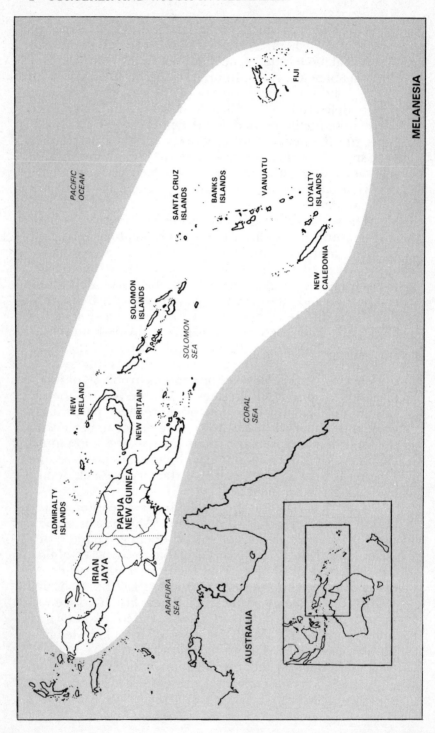

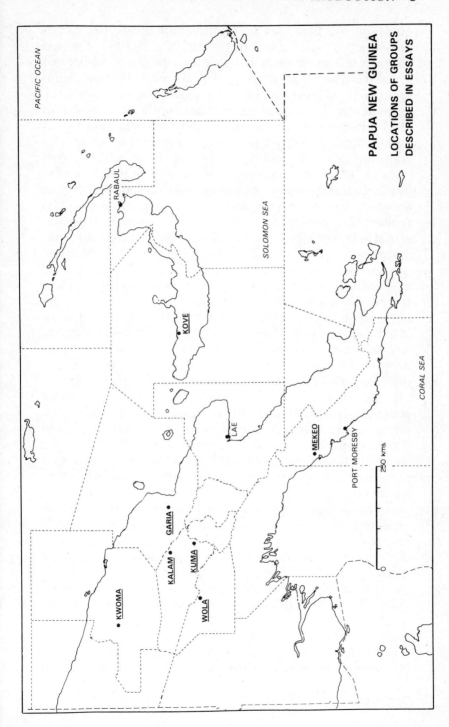

PACIFIC OCEAN

PAPUA NEW GUINEA

LOCATIONS OF GROUPS
DESCRIBED IN ESSAYS

RABAUL

SOLOMON SEA

KOVE

CORAL SEA

LAE

MEKEO

PORT MORESBY

250 kms

GARIA

KALAM

KUMA

KWOMA

WOLA

questions of belief. The micro-sociological approaches developed by Africanists in the 1950s and 1960s focused almost exclusively on witchcraft accusations as indices of social conflict and tension. It has now become commonplace for Melanesianists also to treat sorcery primarily as an 'idiom' for expressing human conflict (Lindenbaum 1981:119), or at least to confine their investigation to this aspect alone. Lawrence tries to go beyond this position by adopting what he calls a cosmic approach, which incorporates not only conventional socio-political but also intellectualist analysis. For the Garia of the Madang subcoast, on whom he bases his argument, the cosmos consists of two realms: the empirical realm or socio-economic structure, actual relationships between human beings; and the non-empirical realm or religion, putative relationships between human and various types of superhuman beings. In the first context, Lawrence's argument is in keeping with a structural-functionalist interpretation. In the second, he takes up epistemological issues raised earlier by Evans-Pritchard, but passed over in more recent discussion. He stresses that we cannot ignore that beliefs in sorcery are deeply embedded in the Melanesian view of man's place in the cosmos and his ability to control it through ritual.

For the Garia, as Lawrence shows, sorcery as a belief system provides culturally meaningful explanations for the universal existential problems of suffering and death, and the reassurance that disease can be controlled through the sorcerer's powers to heal. Garia regard sorcery as an integral part of the corpus of divinely revealed knowledge that enables men to order their world. The Garia sorcerer invokes a deity—possibly with support from other superhuman beings—to accomplish his ends; he is a highly respected ritual expert who also heals, a 'bigman' whose skills are an important criterion for leadership. Lawrence argues—as he has so cogently argued of Melanesian cargo cults—that the persistence of belief in sorcery, despite the many changes brought by colonialism and independence, must be understood in the total context of the Melanesian magico-religious world view.

In another respect African stereotypes seem to have obscured the close relationship between sorcery and religion in Melanesia. Sorcery can be treated as peripheral or even irrelevant to religion in African societies, where one is likely to find priests, prophets, mediums, diviners, healers and religious experts of all kinds attributed with socially valued ritual powers. Sorcerers, where they are thought to exist, are but a despised minority, the gangsters of the supernatural, perverting its powers for selfish, anti-social ends. A very different situation prevails in New Guinea. Professional ritual experts are few; where they are reported, they often turn out to be *sorcerers*—a circumstance which seems to have gone unnoticed in much recent discussion.

The Garia and the Mekeo, of the central Papuan coast, are cases in point. The Mekeo sorcerer is a socially recognized and rewarded ritual expert who commands powers to kill and to heal. Michele Stephen's chapter describes the sorcerer's role as a mediator of sacred power; his interaction with the spirit world—in controlled dreams and trance states—is compared with that of the shaman. Both Lawrence's and Stephen's chapters are of particular ethnographic interest in providing descriptions of sorcery not merely on the basis of what other people allege sorcerers do, but also from the point of view of the practitioner (see also Reay and Chowning in later chapters). The current emphasis on sorcery accusations has turned attention away from the sorcerer, to his accuser. Some writers assume that only beliefs about alleged sorcery activities are at issue, and that no one actually believes him or herself to be a sorcerer (Glick 1973:182). Such is clearly not the case among the Garia and the Mekeo, where the sorcerer is the community's most prominent mediator of spirit and ancestral power.

Part Two examines sorcery and witchcraft in the context of Melanesian warfare. Marwick (1970:291) noted the 'close intertwining in this region of the mystical aggression of sorcery and the real aggression of war', yet this feature of the Melanesian situation has received comparatively little theoretical comment since then. The social conflict theories of witchcraft were developed in societies where tribal warfare no longer existed. In contrast, anthropologists working in the New Guinea Highlands in the 1950s were describing societies only just being brought under colonial control; a unique situation existed to examine the relationship between the mystical expression of conflict and physical combat. Yet even the conflict theory framework formulated by Patterson (1974–75) pays scant attention to examining why communities that can express conflicts in open warfare also direct aggression through mystical channels, beyond noting that attribution of deaths to enemy groups increases the solidarity of the in-group and that in some communities sorcery provides a 'good excuse' for initiating war (1974–75:158–9).

Both chapters in this section describe New Guinea Highlands societies which have resumed tribal fighting in recent years and thus provide particularly interesting ethnographic information. In examining sorcery and witchcraft among the Kuma of the Western Highlands, Marie Reay (whose fieldwork spans more than three decades) challenges the commonly held notion that Highlands warfare is a secular, purely pragmatic affair. Her discussion turns on its head the question of the sublimation of physical aggression through mystical attack, demonstrating that the overt violence of Kuma warfare must be understood in terms of the ideological framework of supernatural beliefs underlying it. The Kuma war sorcerer is a highly respected ritual expert whose crucial function is to enlist the aid of the spirits of the dead and the ancestors in the battle against the enemy. Furthermore, the violence between men becomes the means of placating the ancestral ghosts. In underlining the magico-religious significance of Kuma war, Reay develops in a new direction themes raised in Part One.

Reay also brings to the fore the problems of definition. Recent writers have explicitly declined to attempt to separate sorcery and witchcraft (Zelenietz and Lindenbaum 1981: 13–14; 127 note 1), yet as Reay shows, the Kuma situation necessitates some distinction being made between different kinds of beliefs. The Kuma 'sorcerer' uses his destructive powers only against the enemy; but there are also 'witches', despised, anti-social creatures, who bring about the deaths of members of their own community.

Paul Sillitoe's chapter on sorcery divination among the Wola of the Southern Highlands reveals that by placing warfare in the broader context of Wola beliefs in the supernatural, the very pattern of their feuding can be better

understood. Since the Wola, like the Kuma, attack their
enemies on both a physical plane, and on a mystical plane
by means of sorcery, they are able to appeal to supernatural
agencies—the clan spirits and ancestors of the opposing
sides—to resolve their disputes through supernatural punishment. This recourse to the judgement of the clan spirits,
Sillitoe argues, enables the Wola to bring to an end an
otherwise interminable sequence of violent feuding. Like
the Kuma, the Wola fear mystical harm emanating from
insider 'witches', but attribute sorcery deaths to enemy
groups.

Part Three draws attention to another aspect of the
Melanesian situation noted by earlier writers but obscured
by recent theoretical orientations—the legitimate use of
sorcery within the community. Malinowski's Trobriand
studies described sorcery as a legitimate instrument of
chiefly authority and as a force for social conformity; but
his views have been passed over or found wanting by recent
scholars (Patterson 1974–75:133; 212–14). The postwar
emphasis on sorcery accusations as an attack on the putative
sorcerer has directed investigation along different lines.
The very notion of sorcery accusation as attack rests upon
the assumption that sorcery is socially condemned. Thus
accusation brands the accused as an anti-social being. The
possibility of legitimate sorcery runs counter to this whole
line of argument. Though it has long been recognized that
sorcery is sometimes reported to have legitimate uses in
Melanesia (Marwick 1970; Forge 1970; Zelenietz 1981), an
apparent contradiction here is avoided in the generali-
zation that sorcery attacks are usually suspected from
members of other communities. What is approved as war
sorcery from one perspective may thus be regarded as
unjustifiable homicide by another community. The
legitimate exercise of sorcery powers against members of
the same community is ignored or else explicitly denied by
some recent writers. Lindenbaum (1981:122), for example,
argues that endo-sorcery in general, or fear of it, is the
product of a collapse in the internal solidarity of the group
brought about by social change.

Ann Chowning's chapter on the Kove of New Britain,
and Ross Bowden's chapter on the Kwoma of the Sepik
River region, contest these interpretations. Both describe

societies where deaths are attributed to sorcerers within the local group—and where such deaths are accepted as the expected consequences of failure to meet social norms. The two societies, nevertheless, are very different in social structure, and in their beliefs concerning sorcery. Chowning emphasizes that the Kove bigman openly uses threats of sorcery to intimidate and control subordinates. In contrast, no Kwoma admits to being a sorcerer but anyone is believed to be able to hire a sorcerer to revenge himself or herself against those remiss in their social obligations. Chowning sees Kove sorcery primarily as an instrument of political power manipulated by the bigman, and thus as supporting the social order. Bowden sees Kwoma sorcery primarily as an ideology motivating people to resolve their difference and work towards social harmony. Both authors refer to similar evidence from elsewhere—evidence of the legitimacy of endo-sorcery in Melanesia that has been overlooked in recent discussion.

Part Four deals with an important aspect of the topic that has attracted recent investigation—sorcery and witchcraft in the context of social change. The unique opportunity afforded by the Melanesian situation to study the effects of social change has been the subject of a special edition of the journal *Social Analysis* (1981) on 'Sorcery and Social Change in Melanesia'. Postwar witchcraft studies in Africa were carried out in societies long adjusted to colonial rule (Douglas 1970:xxiii), whereas in New Guinea, anthropologists have observed at first hand processes of change from initial contact with the outside world, to the present problems of a newly independent nation. Most studies have concentrated on the changes wrought by European contact. Inge Riebe's chapter on the Kalam of the Western Highlands is unusual, and particularly valuable, in being able to trace (by combining oral traditions and other evidence) the development of Kalam witch beliefs since their introduction to the region in the late nineteenth century, at least sixty years prior to pacification and colonial rule. Studies with more restricted time spans tend to the conclusion that European contact disrupted stable institutions in predictable ways; for example, pacification resulting in an increase in fears of mystical aggression. Riebe shows the flexibility of Kalam witch beliefs as they responded to internal developments and changes within Kalam society prior to contact, as well as in the years following it. Another novel perspective is her analysis of the close interrelationship between witch beliefs and the Kalam exchange economy. Her account reveals that Kalam witchcraft must be understood not as a stable 'institution' but as a highly flexible, constantly changing ideology.

The final section of the book consists of an overview chapter which discusses the general problems of defining and interpreting the Melanesian ethnographic evidence in its own terms. Drawing together the many themes and sometimes conflicting lines of argument developed by the different authors, this chapter focuses on another commonly held assumption borrowed from African studies—that there is little point in distinguishing between sorcery and witchcraft and that for analytical purposes they can be treated as the same phenomenon. It is argued that while this assumption may be valid for Africa, making the same assumption in relation to Melanesia has, in effect, collapsed Melanesian sorcery into African witchcraft—thus obscuring the essential nature of sorcery in Melanesia.

As a whole, this book represents a contribution to an existing debate. It cannot pretend to offer the final word, nor claim to have tackled all the relevant issues, nor can a single volume do justice to the diversity of Melanesia. The task of rethinking our way through the conceptual categories and explanatory models that have been applied to Melanesian sorcery and witchcraft has only begun. We hope, however, by placing the problem in clearer perspective, and in providing new data and interpretations, that this book will serve to stimulate further debate, and point to some new directions for future research. Many of the arguments presented here have wider implications for cross-cultural interpretations. These broader issues cannot be pursued in depth here, our focus is restricted to Melanesia; we hope that others will take them up, particularly Africanists, who may find in them the stimulus to re-examine their theories, much as New Guinea findings have prompted a reassessment of African descent models—but that is a task we must leave to them. Hopefully, the book will also serve

to encourage new fieldwork in Melanesia. The ethnographic picture is still far from complete, or even adequate.
Much more data is required before the questions we have
raised here can be answered satisfactorily. If the book is
successful in this intent, its arguments will be gradually
refined, reformulated, and possibly discarded, as new
evidence mounts; such is the usual progression of scholarly
discourse.

Yet it is not too much to claim, I think, that this collection will significantly alter our understanding of sorcery
and witchcraft in Melanesia. The images of sorcerers and
witches that emerge here—the Garia sorcerer, healer and
bigman; the Mekeo 'master of souls'; that solid citizen, the
Kuma sorcerer; the Kove bigman publicly vaunting his
destructive powers; the Kwoma striving 'for the sake of
their health' to heal their social ills; the Wola invoking
ancestral spirits to punish mystical aggression and thus end
physical fighting; the self-confessed Kuma witch; the Kalam
witch, regarded as the despised 'enemy within' in one period,
in another as the nub of the exchange system—these force
us to expand our existing understandings, and will remain
to challenge future formulations.

La Trobe University   Michele Stephen
May 1986

NOTES

[1] This volume deals mainly with Papua New Guinea, though references are made to societies in other parts of Melanesia. The
general statements made here should be regarded as applicable
to Melanesia, as a whole, only to the extent that Papua New
Guinea can be considered representative of the whole region.
For stylistic reasons, 'Melanesian' has been preferred to the cum-
bersome 'Papua New Guinean' as an adjective.

[2] I would like to thank Professor Donald Tuzin, University of
California, San Diego, for prompting me to develop this theme
more explicitly here.

REFERENCES

Barnes, J. A.
1962 'African Models in the New Guinea Highlands'. *Man* 62:5-9.

Crick, M.
1976 *Explorations in Language and Meaning: Towards a Semantic Anthropology*. London: Malaby Press.

Douglas, M.
1970 (ed.) *Witchcraft Confessions and Accusations*. London: Tavistock.

Evans-Pritchard, E. E.
1937 *Witchcraft, Oracles and Magic among the Azande*. Oxford: Clarendon Press.

Forge, A.
1970 'Prestige, Influence, and Sorcery: a New Guinea Example.' In Douglas (1970:257-75).

Glick, L. B.
1973 'Sorcery and Witchcraft'. In I. Hogbin: (ed.) *Anthropology in New Guinea: Readings from the Encyclopaedia of Papua New Guinea*. Carlton: Melbourne University Press:182-6.

Karp, I.
1978 'New Guinea Models in the African Savannah.' *Africa* 48:1-16.

Langness, L. L.
1973 'Traditional Political Organisation'. In I. Hogbin (ed.): *Anthropology in Papua New Guinea: Readings from the Encyclopaedia of Papua New Guinea*. Carlton: Melbourne University Press:142-73.

Lawrence, P.
1971 'Introduction'. In R. M. Berndt and P. Lawrence (eds): *Politics in New Guinea*. Nedlands: University of Western Australia Press:1-34.

Lindenbaum, S.
1979 *Kuru Sorcery: Disease and Danger in the New Guinea Highlands*. California: Mayfield Publishing Company.
1981 'Images of the Sorcerer in Papua New Guinea'. In Zelenietz and Lindenbaum (1981:119–28).

Marwick, M.
1970 'Witchcraft as a Social Strain-Gauge'. (First published 1964.) In M. Marwick (ed.): *Witchcraft and Sorcery: Selected Readings*. Harmondsworth: Penguin: 280–95.

Patterson, M.
1974-75 'Sorcery and Witchcraft in Melanesia'. *Oceania* 45:132-60; 212-34.

Zelenietz, M.
1981 'Sorcery and Social Change: An Introduction'. In Zelenietz and Lindenbaum (1981:3-14).

Zelenietz, M. and Lindenbaum, S.
1981 (eds) 'Sorcery and Social Change in Melanesia'. *Social Analysis*, Special Issue, No. 8.

PART ONE:

Sorcery, Sacred Power and Melanesian Religion

1

De Rerum Natura: the Garia View of Sorcery

Peter Lawrence

This paper's primary theme is sorcery beliefs and practices in one small linguistic group or society in Papua New Guinea. I preface the account by discussing two issues: first, the importance of sorcery in Melanesia generally; and, second, the best way in which to study it. This, I hope, will put my ethnographic example in clearer perspective and shed light on the paper's secondary theme: a consideration of the reasons for sorcery's remaining throughout the whole region, after decades of close association with the West and modern administration, a dominant socio-political and intellectual force—in European eyes, a problem.

In the first context, there is, prima facie, a compelling argument that one important consequence of what used to be called culture contact in dependent territories was that it articulated what the subordinate people saw as vital to itself in dealing with its rulers and thus tried to perpetuate. This suggests interesting contrasts, especially in the field of religion. It has always impressed me that, whereas in Africa the post-contact emphasis in religion appears to have been on health—cults to promote human fertility, faith-healing, and the exorcism of devils—in Melanesia it has been on wealth—cults designed to ensure access to the European economy or cargo. For example, Fisher (1971) has outlined the role of the faith-healer in spreading both Christianity and Islam in Africa. By way of contrast, it is now recognized that in much of Melanesia missionaries won souls for Christ because of the popular presumption of ultimate—sometimes immediate—material reward.

This kind of difference is easily exaggerated. It may well be one of degree rather than of kind, so that we are not faced with a dichotomy whereby one type of reaction to external interference completely excludes the other. Although I cannot dogmatize for Africa, it is perhaps worth noting that the northern half of that continent has had for centuries its own kind of cargo cult: alchemy, which is based on the assumption that base metals can be transmuted into gold, and which has its roots partly in Aristotelian science and partly in religion. In its Islamic form, it travelled south in Africa, while, in its Christian form, it went north into Europe, where it claimed many distinguished adherents.

In Melanesia, about which I have greater knowledge, cargoism, although the most prominent, has not been the only post-contact religious interest. Many modern cults, while accentuating the acquisition of European wealth, have stressed also that the achievement of their economic goals depends on social peace to be achieved through the elimination of sorcery and the consequent promotion of health. Nearly twenty years ago the distinguished Papuan missionary Rev. Sir Percy Chatterton (1968:16–18), commenting on my own contribution to the study of cargoism (Lawrence 1964), warned (in my opinion, correctly) that, when converting to Christianity, Melanesians may sometimes have had other than materialistic ends in view. His argument has been supported recently by Wetherell and Carr-Gregg (1984), who have discussed the success of the intensive Moral Rearmament campaign by the Kwato Mission in the Keveri Valley, Papua, in the 1930s. Although they suggest that some form of cargoism may have been a factor, the movement clearly owed its immediate success to the people's desire for stability, peace and good health, and their corresponding dislike of suspicion, warfare, and sorcery. Finally, there is now evidence that Pentecostalism has had a major impact on the peoples of the Southern Highlands of Papua New Guinea, stressing health and salvation rather than material wealth, which plays only a minor role (Robin 1982). In short, we should not be mesmerized by cargoism in Melanesia: even if it has dominated local responses to colonial rule, sorcery and health nevertheless remain subjects of very great popular concern and hence academic interest.

In the second context, it is not enough just to acknowledge the importance that Melanesians attribute to sorcery and, in fact, all aspects of their religion, and then treat them as no more than devious metaphors for everyday mundane behaviour, without attempting to describe and analyse the ways in which their practitioners believe they operate. We must try to understand them as powers or forces that the people accept as real and strive to turn to their own advantage. I state roundly at the outset that I reject, *as a total approach to the problem*, secularist positivism, that derives primarily from Durkheimian sociology, has been coupled recently with Marxist economic determinism, and has been fashionable, in one form or another, in the British Commonwealth since the 1930s. I now set out my position generally in the field of traditional religion—which nowadays is closely associated with cargoism—and then specifically in that of sorcery.

In Melanesian studies it is a commonplace that religion has been presented essentially as a system of symbolic references to the existing state of society, either traditional or post-contact. The best known example is Worsley's (1957) explanation of cargoism as a form of incipient class struggle—an argument which, to be fair, he largely rejected in the second edition of the same work (Worsley 1968). Other scholars—even non-Marxists—have taken up the approach to absurd extremes. In May 1957, a few months after I had taken up my first teaching position in Sydney, New South Wales, I was invited to read a paper at a meeting of a prestigious anthropological society. As I had embarked on a particularly heavy lecturing programme, I chose a subject that I could prepare without too much difficulty: religious syncretism in the southern Madang Province, where I had recently completed my cargoist research. I pointed out the historical accident whereby two religions (local paganism and Christianity), which shared a common theistic assumption that a god/gods had made the world and revealed all essential knowledge to human beings, had confronted each other and eventually amalgamated to provide a cargo doctrine, syncretizing values, concepts and, finally, beliefs. I contrasted this with Read's (1952) report on the Gahuku Gama of the Eastern Highlands, who claimed no myths of origin, politely thanked the missionaries for telling them how everything began, and then thought so little about the matter that they just went on with their everyday pursuits.[1]

The audience received my paper in puzzled silence. The idea that Melanesians engaged in serious theological debate had no place in the tenets of Anglo-Australian social anthropology. Finally, Professor Stanner—ever courteous, even when he disagreed with the case presented—saved the day by remarking: 'This paper is really about cargo cults. Now, cargo cults are really about economics . . .' With a sigh of relief because they had been offered something they thought they could comprehend, the members of the seminar spent the following hour in a learned discussion about economics, to which, being totally devoid of expertise in that field, I contributed precisely nothing. A few days later, I received a charming letter from the chairman, thanking me for my paper: as I could see from the subsequent discussion, everyone had been most interested in what I had had to say.[2]

This persistent refusal to recognize Melanesians' concern for religious exegesis is doubtless well-intentioned: it aims to raise them above 'primitive thinking' to the level of quasi-science. Yet this entirely misrepresents the people's philosophical outlook. They do not envy—let alone share— our secularist viewpoint, as the following incident suggests. In August 1977, when I was staying in a village near Madang, a lad from the Rai Coast told me that he was confused. He was learning science at government school, where he had been told that 'human beings came from animals'. The Lutheran Mission had taught him something vastly different. It transpired that, whereas he could come to terms with The Book of Genesis, which represented the same kind of explanatory mode as the origin myths of his own society, like my own great-grandfather's generation, he found it hard to make sense of the theory of human physical evolution.[3]

In the same way, in much of the Melanesian ethnographic corpus, sorcery and healing practices are set apart
from the rest of traditional religion, of which, in fact, they
are a component. They are presented largely as aspects—
in a sense, as poor relations—of indigenous secular socio-
political systems: sorcery as a reflection of hostility and a
substitute for forms of physical aggression between individuals and groups now outlawed; and healing practices as
a gauge of friendship or solidarity. Hence, although we
know a great deal about their roles in these fields, which
are important to us as external observers, we are often left
ignorant of the people's own understanding and assessment
of them—the theories and beliefs on which they are based—
because relatively few researchers have thought it worth
their while to conduct this sort of inquiry.

In short, to be studied properly, sorcery and healing
practices must be placed within the total cosmic framework
that the people conceive to exist: not only in the human
socio-political structure and not only in the religious system
but simultaneously in both. For this, several kinds of investigation are essential. I have already rejected positivism as
an inadequate total approach. It is an example of *pars pro
toto*. I should say the same of intellectualism: an enquiry
restricted solely to the people's own explanations of the
problem. I believe that positivism and intellectualism must
be combined so that, as Horton (1968:625–34) has cogently
argued, they complement each other. This is the approach
that I have always adopted in my earlier studies of religion
and cargoism (Lawrence 1964, 1965, and 1984), and which
I shall try to use in this paper.

I take as an illustration of my cosmic approach to sorcery
and healing the Garia of the southern Madang District,
Papua New Guinea, who are locally famous for these skills.
In keeping with my earlier comments, my primary aim is
to present their own view of the universe, and the actual
and putative roles of sorcery and healing within it. This
explains the title of my paper, which I have taken from
Lucretius' great poem about the nature of creation. My
secondary aim is to consider why the Garia retain their
belief in the effectiveness of these arts virtually unimpaired
even though, since the mid–1920s, they have been incorporated in a modern administrative system and have come

under strong Lutheran Mission influence. I proceed as follows: first, I summarize the total conceived cosmic order: the people's traditional socio-political and religious systems. Second, I describe Garia sorcery and healing techniques, placing them in this cosmic order by examining them in their socio-political context, and by setting out the religious and intellectual assumptions and beliefs on which they rest. Third, I attempt to answer two questions already fore-shadowed: why do Garia and other villagers like them still regard these beliefs and practices as entirely logical and valid even after sixty years' exposure to the kind of external pressures I outlined above? And what problems will they have to overcome should they opt to discard them because they see them as illogical and invalid? In this context I compare the current Garia situation with that in Britain in the late seventeenth century.

The Garia Cosmos[4]

The Garia, who number approximately 2500, inhabit some 80 to 110 square kilometres of low mountains between the Gogol and Ramu rivers inland from Madang. Broadly, they conceive their total cosmic order as an aggregation of gods, ghosts and men co-existing in this limited physical environment. Within this terrestrial cosmos they recognize two systems of relationships: social structure or actual rela-tionships between human beings; and religion or putative relationships between gods, ghosts and men (superhuman and human beings). They believe that this cosmic order was created by deities. A python god shaped the natural environment. A snake goddess Obomwe gave birth to human beings, but she botched it. She took pity on a boulder that was making heavy weather of the task and herself com-pleted it in a trice. Had she allowed the boulder to complete the job, mankind would have been immortal. Because of her idecent haste, we are all bound to die. Thereafter other gods introduced the material and social culture: artefacts, animals, food plants, initiatory ceremonies, and sorcery and healing. They appeared to men in dreams, or even lived with them, and taught them the relevant secular and ritual skills, which I discuss later. Yet others grouped the people into settlements, and gave them laws of kinship, marriage and descent, and land tenure.

The Garia are a flexibly structured cognatic society with a bias towards patriliny. Because of the fragmentation and dispersal of personal landholdings, they are bound to be migratory. As a result, there are no orderly, permanent, stable, and territorially bounded settlements or political groups but rather irregular and very often ephemeral local aggregations of kinsmen, affines, and even unrelated persons who drift in to exercise their land rights and then move elsewhere when they have temporarily exhausted them. For this reason I have always analysed Garia human or secular society as a series of ego-centric and intersecting networks or security circles, whose members are not corporate groups but merely those people with whom each particular ego has safe relationships preventing resort to serious violence and sorcery, although, under provocation, mild forms of these kinds of retaliatory action are allowed. Ego's security circle consists of his close bilateral kin and affines (in theory up to the fourth ascending generation), exchange and trade partners, and persons with whom he has special associational and initiatory relationships. With persons outside his security circle, he has no safe relationships: he regards them as potential enemies who may plot his death. In the same way, he sees himself as the nucleus also of a superhuman security circle: the deities, rights to whom he has inherited from his father or acquired from his mother's brother; and the spirits of dead persons who were once members of his human or secular security circle. He acknowledges a further category of extrahuman beings: demons or 'wild men' (*norugoiba*) and 'wild women' (*sigiasi*) of the bush. Some are personal doubles, one for each member of the society, while others are impersonal. It is difficult to be specific about putative human dealings with demons. Most informants stressed that an individual could have at best ambivalent relations with his/her personal double but that impersonal demons were invariably dangerous. Yet one informant, who was usually most reliable, claimed that, with patience, it was possible to cultivate positive relationships with both personal doubles and impersonal demons. I refer to this later. Finally in this context, I reiterate that ego conceives gods, ghosts and demons not only as superhuman but also as terrestrial, corporeal and, therefore, as having the same physical reality as men and women themselves. There is no supernatural or transcendental realm.

All this has important implications for what I call ego's political region: the geographical arena in which he has practical dealings with other human and, by implication, with superhuman beings. The situation is analogous to that in modern Northern Ireland: because of their migratory habits, he can never be absolutely sure where his likely friends and enemies, human and superhuman, are located. In this context, we may ignore deities: their sanctuaries are geographically determined and they are said rarely to move from them. Otherwise his kinsmen, affines, exchange and trade partners, associational and initiatory mates, and the ghosts of his departed security circle members may live anywhere—all intermingled with potentially inimical human and superhuman beings.[5] In other words, the men and ghosts whom he trusts and distrusts represent, within his political region, a sort of rag-bag, from which he has to select very carefully to maintain his own security. This may apply even to the inhabitants of his own settlement. I discuss the significance of this later.

From his personal point of view, ego regards the maintenance of order within the cosmos as a function of establishing working relationships with the members of both his human and superhuman security circles. He must forge these relationships by creating a sense of mutual moral obligation that binds the parties to him, one to the other: between himself and other men, himself and gods, and himself and ghosts. He describes this process as *nanunanu täbu* (Pidgin *kisim/pulim tingting*), whereby he can induce the other party to a relationship (man, god or ghost) to 'think on' (*nanunanu*, Pidgin *tingting*) him and do what he wants. He creates moral obligation: with other human beings by fulfilling kinship, affinal, exchange and trade obligations; and with gods and spirits of the dead by performing special ritual in their honour—in the case of deities, by breathing their secret names, the spells that win their favour. Should ego offend any god, ghost or man, he may expect retaliation. Gods, like ghosts and men who do not belong to his security circles, normally show him no mercy. Ghosts and men within his security circles are expected to be moderate.

Garia Sorcery and Healing Practices

I examine Garia sorcery and traditional healing practices against the cosmic background I have sketched (see also Lawrence 1952 and 1984). Yet, initially, I must comment on Garia views about disease and death. Probably like most Melanesians, Garia distinguish between illnesses and deaths that are part of 'the order of nature', and those caused by malevolent agents. In the first category there are boils, sores, skin diseases and so forth, for which there are local remedies. Moreover, because of the snake goddess Obomwe's impetuosity in giving birth to human beings, all men and women must be mortal. Yet Garia are not passive fatalists: they regard only the deaths of old people as 'natural'. They place serious illnesses and deaths of young and middle-aged persons in the second category: they see them as caused by malevolent agents. In such cases ego may choose an explanation from a number of alternatives. The malevolent agent may be either a demon (who, as indicated, is assumed normally to harm human beings), a ghost or a deity whom he has offended, or a human sorcerer. Most informants stated that attacks by demons and, as I have hinted, deities (even those to whom ego has inherited or acquired rights) are irreversible: unless he is lucky, he can find no effective countermeasure. The situation with ghosts is said to be more variable, for the dead, after all, are an extension of the genealogical system: a link between the human and superhuman realms of the cosmos. If ego had a close relationship during life with a ghost he regards as minatory or punitive, he may be able to appease it by suitable ritual techniques.

Sorcery, however, is much more complicated in that human enemies are involved in two ways. First, there are those persons who are scattered at random throughout ego's political region, whom he cannot always immediately identify, but whom, in times of crisis, he may suspect and brand as aggressors. This represents, as I have indicated, especially during epidemics, a rich seed-bed for accusations of sorcery. Second, the sorcerer has to undergo an elaborate training, which, although carried out largely in secret, does not prevent his role from being widely known.

The Garia recognize three forms of sorcery. The first and by far the most lethal is *ämale* (Pidgin *saguma*),[6] which has complementary techniques for healing (*auwobu*, Pidgin *windim sikin*). He who has mastered both techniques is an *au'apu* (Pidgin *man bilong saguma*), a sorcerer-cum-curer: a bigman.

In Garia eyes, *ämale* and *auwobu* are merely one aspect of their religion: they were originally invented and revealed to men by the deity Yeyaguliba, in whose lore the aspiring practitioner must prove himself proficient. Children of both sexes know about sorcery from the earliest years, for public accusations continually occur. Yet only adult males are privy to its inner secrets, and only a few such males succeed in mastering them.

A boy is progressively introduced to religious knowledge, including sorcery and healing, any time after the age of about ten, when he embarks on a series of initiatory ceremonies that may last for about a decade: the Abaiwala and the Oitu (see Lawrence 1984:203–10). First, he is introduced to the Abaiwala as a novice but does not go through the full ceremony. Second, he participates fully in the Oitu. Third, he undergoes the full Abaiwala, during which he has his penis incised. There are three special features of these ceremonies. Boys, who hitherto went naked, now have to cover their genitals with bark girdles. They are segregated from women in a local cult house. Last they have to observe stringent taboos, avoiding all kinds of meat and all contact with water, and eating only roasted vegetable food and sugarcane.

The first training in religious knowledge is very general: broad instruction about deities, ghosts, myths and ritual procedures. But the introduction to sorcery, although its inner secrets may be withheld for a number of years, is always more specific and immediate. As well as having sex ritual lavished on them to guarantee their manhood and capacity to attract wives, the initiands are fed certain medicines designed to induce potency in sorcery: *naguli* (an aromatic tree bark) and *a'au* (a mixture of bush herbs). The leader of the cult house bespells both the *naguli* and *a'au* with the secret names of the god Yeyaguliba before feeding them to the initiands. Most informants told me that *naguli* was traded in from the Ramu Valley but the lone (and reliable) informant to whom I alluded previously told me that this medicine, although quite satisfactory when obtained in this way, became more powerful if it was acquired directly from the demon who was the personal double of the leader's wife and with whom he had been able to create a positive relationship. This applied also to *a'au*. Medicines from this source would 'take' immediately in the initiands' bodies, whereas ordinary medicines would do so more slowly. The importance of this appears below.

At this stage, the initiands are told about the Yeyaguliba myth and the deity's activities during the period of creation. Yet many initiands now decide to drop out of sorcery training or show no interest in it (lacking ambition, ability to master intricate spells and techniques, and so forth). Those who wish to proceed and show promise are apprenticed, after they have completed the initiatory cycle, to big men for special training. They are fed more *naguli* and *a'au*, rehearsed in the Yeyaguliba myth, and finally taught the god's string of secret names. At this point, merely by repeating these secret names and by virtue of the medicines in their bodies, they should be able to turn themselves invisible—a feat they have to demonstrate by stealing someone's property without detection. The implication of my lone informant's claim about deriving these medicines from a female demon is that they would be more likely to induce this condition immediately than ordinary ones.

Those who survive this gruelling course are now taught the final techniques: how to 'shoot' and 'cure' *ämale*. To 'shoot' *ämale* (*ämale wolobu*, Pidgin *siutim saguma*), the practitioner takes his bow, arrow, and a *koli* leaf, hides behind a tree, and waits for his victim to come along the track. Then, after breathing Yeyaguliba's secret names, he becomes invisible and ties the *koli* leaf around the head of his arrow, which he then fits into his bow. He draws the bow but does not let the arrow fly: that would kill his victim in an unseemly manner. Rather, he waits for the god to send *na'oa*, a whistling sound, up from his stomach and out of his mouth. The *na'oa* travels along the arrow-shaft, breaks off the head, and propels it into the body of the victim, who feels no pain because of the *koli* leaf.

As is implicit in my earlier comments, a practitioner may 'shoot' *ämale* either to harm or to kill. He should 'shoot' a member of his security circle no more than once and so make him or her ill but not cause death. The victim should recover quickly if he or she goes to a recognized healer. But should a practitioner attack a person who does not belong to his security circle, he will try to kill him or her by 'shooting' many times. Only a skilful and assiduous curer can save such a victim.

For curing or healing (*auwobu*, Pidgin *windim sikin*), the practitioner is taught to make a funnel of *kemia* leaves and bespell it with Yeyaguliba's secret names. He places the funnel over the painful part of the victim's body, breathes into it once again the appropriate spells, removes it, and lets fall, for his audience to see, the arrowhead or arrowheads he has 'extracted'.

The second and third forms of sorcery, *oi'oi osa* and *se'u* (Pidgin *poisin*) are relatively unimportant in Garia eyes. Both are based on sympathetic magic. I have no detailed information about *oi'oi osa* but *se'u* depends on the principle of contagion made famous by Frazer. The sorcerer purloins a sample of his victim's 'leavings' (such as a discarded cigarette butt or excreta) and places it in a bamboo cylinder, which he heats over or consumes in a fire to cause either illness or death (as for a member of his security circle or an outsider). Once again my lone informant asserted that a sorcerer could get better results if he gave the cylinder to a female demon he had 'domesticated' with an instruction to perform the necessary action on his behalf.[7] Finally, as I have already indicated, mastery of all these skills—especially *ämale* and *auwobu*—is one qualification for traditional leadership.

I shall now illustrate my general description with an example of a Garia sorcery (*ämale*) feud which lasted from 1944 until 1949, when the people suffered very bad health partly because of wartime neglect and partly because of a postwar influenza epidemic. The feud involved people who lived in four settlements within twenty minutes' walking distance of each other and most of whom were unrelated. It began towards the end of the Pacific War, when Maunime of Sogumu patrilineage (Iwaiwa village) was betrothed to Nulua of Waipa patrilineage (Somau village), who was then recruited to work for the Australian Army. During his absence, she carried on with a number of men, one of whom, Liwai of Ulawa patrilineage (also of Iwaiwa village), announced that he would make her his second wife. Nulua came home and broke the contract. Her brother Watutu then arranged for her to marry Sinene'uma of Olei patrilineage in Onea village. About three years later Sinene'uma died. His close kin suspected that Liwai had 'shot' him with *ämale* out of jealousy, although they made no formal charge. Then Liwai himself died and the affair came to a head. On the day Liwai fell ill Sinene'uma's Olei parallel cousin, Noloba of Onea village, was seen with a bow and arrow near Iwaiwa. He was immediately charged with Liwai's 'murder' and summoned to a moot.

It was agreed that the case was 'not proven', and that it should be settled by an exchange of pigs between Ulawa and Olei agnates and other interested kinsmen. But thereafter the influenza epidemic hit Garialand and tragically, but alternatingly, carried off a number of people in Wailagime and Ulawa patrilineages, in Yaniba, Somau and Iwaiwa villages. As the first Wailagime 'victim' was a close 'affine' of Sinene'uma, his fellow agnates and other kin accused Ulawa of killing him to avenge Liwai. The other deaths followed a 'logical' succession until mid–1949, when Salapu of Ulawa patrilineage (Somau village) fell ill. He was quickly 'cured' by his true mother's brother, Labaia of Mosoli patrilineage (also of Somau village). What was important, however, was that people murmured that he had been 'shot' by Polilipa of Wailagime patrilineage in Yaniba village, his close 'mother's father'. Polilipa did not wish to be held guilty of such an immoral act and, with the aid of neutral kin, brought the feud to an end.

Garia Sorcery as a Logical System: its Persistence in the Present Era

I now take up my secondary theme: the endurance of Garia sorcery as a socio-political and intellectual force in the colonial and post-colonial situation. I address myself to the two questions I have already posed: why do villagers such as the Garia continue to regard sorcery as a fully logical system and conform to its tenets even in a changing world? And, should they ever wish to abandon it, what issues would they first have to settle?

The answer to the first of these questions, I suggest, is partly that nothing has happened in the experience of the Garia to persuade them that the cosmic order they have always conceived is ontologically groundless and that, paradoxically perhaps, in these circumstances sorcery is still a social and psychological necessity. In a word, sorcery still makes sense to Garia villagers in terms of both their social system and their religion. Despite modern administration, an airstrip, motor roads, and recently a marked increase in European goods, the social system is still as it was, certainly in 1949 (when I first knew them) and probably in the traditional past. They are still migratory and their local organization remains kaleidoscopic: indeed, motor transport has only intensified these features. People still quarrel and die, so that ego's political arena remains a fertile seed-bed for sorcery accusations. They still conduct sorcery feuds until conflicting kin loyalties force settlement.

Again, there has been little to undermine the primordial conviction of the Garia that their gods ordained the cosmic order and that, provided men gain their *nanunanu* by ritual techniques, they will keep it operating as it did of old—in the fields of agriculture, initiation, human life and death, and so forth. As I have argued elsewhere (Lawrence 1964:31–3; and 1984:242), this implies not mysticism but utter pragmatism in Garia thought. As there is no conceived transcendental realm in the cosmos, superhuman beings are part of the order of nature: essentially terrestrial powers or forces that man can harness to his serious undertakings. They are as real as men and women themselves, so that religion is a matter of conviction, which represents unquestioning acceptance, rather than faith, which allows the possibility of doubt. Any major task demands co-operation between gods, ghosts and human beings, all of whom live virtually as neighbours in the same earthly realm.

Mission and government education has made little lasting impact. In the interwar years, when the Garia came under Lutheran influence, they swiftly assimilated sorcery, like the rest of their religion, to Christianity. The missionaries told them that all their ritual was *Satan po sapi* (Pidgin *samting bilong Satan*)—'the gift of Satan'. Logically, therefore, as the traditional deities had taught them their ritual at the time of the creation, these had to be 'satans' who became the property of the people's first ancestor Ham, when God cursed him for his unfilial behaviour on the Ark before despatching him to Papua New Guinea—bad, perhaps, but still ontologically true (Lawrence 1964:79). The god, or 'satan' of sorcery, far from being debunked, was still a cosmic reality, so that European missionaries who reproved their indigenous followers for resorting to traditional healers by saying in Pidgin *'Satan iholimpas yu pinis'* were quite innocently reaffirming traditional belief. Again, even in the late 1970s, Garia students at the government high school in Madang explained to their parents in the villages that, after living with them as an impecunious and unimportant youth, I had achieved my present affluence and eminence because I had learnt Garia secret ritual, which, quite obviously, I had turned to my private advantage.

In view of this, it is hardly surprising that the people still regard sorcery and traditional healing techniques as providing ultimate medical explanations. Hamnett and Connell (1981) elucidate this very well for the people of the North Solomons Province, who go either to Western or to tribal medical practitioners for treatment. But for explanations of illness and death, they rely almost exclusively on tribal practitioners for obvious reasons. Western doctors treat but do not bother to discuss the nature of their patients' diseases. Even if they do, their patients almost certainly will not understand the technicalities described, whereas traditional healers can give answers that conform to the people's culture. Indeed, I doubt whether nationals on the lower rungs of the Papua New Guinea medical service ladder, who represent Western practice in the eyes of most villagers, really understand very much of their acquired trade. I suspect that many of them merely go through the motions and, certainly in the last analysis, seek explanations in age-old lore. In 1956 a Madang medical assistant, trained for twelve years by the administration, and able to lay out an operating theatre faultlessly in five minutes and distinguish between malaria, hookworm, and other bugs under a microscope, told a European doctor who had unsuccessfully tried to save his child's life that he should not have wasted his time because he (the medical assistant) had recently quarrelled with his Sepik colleague. That was twenty-six years ago, but what I have seen in modern Garia aid-posts leads me to suspect that the situation is little different today.

Finally, in this context, the logic of both sorcery and traditional healing practices—even though sorcery is nowadays widely condemned—is reassuring to villagers. The need to *understand*, as well as the desire to be *cured*, is very real for them. Just as some Europeans use the *In Memoriam* columns of newspapers to proclaim, often in idiosyncratic verse, that deaths, whatever the medical explanation, are part of God's ultimate cosmic plan, even so Garia prefer to be able to say, 'He died and we know who did it' to 'He died and we just don't know why'. At least, man is master of his own fate. There can be no doubt that traditional curing practices have a psychosomatic effect. I have seen one lad very ill indeed—literally foaming at the mouth with fear because he was convinced that he had been 'shot' with sorcery—recover very quickly when a local practitioner publicly 'removed' an arrow-head from his chest. This introduces the old chestnut about the obvious faking of cures. I do not really know what Garia say about this but it is probably pertinent to quote Tuzin (1980:261–3) on an Ilahita Arapesh expert who justified such tricks on the grounds that 'if people did not see something happening, they would not believe that the magic was working'. The expert clearly recognized his psychosomatic role and enjoyed the prestige that it gave him.

Conclusion

I conclude by attempting to answer the second of my two questions: what issues must the Garia and people like them settle if they *opt* to abandon sorcery as a logical system? I have phrased this carefully because, in my opinion, such a decision must be made by the people themselves. Legislative decrees from the National or Provincial Parliaments on their own will have little effect. The repeal of the Witchcraft Act in England in 1736 was possible only after belief in the Black Art had been so discredited during the previous century that at the last witchcraft trial held in 1718, just eighteen years beforehand, the judge remarked in response to one lurid piece of evidence that he knew of no law against flying (Thomas 1971). To rephrase my question: what changes must the Garia accept before a comparable pronouncement makes sense to them?

To state my case succinctly, I do not see the belief in sorcery withering *merely* because of change in the structure of Garia secular society any more than greater access to European wealth on Karkar Island has led to the sudden disappearance of cargoism (McSwain 1977). As I have suggested, Garia social structure has been little altered by contact with the outside world for some sixty years, and I predict that this will continue. Unless there is a sudden pacifist millennium, villagers will go on quarrelling, dying, and suspecting the worst of those of their neighbours unrelated to them. Indeed, like other peoples, Garia claim that sorcery is used now more frequently than in the past because of the elimination of traditional fighting. In a word, I argue that the revolution must be intellectual as, according to Keith Thomas (1971), it was in seventeenth century England, to which I now turn.

In discussing the decline of the magical aspects of Christianity, in general—alchemy, astrology, chiromancy and so forth—and of sorcery and witchcraft (the Black Arts taught man by Satan), in particular, Thomas (1971:656–7 and 577–8) is quite explicit. Arguing against 'sociologically-minded historians', he says that the process was not due to improved technology. Rather, the reverse was true: 'the abandonment of magic . . . made possible the upsurge of technology, not the other way round'. Briefly, natural science began to replace magic as a theoretical or logical system because thinking men saw it as intellectually superior. Hence, belief in witchcraft gradually withered in the face of 'the assumption of an orderly, regular universe, unlikely to be upset by the [caprice] of God or Devil . . . consolidated by the new mechanical philosophy [and] prepared by the emphasis of the theologians upon the orderly way in which God conducted his affairs, working through natural causes accessible to human investigation'. Thomas quotes John Webster: 'it is . . . simply impossible for either the Devil or witches to . . . alter the course that God hath set in nature'. Finally, Thomas argues, there 'was the optimistic conviction that it would one day be possible to uncover the natural causes of those events which still remained mysterious'.

Clearly, if villagers like the Garia opt to abandon sorcery, they must achieve a comparable transformation of their view of the cosmos. Yet here, I think, Melanesians are culturally handicapped. What became the Scientific Revolution in the seventeenth century was not a new phenomenon but had its roots deep in the soil of ancient European civilization. To change the metaphor, the scientific horse was always in the stable, ready for Western man to ride when he was so minded. Western Christianity inherited and came to terms with two distinct epistemological traditions: the Judaic and the Graeco-Roman. The Judaic tradition was based on the assumption of total divine revelation: all knowledge came to man directly from God. The Graeco-Roman tradition, hymned of course by Lucretius, was that man had to win knowledge by means of his own secular intellect. It was perpetuated in its Christianized form by St Thomas Aquinas, the Dominican Professor of Theology at the University of Paris in the thirteenth century, and paradoxically the alchemists, who tried to syncretize the theory of the divine origin of knowledge with Aristotelian science. The two traditions competed until the Renaissance, after which the Graeco-Roman took the lead. It became at least the dominant partner after 1600.[8]

To cut a long story short, the essential feature of the Scientific Revolution was, I believe, the progressive transformation not of logic but of the perception of what was fact: a shift from religious to secular or natural assumptions, in which especially Protestant churchmen played a major part. Unlike Tertullian, who is said to have defended his belief in the Resurrection on the grounds that *certum est quia impossibile est*,[9] and even more than the Thomist schoolmen, these divines always rationally weighed their faith and applied the same techniques to the new learning. Hence, even before the effective establishment of the mechanical philosophy, they contributed much to the scepticism that undermined belief in witchcraft: they reasoned that, although it might be true in fact, the Black Art 'had no Biblical justification' and that satisfactory proof of any accusation was almost impossible to provide (Thomas 1971:570).

How does the Garia situation compare with this? For a start, if we accept the basic assumptions from which they reason, there can be no doubt about the people's capacity for logic, as is attested by the sensible way in which they incorporated their old gods in Christianity as 'satans'—or should I put it the other way round? I could offer many comparable examples from the whole southern Madang Province. Obviously, what we must consider is their perception of what is fact. Again, there is no question of their possession of secular or empirical knowledge: their skill in agriculture alone bears witness to this. Yet, as I have argued elsewhere (Lawrence 1964:30–3; and 1984:240–4), they have no immemorial usage whereby they can forge such knowledge into an explanatory system leading to further secular discovery in its own right. Rather, they have always tended to sweep such knowledge under the carpet of religion, as it were, validating it as afflatus from a deity. It is not a product of their own unaided intellect but something divinely revealed to them in dreams or comparable experiences. Thus, as I have suggested, in any race towards the goal of secular scientific explanation, they must start well behind scratch, for they lack the tradition that European man, when the time was right, could exploit. (I should add in parenthesis that this is one factor that has made it so difficult for Europeans to understand Melanesians: insensitively, we have failed to recognize that they have not been subjected to the process of secularization that has been the leitmotif of our history for the last four hundred years.)

I do not wish to end by leaving the impression that I see this as an *eternally* irreconcilable situation. In Western Europe, even our most illustrious forebears did not make the epistemological change I have described as swiftly and totally as my short account might suggest. Sir Isaac Newton, the father of modern physics, had, at the very least, a serious interest in alchemy, which the Royal Society finally dismissed as baseless only in 1783. In the 1780s 'rational' Parisians flocked to the necromancer 'Count' Cagliostro and other quacks, while doctors still prescribed hartshorn. You could buy moss from a dead man's skull in English chemists' shops as late as 1852. Reputable Enlightenment scientists believed in phlogiston, while those in Frazer's (1971:16) day still accepted the possibility of an invisible ether that could 'explain how things can physically affect each other through a space which appears to be empty'.

By the same token, in Papua New Guinea there are signs that the ice age of traditional religious epistemology may be beginning to thaw. An American anthropologist, M. F. Smith (1980), reports that the people of Kairiru Island off the north mainland coast, who became devout Catholics at the turn of this century, were disillusioned by post-Vatican II theology, which eschewed sacramentalism and other fundamental beliefs, and suggested that Christianity was not so much literally as symbolically true: a sort of personal socio-spiritual condition. Essentially hard-headed, the islanders replied to the new missionaries that if Christianity was not literally true, they saw no reason to assent to it any longer: some who had been to government schools said that they would opt for secular humanism, which provided an acceptable cosmic explanation. Romola McSwain (personal communication) has told me that the Karkars are now beginning to show interest in what they call in Pidgin *as bilong saiens*—natural science.

Nevertheless, with due respect to them both, I regard Smith's and McSwain's information, however positive, as at the moment no more than a small beginning. I should wish to see definite evidence that the peoples of Kairiru and Karkar were not merely expressing pique and frustration but were really beginning to turn to science. I should like it demonstrated that the Keveri people, who embraced Moral Rearmament, and the Southern Highlanders, who were swept up in Pentecostalism, rejected sorcery not only as socially objectionable but also as intellectually fraudulent. In my opinion, it will take an exceptionally strong educational assault to win over the Garia and many other Melanesian villagers quickly to a secular interpretation of disease and death—indeed, of their whole cosmic order. We may expect the belief in sorcery and traditional healing practices to stay alive and well for some time to come. For the Garia, the ultimate logic will still be that Noloba of Olei patrilineage and Onea village was seen with a bow and arrow near Iwaiwa village on the day that Liwai of Ulawa patrilineage became fatally ill, and that subsequently there was a series of deaths alternating between persons who could be classified as mutually hostile or potentially so. Clearly, sorcerers had used the god Yeyaguliba to cause these deaths. Western medical explanations through the microscope are still mumbo-jumbo: they leave a social and intellectual vacuum which—as does nature itself—the Garia abhor. Like the Rai Coast schoolboy who talked to me in 1977, Garia will continue to feel more comfortable with the explanatory mode of The Book of Genesis or its traditional equivalent.

NOTES

[1] I refer here to the situation around Goroka only as it was described in the early 1950s. I cannot say whether or not more recent research would present it differently.

[2] The following year Professor Stanner (1958) published his paper, 'On the Interpretation of Cargo Cults', in which he reasserted positivist dogma: that it is useless to study belief because we cannot assess its ontological validity. We must concentrate rather on examining secular social values through the sole medium of observed behaviour. I, meanwhile, began to satirize positivism in a set of verses, *Don Juan in Melanesia* (Lawrence 1968/1964).

[3] Precisely thirty years earlier Yali, who was the figurehead of the regional Cargo Movement and also came from the Rai Coast, had comparable problems with the concept of evolution (Lawrence

1964:173 ff.). I should stress also that none of my comments in this or later contexts, in which I contrast religious and secular scientific thought, is meant to imply stupidity on the part of those who endorse the former. Religious thinkers—among whom I number Melanesians—can be placed among the most intelligent human beings.

4 For a more detailed account, see Lawrence (1984).

5 During field work on the Rai Coast in the 1950s I was struck by one particular difference between Ngaing and Garia. The Ngaing lived in relatively stable villages, most inhabitants of each one being in some way interrelated. They had no fear of leaving their settlements at night (for example, to hunt in the bush) because the ghosts in the area were bound to be friendly. They would not, however, stray at night from distant villages which they were temporarily visiting because they were unwilling to entrust their safety to 'foreign' (that is, unrelated) ghosts. Garia rarely ventured out at night even from their own settlements: because of the kaleidoscopic nature of local organization, spirits of former enemies as well as friends might be roaming the local bush.

6 More usually Pidgin *sangguma*. Garia have no 'ng' in their own language and appear to avoid it in Pidgin whenever possible.

7 I cannot say to what extent my older informants in the 1940s and 1950s would have supported these claims for the roles of female demons in either *ämale* or *se'u*. They are now all dead. Yet the claims are interesting in one respect. They emphasize the Garia view that success in serious enterprises depends on harnessing other than human powers: on winning co-operation from superhuman beings—the more the better.

8 I do not wish to leave the impression that the switch to the scientific epistemology was immediately total or clear-cut. As Webster (1982) points out, the older magico-religious epistemology remained influential at least until late in the seventeenth century. There was considerable continuity between the two. To return to my earlier metaphor, the scientific horse was not the only one in European man's stable, and he did not ride it all the time (cf. Lawrence 1975).

9 'It is certain because it is impossible' (my translation).

REFERENCES

Chatterton, P.
1968　'The Missionaries'. *New Guinea and Australia, The Pacific and South-East Asia* 3:12-18.

Fisher, H.
1971　'Hassebu: Islamic Healing in Black Africa'. In M. Brett (ed.): *Northern Africa: Islam and Modernization*. London: Frank Cass:23-47.

Frazer, Sir J. G.
1971　*The Golden Bough: A Study in Magic and Religion.* London: Macmillan paperback.

Hamnett, M. P. and Connell, J.
1981　'Diagnosis and Cure: The Resort to Traditional and Modern Medical Practitioners in the Northern Solomons, Papua New Guinea'. *Social Science and Medicine* 15B:489-98.

Horton, R.
1968　'Neo-Tylorianism: Sound Sense or Sinister Prejudice?' *Man* 3:625-34.

Lawrence, P.
1952　'Sorcery among the Garia' *South Pacific* 6:340-3.

1964　*Road Belong Cargo: A Study of the Cargo Movement in the Southern Madang District.* Manchester and Carlton: Manchester and Melbourne University Presses.

1965　'The Ngaing of the Rai Coast'. In P. Lawrence and M. Meggitt (eds): *Gods, Ghosts, and Men in Melanesia: Some Religions of Australian New Guinea and the New Hebrides.* Melbourne: Oxford University Press:198-223.

1968　*Don Juan in Melanesia.* St Lucia: University of Queensland Press (first published in *Quadrant* 1964).

1975　'European Cultism: The Skeleton in the Scientific Cupboard'. In J. Brammell and R. J. May (eds): *Education in Melanesia: Papers delivered at the Eighth Waigani Seminar.* Canberra: University of Papua New Guinea and Australian National University Press:339-45.

1984　*The Garia: An Ethnography of a Traditional Cosmic System in Papua New Guinea.* Carlton: Melbourne University Press.

McSwain, R.
1977　*The Past and Future People: Tradition and Change on a New Guinea Island.* Melbourne: Oxford University Press.

Read, K. E.
  1952   'Missionary Activities and Social Change in the Central
         Highlands of Papua New Guinea'. *South Pacific* 5:229-
         38.
Robin, R. W.
  1982   'Revival Movements in the Southern Highlands
         Province of Papua New Guinea'. *Oceania* 52:320-43.
Smith, M. F.
  1980   'From Heathen to Atheist: Changing Views of
         Catholicism in a Papua New Guinea Village'. *Oceania*
         51:40-52.
Stanner, W. E. H.
  1958   'On the Interpretation of Cargo Cults'. *Oceania* 29:1-
         25.
Thomas, K.
  1971   *Religion and the Decline of Magic: Studies in Popular
         Beliefs in Sixteenth- and Seventeenth-Century England.*
         London: Weidenfeld and Nicolson.
Tuzin, D. F.
  1980   *The Voice of Tambaran: Truth and Illusion in Ilahita
         Religion.* Berkley: University of California Press.
Webster, C.
  1982   *From Paracelsus to Newton: Magic and the Making of
         Modern Science.* Cambridge: Cambridge University
         Press.
Wetherell, D. and Carr-Gregg, C.
  1984   'Moral Re-Armament in Papua, 1931-1942'. *Oceania*
         54:177-203.
Worsley, P.
  1957   *The Trumpet Shall Sound: A Study of Cargo Cults in
         Melanesia.* London: MacGibbon and Kee. (Repub-
         lished in 1968 by Schocken Paperbacks, New York.)

2

Master of Souls:
the Mekeo Sorcerer

MICHELE STEPHEN

The experiential aspects of shamanism have attracted much anthropological attention ever since the appearance of Eliade's (1972) classic comparative study. The importance in shamanic practice of visions, dreams, ecstatic trances, spirit possession, drug induced states and similar experiences is now well established (Peters and Price-Williams 1980). No comparable interest has focused on experiential aspects of sorcery.[1] There are, nevertheless, many scattered references throughout the literature to suggest that Melanesian sorcerers and magicians make a similar use of visions, dreams and other alternate states of consciousness. For example, the spirit familiar of the Orokolo sorcerer revealed itself to him either in a dream, or in waking visions brought on by fasting (Williams 1940:105). Dobuans believed that 'In sleep the spirit goes forth; the spirits of witches and sorcerers go on their evil errands . . .' (Fortune 1963:181). At Bartle Bay, in the Southern Massim, it was said that death might be caused 'by means of a "sending" projected from the body of the sorcerer or witch' (Seligman 1910:640). Among the Koita it was reported that spirits of the dead 'are seen in dreams and a few men who would probably be called sorcerers have the power of seeing them in the waking state' (Seligman

1910:190). Similar references can be found to the ritual role of alternate states of consciousness in many Melanesian societies (Stephen 1979).

This chapter describes the role of the Mekeo sorcerer as a mediator between the living and the spirit realm.[2] It focuses on the nature of his interaction with the spirits, the rituals he employs to contact them—and the inner states he experiences. Examined from this perspective, striking similarities with the shaman emerge, though it is clear that the two roles are by no means identical (see Herdt 1977 for a discussion of the applicability of the term 'shaman' in Melanesia).

Who has Mystical Powers?: Ideology and Practice

The Mekeo, who speak an Austronesian language, number approximately seven thousand. They live in fourteen nucleated villages situated on a rich, riverine plain within the Central Province of Papua New Guinea, approximately 110 kilometres to the north-west of the capital, Port Moresby. Ninety years of European contact have not radically altered, though they have modified, traditional political and social structures. A Mekeo village is composed of several localized segments of named, patrilineal descent groups, each with one or more hereditary leaders, the *lopia*. Despite the changes over the colonial period and in more recent years, the traditional holders of authority are still influential and the respect they command is to no small extent related to the mystical powers to which they are believed to have access (Hau'ofa 1981; Stephen 1974).

So much subterfuge surrounds the whole matter that it is no easy task to establish who in fact possesses mystical powers.[3] It is, however, quite clear-cut who should possess them. An outsider is not likely to spend more than a few hours in any Mekeo community without hearing some reference to 'sorcerers' (*ugauga*) and their nefarious actions. One soon learns that these men—for no women are accused of such activities—are not merely suspected by the rest of the community of wielding death-dealing powers; they are publicly recognized as the force backing the authority of the village leaders of descent groups, the *lopia*. Moreover, their position is one determined by inheritance and descent. People often remark that the sorcerer is the *lopia*'s 'policeman', and his position is socially acknowledged and defined; but he is, for all that, no less feared by the ordinary man and woman who attribute to him all death, major illnesses and misfortune in the community.

There is always much talk about the dangerous powers of the sorcerers and people's fears of them. Though he is, of course, never to be seen practising his arts in public, the sorcerer is an easily identifiable and publicly acknowledged figure at feasts and other important social occasions. While preparing his magic, he must seclude himself from the rest of the community and observe a rigorous regime of fasting and sexual abstinence; when he does appear in public, his emaciated frame, black attire (he is usually in mourning for only widowers usually practise sorcery), and aloof, forbidding presence immediately set him apart from ordinary men, who are careful to keep as far away from him as possible for fear of the powers emanating from him and the objects he is likely to be carrying.

In contrast to the interest that always seems to surround the topic of 'sorcery', one hears little about 'good' magic, and even less about healing. People do talk about the families of sick individuals approaching various sorcerers to persuade them—by means of heavy payments in cash and traditional valuables—to remove their evil influence; but no one speaks of this as 'healing'. Nor are there individuals publicly identified as 'healers'. Some people are said to be able to divine (through dreams and other methods) the causes of illness; and occasionally it may be admitted that someone has a particularly effective spell to cure some ailment, such as ulcers or fever; but these 'experts' are never to be seen practising their arts in public. In contrast, every day there is a steady stream of people seeking outpatient treatment at the Mission hospital; and any European with certain basic medical supplies on hand can expect constant requests for aspirin, bandages and the like. On the surface, it would appear that people today rely primarily on European medical services, and that only in the case of an illness which does not respond to treatment do they begin to look for the sorcerer responsible. Once again, though there is much talk of anxious relatives seeking out different sorcerers in the hope of saving the patient, such affairs are conducted in the strictest privacy.

Though there are no public rituals connected with either sorcery or healing, sorcery is more often discussed and more visible—at least in the person of the 'sorcerer' who is a socially recognized and identifiable figure. The Mekeo emphasize that mystical powers are concentrated in the person of the sorcerer, and that these powers are dangerous and destructive—though used under the direction of the descent group heads to maintain social order. There is a sharp ideological separation of the social, familial authority of the chiefs (*lopia*) and the mystical, destructive powers of the sorcerers (*ugauga*). People consciously articulate this division and it is reflected in complex cultural symbolism. As Hau'ofa (1981) shows, it is revealed in the spatial symbolism of the layout of village settlements. The chief, the *lopia*, is associated with the central, safe, domestic space of the settlement—the 'belly of the village' (also 'womb')[4]—where his house and his descent group clubhouse are situated. The sorcerer, the *ugauga*, must walk only along the paths circling the periphery of the village; lives, when he is practising, away in the bush (untamed nature); is celibate (i.e. removed from normal, domestic ties and sentiments); is associated with the night, the unseen, the threatening and the dangerous. Accordingly, sorcerers are always segregated from both chiefs and commoners at feasts and public occasions, and their share of meat from feasts is, it is said, sent to them at night, secretly along the hidden back paths of the village.

This forcefully articulated and pervasive dualistic ideology masks the complexity of social practice. In the first place, it obscures the fact that not only those individuals designated as 'sorcerers' possess mystical powers—many others, both chiefs and commoners, possess such powers. In the second place, it obscures the fact that those who are referred to as 'sorcerers' (*ugauga*) possess not only death-dealing magic but other powers as well, and that a 'sorcerer' may well spend far more of his time in healing than in doing harm. Thirdly, it obscures the fact that there is no simple categorization of 'good' or 'bad' powers, rather there are many different mystical powers, each of which has both a positive and a negative aspect.

The range of magical knowledge (*ikifa*) is wide (and its branches are complex and far-reaching).[5] For the purposes of making some sort of systematic description, it can be divided into the following areas of activity: hunting, fishing, gardening, love and courting, war, weather, inflicting sickness and curing, protection, divination and signs, competition in sport and gambling, acquiring attention and favour from others. While this bare listing would suggest that most Mekeo magic is primarily productive in nature, such is not the case. Most forms of magic, except for the very minor techniques, may be used destructively. Thus love magic may be used to attract a lover or to drive a woman mad with sexual desire, shaming her and her family in the eyes of the community. Garden magic may be used not only to make crops grow but to cause them to wither and die. Weather magic may be employed to devastate the region with floods or kill young, tender crops with a burning sun.

Commoners who have knowledge of one or more magical techniques—for example, the dream divination of illness—may, covertly, operate a small practice and charge clients a fee for their services; but they are very wary of making this too public for fear of arousing the resentment of the holders of more powerful techniques. One woman told me about her knowledge of dream divination, then later said that her husband had been very angry with her for doing so, warning her that if I revealed her confidences to the sorcerer who was known to be my teacher, he would have no hesitation in striking her down for her presumption in claiming esoteric knowledge. Nor was this an isolated incident, many people indicated similar fears. Clearly the 'sorcerer' is the one socially recognized figure who is paid to use his powers, and smaller fry had better take care not to compete openly.

Many chiefs (heads of localized descent groups) possess major mystical powers which can be used destructively. It is true, however, that they rarely profess knowledge of the particular form of destructive magic exercised by the sorcerer, the *ugauga*. There is a sort of terminological trick involved here—people commonly speak of all destructive mystical powers as *ugauga*, translated into English as 'sorcery'. In fact, *ugauga* is only one specific form of death-dealing magic—there are many others, and, as I have already indicated, most magical techniques can be used destructively. Thus it is quite true to say that the chiefs do not usually have *ugauga* powers, but this does not mean that they lack other mystical means to kill or punish their people in various ways. While laymen loosely use the term *ugauga* as a general category under which is subsumed all destructive powers, and refer to the holders of such powers as *ugauga aui*, the adept discriminates much more carefully.

My determined insistence that I wanted to be taught *ugauga* puzzled my key instructor in esoteric lore. He assured me that if I had enemies or rivals I wanted to dispose of by mystical means he could teach me many ways of swiftly and efficiently achieving my ends, without having to undergo the privations involved in practising *ugauga*. This technique, he explained, was only necessary if one wanted to make money: one used it to make people sick and then demanded hefty fees to cure them. If you merely wanted to kill someone, there was no need to employ such a burdensome technique.

Since, for the adept, *ugauga* is not a general category but a specific technique, he does not generally refer to himself or others as '*ugauga aui*'. He will, if asked, specify that he or someone else 'knows *ugauga*' (*ugauga e logo*), along with various other mystical powers. The term he uses to refer to himself and other adepts is *ikifa aui*. '*Ikifa*' is the general term applied to magical knowledge. While it may be glossed as 'clever', it means more than innate ability, implying instruction in specific procedures. For example, a child who has been taught certain household duties is '*ikifa*' while another, who is no less intelligent but has not been taught how to perform these tasks, is not *ikifa* in that context. *Ikifa* is in effect 'knowledge', and though it may be used in a general sense, it usually implies ritual or magical knowledge. The adept thus regards himself and his colleagues as 'men of knowledge'—and this does not necessarily indicate the knowledge of 'heat sorcery' (*ugauga*) though it may include it. The most renowned 'men of knowledge', nevertheless, invariably possess one or more techniques of death-dealing magic—of which, as already indicated, there are many in addition to *ugauga*.

The man or woman of knowledge (women also possess esoteric knowledge of various kinds) may know one or many magical techniques. A spell to treat ulcers or fever, dream divination, a particular technique of gardening or hunting magic, or an effective love charm—any of these would be sufficient for an individual to have a reputation as a man or woman of knowledge, while some would have competence in many of these areas. In a large community (such as the one I worked in which had a population of just under a thousand) there are likely to be several individuals with a knowledge of one or two important magical techniques that they might use on behalf of others for a fee; but there will be only a few individuals who have a deep knowledge of several areas of magic, those who are the real masters of esoteric lore. These 'grand masters' are invariably men, and are usually the genealogically senior members of their descent group or lineage. Major magical powers are the prerogative of the socially powerful.

Despite the ideological insistence on the separation of powers—the mystical destructive powers of the sorcerer and the human, social authority of the chief—the social reality is more complex. There are in fact many men and women of knowledge, including commoners and chiefs, who possess many different kinds of magical knowledge—none of which are unequivocally 'good'.

Relations with the Spirit Realm

Magic as the Means of Altering the Natural Order

Though it appears to be a very sweeping assertion, I believe it is true to say that the Mekeo undertake no ritual actions directed towards spirit entities other than manipulative magical acts with a specific end in view. There are no rites of general propitiation of spirit entities, no celebration of the perpetuation or maintenance of the natural order, no rituals concerned with ensuring the continued fertility of crops, animals or men, no rituals directed to the guidance or welfare of the souls of the recently departed. There are public rituals of food exchanges and distribution associated with the death of a member of the community, and with such events of social significance as the installation of a new chief or the inauguration of a new clan clubhouse; yet these ceremonies are not consciously articulated as having anything to do with spirit entities nor, even in the case of mortuary ceremonies, with the soul of the dead. An exhaustive symbolic analysis might well reveal deeper levels of meaning and referents other than purely social ones, but this would not obviate the fact that at the level of conscious awareness of what is going on, spirit entities are not involved.

That the natural order is taken for granted is reflected in the fact that there is no commonly known myth to explain the origin of the physical universe or even of man himself. The most important myth cycle is concerned with the establishment of the social order and the revealing of the esoteric knowledge which is its concomitant. The existence and continuation of the natural order asks for no comment; what needs explanation is any marked deviation or change, and this is sought in the manipulation of the external world by a human agent, the magician (cf. Weiner 1977:217ff). Mekeo magic is not creative in the sense that without it crops would not grow or canoes would not float. It is only if one wants to produce more than anyone else, or desires to make others suffer by blighting their crops, that garden magic is necessary. When people go hunting they usually return with something; it is only if one wants to shoot more than anyone else, or spoil someone else's catch, that magic is necessary. The magician has no effect on the amount of game or fish or garden produce in any absolute sense; all he is able to do is put controls over the individual's access to these resources. There is thus a high degree of ambivalence in relation to magical powers—a real sense in which the magician's power to change the existing order is a *perversion* of it.

According to the myths which relate the founding of the social order, men were given political rank and magical powers along with jealousy and death—the first two are the concomitant of the second. Without jealousy and death, there would be no political rank or mystical powers; without mystical powers and political rank, there would be no jealousy or death. It becomes clear why death, though accepted in the abstract as the eventual end of all men, is, in the concrete, always attributed to magic. Death is an interruption of the natural order of things; had death not been introduced along with magical knowledge, men would not need to die.

Since the mystical powers of the man of knowledge are not seen as necessary for the maintenance of the natural order, but rather as a means of changing this order to suit the desires of a particular individual, it is little wonder that such powers are highly valued by those who possess them but at the same time are regarded with suspicion and fear by those who do not. In fact the layman tends to regard *all* magic as sorcery—that is, as potentially dangerous and destructive.

Though spirit beings are not thought responsible for, nor concerned with, the maintenance of the natural order, through magic they can be called upon to help bring about *changes* in it.

The Nature of the Spirit Realm

One cannot rely on formal, consistent cosmological statements to understand how the spirit realm is conceived. Even the man of knowledge has little taste for purely metaphysical speculation, his concern is with concrete experiences of the spirit realm. The layman, of course, is even less occupied with speculative cosmology. One must thus attempt to discern what is *experienced* of this other world. Certain cosmological oppositions may, however, be inferred from general statements made in particular contexts.

The spirit beings most often referred to are the *isage*: these include the spirits of the dead (both recent ghosts and distant ancestors) and various powerful beings whose exploits are recounted in the myths (*isonioni*). The most important of these myth heroes is A'aisa, the originator of the present social order and of many techniques of magic including sorcery (*ugauga*). A'aisa cannot be described as a creator deity—he is not attributed with the creation of the natural order, nor of specific parts of it, nor with the creation of human beings. He once was a man—or at least lived among men, giving them important esoteric knowledge and setting some in authority over others. He then journeyed westwards along the coast to a hill called Kariko—this is the abode of the dead. Various relics of his physical presence—for example, his footprints—have become transformed into stones and other natural substances which are now employed by human magicians. Many other myth heroes (referred to in general as *isonioni papiau*, the 'myth people') also lived among men, endowing them with specific techniques of different kinds of magic. Their physical remains also were transformed into natural substances or species of plants or animals which are now used in magic. Like A'aisa, all these heroes have become *isage*—spirits.

The other important class of spirit beings are the *faifai*, who live under water and may appear in the form of snakes, eels and other aquatic creatures, or as men and women with white skin and long, straight hair. Whereas people live on land, the *faifai* live in water; they need cold while people need warmth; they herd fish while people herd pigs; their skin is white, the skin of human beings is brown. Though the *faifai* are not thought to be deliberately malicious in their actions towards human beings, any contact with them is inherently dangerous. They are said to fall in love sometimes with humans, drawing their lovers' souls under water with them and thus bringing about their death. Many illnesses are attributed to contact of some sort with *faifai*.

The *isage* are similarly cosmologically opposed to the living, though in different ways. They possess a powerful heat (*isapu*) which is as dangerous to men as the cold water element of the *faifai*. Like the *faifai*, the spirits of the dead are not thought to be ill-disposed to the living; indeed it is rather attachment for living relatives which is likely to cause the recently dead to reappear in the world of the living; nevertheless any contact with them is potentially dangerous. If a child is left crying unattended, grandmother's spirit may come to comfort it, but her touch will cause sickness that may even prove fatal. A mother who has recently died may appear in dreams to her children and spouse and offer them food, but if they accept it they will fall sick. Likewise physical contact with dead bodies, graves and relics of the dead is dangerous and likely to result in illness.

On death, the spirit is said to reside in the village of the dead, Kariko. The hill on which Kariko is situated is not, however, located in some other world but in this one. Some adepts claim to have visited the hill and slept the night on its slopes from where they could plainly hear the noises and see the lights of the spirits' village, but no one claimed to have approached any closer than this. Men occupy the earth; *faifai* the water beneath it; Kariko, the abode of the spirits of the dead, is to be found on the summit of a hill above the earth. This suggests a cosmological opposition of three elements—water, earth and air (or perhaps fire).

As Lawrence and Meggitt (1965) have pointed out for Melanesia in general, it would be false to suggest that the spirits represent a supernatural or transcendent realm. Nevertheless, they are thought to inhabit realms conceptually and symbolically opposed to and separate from the earthly plane of human existence. In the ordinary course of things, these other realms are hidden from humans' view and do not impinge upon their consciousness. When the boundaries are breached, the event is characterized by the abnormal, the uncanny or by non-ordinary states of consciousness, including dreams and temporary insanity.

The Layman's Experience of Spirits
The ordinary man or woman does not deliberately seek encounters with spirits but he or she inevitably experiences a certain degree of involuntary contact with them. Sightings of ghosts, particularly of the recently dead, are not uncommon yet neither are they regarded as ordinary; their appearance, no matter how brief, is a disquieting glimpse into other realities where the predictable order of normal reality is swept away. People are often physically ill for some days after such an encounter. Spirits sometimes appear in the form of animals or reptiles of unusual size or uncanny behaviour, their strangeness revealing their true identity. More rarely, people catch sight of a water spirit in its human form, an experience that leads to temporary insanity or unconsciousness. Individuals known to be subject to periodic bouts of violent insanity explain that during their seizures

they are goaded on by angry spirits of the dead to attack anyone they see.

The most common experience of the spirit world, shared by all, is the dream. Dreaming is interpreted as the actions of the dreamer's soul which is able to leave the body during sleep and, by virtue of its non-corporeal nature, commune with the spirits and visit the underwater realms of the *faifai*. Persistently bad or frightening dreams are invariably associated with an approaching illness and even ostensibly pleasant dreams may indicate danger. The soul (*lalauga*—the same word is used for 'shadow' and 'image') is distinguished from conscious thought (*opo*). In its dream journeys the soul is exposed to many dangers that conscious thought cannot shield it from, for one is usually not aware of what one's soul is doing. Many people would simply prefer to forget their dreams and close their conscious minds to their disturbing messages. Lacking the knowledge to interpret the meaning of their dreams, they are usually uneasy about consulting someone else's opinion for fear of the secrets the dream might reveal. Though it is widely recognized that dreams may provide valuable knowledge about the future and other matters, nevertheless many laymen take a highly negative view of dreaming.

When troubled by ghosts, persistent dreams and similar inruptions from the other world, the layman usually takes steps to remove the dangerous influence. The spirits may be formally addressed and asked to leave; spells may be said to counter the effects of the visitation; protective charms may be worn. But not all take such a negative view. Some people unversed in esoteric lore regard their dreams in a positive light, but emphasize that this interaction with the spirit realm is spontaneous and not solicited on their part.

The Adept's Interaction with the Spirits

In contrast to the layman, the adept intentionally seeks contact with the spirits. Lesser practitioners move freely between the ordinary world of human society and spirit realms; while the master of knowledge seems to live in a state of continuous awareness of other realities.

It should be kept in mind that varying degrees of inter-action are experienced by different practitioners; I will describe here the more extreme form as exemplified by a man described by his community as a 'sorcerer' (*ugauga*) and widely renowned as one of the most knowledgeable and powerful magicians in the whole region. I will refer to him as Aisaga, which is not his name. Aisaga was my constant mentor during the fieldwork on which this paper is based. I spent several hours with him every day, and as my house was built next to his, I was able to observe many of his actions even when not actually conversing with him. Arrangements for this fieldwork had been made with Aisaga on a brief return visit to the Mekeo in the 1978–79 summer vacation; he had agreed to build a house for me and stated that if I had gained sufficient competence in the language to converse with him without any intermediaries, he would instruct me in the esoteric traditions of magic and sorcery. I was not certain that either promise would ever be fulfilled, but when I returned in October 1980 I found my house finished and over the next eight months I was methodically introduced to the main areas of magic. When it was realized that Aisaga was instructing me in magic, other friends, who previously had always declined to give more than generalized information on the topic, now told me the esoteric versions of myths, taught me spells and identified for me the magical medicines. I thus had good opportunity to compare traditions and techniques, but my most comprehensive experience of the rituals of magic was provided by Aisaga, who in any case was the most knowledgeable teacher available.

In his own estimation, Aisaga is a 'man of knowledge' (*ikifa auga*) whose command of hunting, gardening, weather, love and other magic is no less than his knowledge of death-dealing techniques. It is not to be supposed, however, that he denies his destructive powers: these include means to bring about death by snake bite; by attack from wild animals; from accidents; in fights; as the result of numerous diseases, including internal haemorrhaging, dysentery, disorders of the womb, pneumonia, fever, swellings, ulcers (each of which requires a different technique and which he can also cure), to name but a few. He claims powers to blind his victims, to send them insane, to destroy their reproductive capacities, to blight their crops and to impose numerous other hardships upon them. The community at large is not aware of the details of these powers, people know only that he holds power of life and death over them. It is sometimes said in awe of such men that not only can they destroy you but—more insidiously—they 'have the power to change your mind'.

Aisaga is a man in his mid-sixties—though he is capable of appearing much younger—tall, erect, bone thin and conveying a commanding dignity of presence in every line of his face and controlled gesture of his body. His fine, slightly hooded eyes are at once arresting and calm. One does not feel like laughing in his presence—it was difficult even for me to see him as entirely human—yet I was eventually to discover that he has a keen, playful sense of humour. He has been a widower for almost twenty years and lives alone in a small house (*gove*) separate though not far from the family house (*e'a*) occupied by three of his married sons, their wives and numerous children. Meals are usually brought to him by his sons' wives, but the food rarely meets with his fastidious standards and he prefers to cook for himself. His house is situated right at the back on the outer periphery of the village and abuts on to the surrounding bush. The house is encircled by a fence and many trees, shrubs and flowering plants. In contrast, the village space is kept clear of all vegetation and people express abhorrence of plants and creepers overgrowing and rotting their roofs and house timbers. My house is situated to one side of his, only a few feet apart, where we can keep a sharp eye on each other. He eats separately from the rest of his family, never goes to sit and talk with them on their platform and never enters their house, which in any case is only for sleeping. His sons occasionally come to consult with him about the day's activities, but never stay long; his younger grandchildren are not permitted to sit with him and the adolescent boys do not care to do so.

Outside his immediate family he has even fewer visitors; those who come are on some specific errand and do not dally. Never on any occasion does he visit the men's houses of other descent groups nor does he attend feasts or other public activities in the village. The only time he appears in public in his own village is when hospitality is being offered in his own descent group's clubhouse to guests who have come to see him—he is the chief of the lineage. Nowadays he rarely visits other villages. Nor does he go to the garden to work or the bush to hunt. This inactivity is not due to physical decline as he is still evidently agile and swift in his movements. He spends hours alone every day singing softly to himself on his veranda or silently pottering around among the flowers growing around his house, which, he will demur with a half smile, are merely for 'decoration'. Though the village abounds with rumours of the nefarious deeds of this man, the outside observer would see little to suggest that he was anything other, despite his commanding appearance, than a harmless old man who prefers to be left to himself. But this would be a total misunderstanding of the situation.

Though not in any way apparent to the casual observer, this man's contact with the realm of unseen powers is such that it has rendered his very person a source of danger to all who come near him—including his own children and grandchildren. It is not merely that the community shuns him because of its suspicions of nefarious dealings, but that he himself is well aware that his mere presence is sufficient to bring harm to others, regardless of the absence of any intention on his part to do so. His solitary hours—which seem so empty—are in fact filled with a subtle but continuous interaction with the realm of unseen powers. The plants that he tends in his house garden are not 'just for decoration'; they provide the necessary ingredients for magical potions, like the insect tied up by one leg hanging over his fire and the dried bird's wing, and the lizard skin, thrust into the thatch over his veranda. The songs he sings to himself for hours on end are spells of various kinds; the soft muttering which can be overheard from my veranda when he retires for the night is not the old man talking to himself, as one might surmize, but a ritual invocation of the spirits of his fathers and grandfathers. The cries of birds, the chirps of insects, the sudden appearance of a firefly or a bat in the evening gloom, are all communications from the other world for a 'man of knowledge', imbuing his waking consciousness with constant awareness of other realities. This morning he has heard, for the third time in a row, the bird *ifi* calling in the bush towards the near end of the village; this is a sign of imminent death for someone in his clan. In the early evening a cicada shrills from the roof of the veranda, or a bat swoops low overhead; they are A'aisa's messengers. A sneeze, ringing in the ears, a throbbing of the veins in one's upper arm, all are meaningful to the 'man of knowledge'.

The signals are magnified at night, when he might hear the rapping of spirits within his house, smell their presence, or glimpse them in the form of snakes coiled in pools of shadow around the veranda or in overhanging trees, or hear their voices murmuring beneath his window in the early hours of the morning. At night, in his dreams, he will receive further communications, particularly if he has been reciting spells during the day. Today he has been singing hunting spells to himself all afternoon; accordingly he dreams early in the night of spearing a child and a man from the coast who have come to visit him. Before it is light, he is roused by his son who has just returned from a night's hunting with a small pig he has shot and the news that he has also bagged another too large to carry back by himself— just as the dream had indicated.

If a patient is under treatment, dreams will reveal the outcome of the illness. Aisaga almost invariably attributes his dreams to the effects of the spells said that day or of the magical potions he has prepared. When the message of the dream is not clear enough to satisfy him, he resorts to divination—an activity he is often to be found engaged in first thing in the morning.

Divination is another means at his disposal to communicate directly with the spirits. He often uses it in conjunction with dreaming, testing the possibly ambiguous message of the dream against the simple yes/no answers provided by divination. After reciting a spell invoking his ancestors, he states the question and then takes a small bone covered in clay (a fragment of a human bone from the lower arm), about the thickness and length of a biro, and with one movement of his hand attempts to stand it upright on the curved back of a small cowrie shell. If the answer is affirmative, the spirits will 'hold up the bone'; if it is negative they will let the bone fall. The questions are always repeated two or three times in different ways to test the result.

In addition to the many powerful objects he needs for

his rites, he keeps with him the relics (bones, teeth, hair) of his patrilineal ancestors, who are also the ancestors of the whole lineage, since he is its most senior representative. He is thus in constant communion with them through dreams, signs, divination and his nightly invocation of them to assist him and watch over the members of the lineage. To withstand their presence and that of the other powerful beings he invokes, he must be in a constant state of ritual preparation (*gope*), though he does not follow as strict a regime as he would if practising heat sorcery (*ugauga*). Most importantly, he never washes in cold water, consumes any cold foods or cold liquids, he eats sparingly and lives alone. The effect of his constant fasting, long celibacy and advanced age is to make him *lolova*—dry, light, pure. Heavy, moist flesh has been reduced till his frame is little more than dry skin on empty bones (*unia mai'ini*). One is reminded of Carmen Blacker's (1975:87ff.) description of certain Japanese shamans and saints called 'tree eaters', who attempt to limit their food intake to the point that all corruptible elements of the body are wasted away and on their death their corpses become natural mummies without further treatment. The common aim is clearly to purify the self of all that is human and thus corruptible, thereby entering the realm of the spirits in life.

The Mekeo 'man of knowledge' who has become *lolova*, becomes more spirit than man, though he still exists on the human plane. Hence his very presence is so imbued with the power of this other realm, that he becomes dangerous to other human beings and he spends less time in their company than he does in contact with spirits. Once, when severely provoked by some insufferable arrogance on my part, Aisaga quietly warned me not to underestimate his powers as his ritual practice had long since transformed him into a being 'like a *faifai*'. Despite the suspicions of the community, this 'master of knowledge' in fact spends most of his time using his dearly bought powers for the good of his family and lineage—in performing healing magic and hunting and gardening magic (though this is not to deny his powers to bring death and destruction).

There is a very wide range in experiences of the realm of unseen powers—from the ordinary man who attempts to shut out its influences, to the master of knowledge who is in such constant communion with it that he becomes more spirit than human—nevertheless the differences are of degree rather than kind. By its very nature, the unseen is known in states of non-ordinary reality—in waking visions, in premonitions, in hallucinations and perceptions of the abnormal, and particularly in dreams (cf. Malinowski 1974:150–66). The man of knowledge's experience of this realm is different only in that he deliberately employs ritual means to magnify, instead of shut off, these influences.

The Rituals of Sorcery and Magic

I now wish to examine the nature and intention of the rituals employed by the man of knowledge. Current anthropological approaches to the analysis of ritual stress the elucidation of the specific cultural meanings expressed in symbols which compose the rite. My aim here is avowedly different. Putting aside for now the specific cultural symbolism, I will describe the general structure of the rituals performed by the adept and explicated by him. In the final section of the paper I will discuss the possible psychological effects of these rituals.

The Components of the Ritual

The magical rite—regardless of whether its intent is creative or destructive—follows the same basic pattern. It requires a knowledge of five separate possible components: the magical 'medicines';[6] the spells; the powerful relics; the ritual regime; the myths. It should be emphasized that as far as the practitioner is concerned magic consists of a set of practical procedures which have been tested in long practice; he does not theorize about its operation, though he does articulate certain basic principles.

In its simplest and least dangerous form, the magical act may involve no more than the use of a particular medicine (fu'a). The range of medicines is enormous and there are myriad combinations to be used for all types of magic. Even the ordinary man or woman is likely to know a few of the minor medicines; yet this knowledge is so jealously guarded that it is difficult to be sure what is known to the 'average' person. The medicines are made from various plants, certain types of earth and clay, and from insects, birds, animals and reptiles. They may be administered as potions or rubbed on the skin, clothes and other objects (either of the practitioner or the subject), depending on the intention of the rite. The adept will usually point out some link of similarity between the medicine and the intended aim of the magical act; for example, a spotted, brightly coloured leaf is the appropriate medicine to use when hunting the spotted cuscus. In the case of the more powerful potions, he reveals that they are connected in some way with one of the myth heroes. A'aisa's canoe, for instance, was made from a variety of wood which is now employed as a medicine for various magical purposes. Most of the medicines are not thought to be dangerous in themselves, and no ritual preparation is necessary if they alone are used.

The man of knowledge more often uses the medicines in conjunction with spells (*mega*). That the spell is considered to be the more powerful element is indicated by the normal procedure of imparting esoteric knowledge: usually the medicines are taught first, then later, if the instructor can be persuaded, he will give the spells and other necessary information. It is said that while the medicines alone may be sufficient to achieve one's ends, the magician who knows the other elements will have the advantage over one who does not.[7]

The spell is believed to be the words spoken by the myth hero or water spirit (or occasionally the spirit of a dead relative) who initiated that particular magical technique and taught it to men. It is usually preceded by a list of names beginning with the originator and ending with the name of the person who taught the spell to the adept, indicating the chain of transmission. The spell itself consists of a stating of the aim of the rite in various metaphorical repetitions, or, alternatively, a dramatization of the event to be achieved by the spell. The structure is always highly repetitious, with usually only one or two words altering in each verse, and very rhythmic and alliterative. Many are not spoken but sung in what is said to be an archaic form of the language not understood by laymen. The spoken spells are always muttered inaudibly under the breath to prevent anyone else learning them. Though the spell is considered efficacious because it represents the words of some powerful spirit being who used it to achieve his ends, it is not an explicit invocation of this spirit. In some cases, however, in addition to reciting the spell, the adept makes a separate invocation of the spirits and calls upon them to assist him (*isage e pamagogo*).

Many magical procedures, especially the major ones, require certain powerful objects in addition to the medicines. These objects can be divided into two categories: actual physical relics of the dead and objects which are believed to be the relics of the myth heroes and water spirits. The relics of the dead (*faga ofuga*—literally 'body dirt') include bones, teeth, hair and dried organs and various powders said to be made from these ingredients. The relics of the myth heroes and water spirits are usually referred to as 'stones' (*kepo*). These stones (there are many kinds and they have various names) are believed to be the actual bodily substance, now petrified, of the spirit beings who were the originators of the different magical techniques; they are considered to be highly dangerous. The bodily relics of human dead are likewise thought to be very potent. Whenever these dangerous relics are employed the practitioner must undergo some ritual preparation beforehand, otherwise he, himself, would be overcome by their power. Though used in heat sorcery (*ugauga*) and war magic, the relics and stones are also required in the major forms of love magic, gardening magic, hunting magic and weather magic.

The regime which constitutes the ritual preparation for the magical act (*gope*—which has the further meaning of 'tie up, restrict') varies in severity according to the nature of the rite to be undertaken. Sexual abstinence is the most important restriction and this may be necessary for only a few days, several weeks or many months. It is also essential not to immerse the body in cold water, wash in it or drink it. Hot water must be used for washing; and in the most rigorous forms of *gope* no washing at all is permitted. Only hot liquids may be drunk; and under rigorous *gope* one drinks as little as possible. Cold foods, particularly watery or juicy vegetables and fruit, must be avoided, as must coconut oil and animal fats. Lean meat is permissible, according to some adepts, but all food must be eaten as sparingly as possible and it should be roasted over the fire (Mekeo food is usually cooked by boiling in water or water and grated coconut). What little food is consumed must be taken with plenty of ginger or chilli to make it 'hot'. This regime is said to render the adept's body light and hot and dry—whereas the ordinary person's body is heavy, moisture filled and cold, and thus weak and vulnerable.

Though minor magic rites do not require such preparation, it is essential for all the major forms of magic which involve the use of powerful relics and the invocation of spirits. Different practitioners tend to give slightly different versions; my description here is based primarily on observation of the regime followed by Aisaga. Whereas he tended to stress the importance of *gope* in strengthening the adept to withstand the dangerous forces he exposes himself to, others emphasized the importance of fasting, celibacy and seclusion as a means of attracting the spirits' presence. In certain procedures, total seclusion from society is necessary; but a master like Aisaga maintains a constant state of partial preparation which precludes the necessity of living away from the village, though he does not mix freely with others.

Many, though not all, magical procedures are associated with a particular myth (*isonioni*) which explains the origin of the rite. The myths recount the deeds of the myth heroes and water spirits who revealed the various techniques of magic to men. Public versions of these tales are widely known and are often told merely for entertainment. Consequently everyone knows that A'aisa taught men sorcery, that Gava (the moon) was a great lover, that Foikale was a great hunter. Only the adept, however, knows the esoteric versions of these myths which provide the key, as it were, to the magical act—incorporating the spell to be recited, identifying the medicines to be used and the powerful relics essential to the rite. It establishes that the spells are the words spoken by the hero (or water spirit), that the medicines are transformations of objects he used or were associated with him, and that the powerful relics are the actual physical substance of the hero (or water spirit) himself. Knowledge of the myth, however, is not necessary to the performance of the rite providing one knows the other elements. Though there is a vast body of magic considered to have come from the myth heroes and water spirits via human ancestors, many people also claim to have received personal revelations of spells and medicines in dreams (Stephen 1982).

The Implementation of the Ritual
The performance of the rite involves little in the way of a sequence of ritual actions; the key symbolic and ritual elements of the rites are the substances employed and the words said. The only essential context of action is the ritual preparation which must precede the putting together of the magical ingredients and the recitation of the spell. In the case of the most dangerous forms of magic, the practitioner also performs certain ritual actions while he is preparing his potions to protect himself from the powers he is conjuring. In no case is there any sort of public performance; all is conducted in secret by the practitioner on his own.

The stated aim of the spell, the medicines and the powerful relics is twofold: (a) to draw out and attract the soul, or dream-image, of the subject (*oge e ila'a*); (b) to send out the soul, or dream-self, of the practitioner (*lalauga e papealai*), which then acts upon the subject's soul.[8] The principles underlying love magic, hunting magic, heat sorcery and war magic—as my instructor so frequently impressed upon me—are exactly the same—to attract and then control the *soul* of the victim. The inflicting of serious illness, injury and death differs from other magic only in that the sorcerer deals with more dangerous entities—the angered spirits of the dead and the beings who originated sorcery, whose physical relics he manipulates and whose souls, *lalauga*, he summons—and he must prepare himself more stringently for the task.

It is important to realize that the adept understands the magical act as an action performed on another level of reality, by a part of himself over which he can have only indirect conscious control. He is aware of two distinct and separate realities—the world of physical bodies and objects, which he knows in waking consciousness, and the world of visible but non-corporeal entities he experiences in dream consciousness—here he encounters the souls of both living persons and of the spirits. (Spirits, *isage*, have a *lalauga*, a soul or dream-self, but no physical body, *imauga*.) The dream reality is experienced as a realm of power unconstrained by the limitations of physical reality; furthermore, it is seen to underlie physical reality and to be capable of changing it. What occurs in the dream reality eventually affects bodily reality, and the experiences of the soul or dream-self are later realized in the body. Thus if the soul is attacked or suffers injury, the body will sicken; if the soul has an amorous encounter, the body will later experience desire. The adept uses the rituals of magic (a) to guide his soul to implement actions in the dream reality and (b) to gain knowledge of what is occurring in the dream world, as this will reveal what is later to eventuate in physical reality. But he can never have complete control over his soul nor total knowledge of the happenings in the other realm.

The rituals of heat sorcery are directed at arousing the souls of the sorcerer and various spirits to attack the soul of the victim. The sorcerer begins his rituals with the gathering together of all the medicines and other substances he requires. This may take weeks or months as there are many ingredients and some are rare and difficult to obtain. The experienced practitioner, however, takes care to have a good stock on hand and those which he cannot grow or find easily he keeps in dried and powdered form. Having ensured that all that is necessary is at hand, he will begin his ritual regime; since the experienced practitioner remains in a constant state of partial preparation, he does not need to wait long. When the regime is sufficiently far advanced and he judges it safe for him to handle the powerful substances, he takes them out (up to this point they have been stored separately) and places them together in a container made from two half coconut shells (*polo*) or a tube of bamboo stoppered with wood (*wala*). When combined, the medicines and the powerful substances become highly potent and dangerous and the sorcerer must take the utmost care not to injure his own soul. Once the charm is prepared, he proceeds to sing the spells intended to drive the spirits of the dead to fury and to arouse his own soul, or dream-self. That night, before retiring, he then invokes the spirits of his fathers and grandfathers (whose relics he has taken out) and asks them to accompany him when he goes to seek out his victim and to strike him once he is identified to them. That same night he will dream, or see some sign indicating the presence of the spirits; if not, he will wait until he receives such a sign, then he prepares to take the charm to the victim, confident in the knowledge that the spirits will be with him to help his soul accomplish the magical task.

The charm (*polo, wala*) employed varies in potency according to what is put in it and how it is to be used. A less powerfully charged container can be given to an accomplice, once it is properly prepared, who places it in the bag in which he carries his personal belongings and then goes to pay a social call on the intended victim. The soul of the sorcerer who prepared the charm, accompanied by the spirits of the dead he invoked, follow the charm as it is taken to the victim. When the bag containing the charm is placed near the unsuspecting victim, its mere proximity is said to jolt his soul from his body, whereupon the soul is beaten and seized by the soul of the sorcerer and the accompanying spirits.

In other circumstances, the adept may concoct an even more dangerous charm which he, himself, will carry by stealth at night to the house of his intended victim. He then waits for the opportunity to startle the victim, for example, by seizing hold of his leg as he climbs down the ladder from his house, causing him to stumble or fall. In this brief moment, the sorcerer must expose the charm to the victim. Before the victim realizes what is happening, the sorcerer has slipped off into the dark, leaving him to assume that he simply stumbled of his own accord and that nothing is amiss. During these few seconds his soul is said to be propelled out of his body by the brief shock he experiences, and at that vulnerable moment is exposed to the power of the deadly charm. Driven out in weakened confusion, the soul is then set upon by the angered spirits of the dead and the soul of the sorcerer, who quickly overpower it, beat it, tie it up and bring it to the sorcerer's house. There the soul of the victim is imprisoned inside the container, which is placed over the fire to intensify the heat; and as the captured soul begins to writhe in agony, the victim begins to feel sick.

It should be stressed that while he is performing his rituals, the adept is *not consciously* aware of the actions of his soul or of those of the other parties involved. His ritual actions are intended to produce certain results in the dream reality, but he must wait for dreams and omens to gain conscious knowledge of what actually transpired and whether the efforts of his soul were successful.

To cure the victim is simplicity itself for the sorcerer who has imprisoned the soul. All he has to do is take the container off the fire and open it, thus freeing the captive soul. Once the soul is allowed to return to the body, the body quickly begins to heal. Laymen commonly state that only the sorcerer who has ensorcelled the victim can cure him; the adept knows that this is not necessarily the case, though certainly the easiest way to achieve a cure is to persuade the sorcerer responsible to free the soul. Spells are known to a few powerful adepts which can render cold the heat of the charm and can split open the container holding the soul captive. Yet no matter how the cure is effected, the victim will not be privy to the ritual action taken. Whether he is removing his own influence, or attempting to counter the influence of another, the practitioner will merely bespell some water or tea for the patient to drink and send it to him. This is the only sign the patient has that anything is being done for him. If the sorcerer is adamant in his intent, or denies any responsibility, he will refuse to treat the patient; there is, however, always the possibility that he may dissemble and pretend to say curing spells when in fact he is reciting harmful ones. The patient and his relations cannot know for certain where they stand, or really have any confidence in what the sorcerer is doing.

In addition to removing the effects of his own sorcery, Aisaga is an expert in healing magic in general. The task he was most often called upon to perform during my fieldwork was healing ailments that were not, in his estimation, the result of his sorcery—though undoubtedly many of his patients thought otherwise. The sorcerer, as already described, merely has to free the imprisoned soul of his victim. The healer who is not responsible for causing the complaint must rescue and restore the patient's soul; and this must be done through the action of his own soul in a dream. Having made enquiries about the nature of the complaint and its symptoms, Aisaga would select an appropriate spell—for example, a spell to cure headache—and then bespell some water or tea for the patient to drink. Often he did not even see the patient but was approached by a relative of the patient who acted as an intermediary. Depending on the nature of the complaint, he would sometimes prepare potions of various medicines to be drunk or rubbed on the afflicted parts of the body. In cases of serious illness, he would, after himself bespelling the patient, later invoke the spirits of his forefathers and ask them to add their power to his to help the patient recover. Following this, he would expect to dream. Sometimes the dream might vividly represent his soul flight to the spirits' village or to the *faifai*'s dwellings and the struggle there to free the patient's soul; but more often the dream revealed in fairly cryptic, symbolic terms the success or otherwise of his soul's mission. Some men and women, who are not sorcerers, have knowledge of healing and employ techniques similar to those just described; but in general they deal only with minor complaints.

The Sorcerer and Altered Consciousness

Like the shaman, the Mekeo sorcerer gains knowledge of the spirit realm and interacts with it by means of alternate states of consciousness; but whereas the shaman's states tend to be physically active, or violent, possession and mediumship (or at least are acted out in some way for an audience to witness), the sorcerer's experiences are private and quietistic. Visions, auditory and olfactory hallucinations, signs and omens, 'automatic' divination, and especially dreams, are the sorcerer's windows on to another world.

In order to induce his ecstasies, the shaman is usually reported to rely on some form of sensory overload—loud music (particularly drumming), wild dancing, hyperventilation, the use of psychoactive drugs (Ludwig 1972). The sorcerer uses sensory deprivation; his quietistic states—

aided by fasting, celibacy and isolation—resemble those of the meditative mystic (Peters and Price-Williams 1983:15–19; Ludwig 1972). In these states he, too, is in touch with an 'inner' reality;[9] and it is certainly his belief that he thereby gains knowledge and power hidden from ordinary men (cf. Elkin 1977:37–66).

Sensory deprivation is employed by him mainly to create a state in which he is sensitive to this inner world— or, as the adept himself puts it, a condition in which the spirits feel attracted to him. He becomes aware of shadowy presences, whispered communications, strange scents; he is alert to subtle signs and omens. Such signs—the cries of certain birds, the sighting of particular insects, reptiles and animals, and other indications—formed an important part of Aisaga's continuing interaction with the unseen. For him, they seemed to act as cues to fasten his attention on a different level of awareness (cf. Deikman 1972).

In addition to the sensory deprivation he imposes on himself, the adept attempts to guide and control his interaction with the spirit realm through the recitation of magical incantations and the manipulation of magical substances and relics. While the psychological effects of sensory deprivation are well established, it is rather more difficult to pinpoint the effects of these other elements of the ritual. But there are grounds to argue that they, also, are used to practical effect in inducing and influencing alternate states of consciousness.

In the anthropological literature, these states tend to be associated only with dramatic instances like drug-induced visions and violent forms of spirit possession. Consequently it is easy to overlook more subtle forms. A hypnotic trance, for example, may be easily and quickly induced; a few passes of the hands or gazing briefly at a moving object may be sufficient. The form of divination described earlier, in which a bone is balanced upright on the back of a small cowrie shell, seems to involve an automatism analogous to the 'automatic writing' of Western spiritualistic mediums. This is suggested on the basis of my observations of the adept's hand movements and his statements to the effect that he experiences the placing of the bone as determined by hands other than his own. Before posing his questions he recites a spell calling upon his ancestors to reveal the truth. The recitation of the spell, I suggest, induces a light trance (or brief dissociation) in which his hand movements seem to become independent of his own volition.

There are said to have been in the past adepts who could induce controlled, waking visions (*laulau isa*—'to see souls') by means of spells and magical medicines rubbed on the eyes; but to my knowledge no one today claims such feats. The usual intention of the rituals, as already described, is to influence dreaming. Aisaga's claim to be able to control his dreaming certainly appeared to be borne out by dreams recorded in sequence over a period of several months.[10] Even my own dreaming during fieldwork supported the correlation between ritual performance and dreams; though I am not normally a particularly vivid or prolific dreamer, I found that disturbing, or simply persistent, dreams followed instruction in spells. This of course may be put down to suggestion, though at first I was not aware of the correlation—but even so, what was the suggestion that was powerful enough to produce the dream? One cannot normally control one's dreaming; it is by its very nature beyond normal conscious control. It seems to me that this powerful suggestion is quite simply the spell itself, as the adept states. The spell, as already indicated, is a highly repetitious, rhythmic and alliterative metaphorical statement of the intention of the magical act. These characteristics, which are common to all the spells recorded from Melanesia that I have seen, are often explained as mnemonic devices. No doubt they do aid memory; I found that when I was told a spell even quite meaningless (to me) phrases would stick in my mind and I would find myself repeating it over and over again. On reflection, this suggested to me that the spell, by means of its alliterative and rhythmic structure, is able to penetrate to subliminal levels of consciousness, and thus to dreaming. Furthermore, many magical procedures require the adept to sit up all night singing his spells until he finally falls asleep in the early hours of the morning, when he will expect to dream.

Certainly the spell employs what Eric Fromm (1951) terms the 'forgotten language'—the metaphorical, repetitive, symbolic language of dreams (and myth) in which the unconscious, or dream consciousness, communicates with the waking consciousness. Like dreaming, which characteristically reiterates the same message in a series of several symbolic transformations, the spell states an intention in a repeated series of metaphors. A spell to cure headache, for example, calls upon the tears of the morning star (the dew) and its coldness, then names every stream of cold running water coming from the mountains, then calls upon the river and invokes its coldness, and finally commands the patient's head to be cool like them; that is, to stop aching. The similarity between the language of the spell and of the dream becomes even more persuasive, I think, when it is remembered that some adepts claim to have received spells in dreams, and that many spells and other esoteric knowledge that have been passed down for generations are said to have been originally revealed in dreams. Here we have more than a strong hint that the conscious mind is able to make use of messages from the dream consciousness to communicate back to it.

The spell can be seen to function as a means of auto-suggestion or autohypnosis which not only may allow the adept to influence his dreaming (cf. Tart 1972(a):143) but presumably affects other subliminal and unconscious levels in himself. Aisaga often used healing spells to treat himself; and both he and other people who taught me spells told me to use the spells on myself. The use of the spell in self-healing—for example, the headache spell just described—is very similar to modern psychotherapeutic techniques in which the subject induces a relaxed, trance-like state in himself and then recites a simple, repetitive formula incorporating certain suggestions or instructions relating to bodily states (cf. 'autogenic' training, Luthe 1972; Meares' self-help therapy, 1982: Singer 1974).

My argument that the spell provides a means of relaying messages to the dream consciousness is, of course, in accord with what the adept asserts is its function—to send out his soul, or activate the entity that dreams.

The medicines and powerful objects employed by the adept, like the spell, represent symbolic statements of the intention of the rite—but in a concrete, physical form. For example, in order to prepare a love potion, he would collect various flowers, fruits and leaves from plants which are revealed in the esoteric versions of myths to be the transformed genitals or sexual secretions of the myth heroes. The adept explains that the spell and the medicines 'help' each other and that both act to 'send out the soul'. Collecting the necessary substances, a task that may take many weeks, serves to focus the sorcerer's conscious attention over a period of time on the intention of the ritual. The combination of the substances—it is only when they are placed together that they become really potent—is a symbolic statement in concrete form made by the sorcerer to himself, and then reiterated in the verbal formula of the spell.

In addition to the adept's use of autosuggestion, there are also indications that his rituals may involve the communication of subliminal suggestions to his victims. The use of strong-smelling medicines is particularly characteristic of love magic and sorcery. The smell is said to startle the subject which causes his or her soul to leave the body— any minor shock or sudden surprise is said to act in this way. When he moves silently through the dark to attack a victim, the sorcerer wears on his body a distinctive combination of strong-smelling leaves; his victim is unable to see him in the dark but as he draws near will suddenly smell his presence. Aisaga related that he had in the past affected many people in this manner, though his intention had not been to hurt them; they had by chance been near him when he passed unseen through the bush at the back of the village on his way elsewhere. Merely by smelling the charms he wore, he claimed, their souls were jolted from their bodies and they became ill.

As Gell (1977) observes, perfume, or smell, is an admirable symbol of the pervasive yet intangible influence of magical power. I found that charms I was given to induce dreaming succeeded not in making me dream, but in bothering me all night because of their pungent scent. This suggests that some medicines may well act as subliminal cues for the dreamer, as sense stimuli which would not be strong enough to keep the dreamer awake (as it did me), but would be present and perceptible to the sleeper (for we know that though the conscious mind is in abeyance the sleeper is still responsive to some sense stimuli), a reminder to the dream consciousness from the waking consciousness.

The adept's employment of subliminal suggestion is also evident in the fact that though performed in the utmost secrecy, most forms of magic require some covert contact between the practitioner and the subject, or at least the existence of some indirect link. The sorcerer's lethal charm must be carried to the victim and placed in close proximity to him. Though this may be done by an intermediary, he is very much aware of the dangerous object he is carrying, to the extent that he is said to feel it get heavier and heavier at every step until he feels he will be unable to carry it further, or else the side of his body on which he carries the bag containing the charm begins to burn like fire. The carrier is probably communicating, unconsciously, all kinds of subliminal cues to the victim. Suggestion of this kind is even clearer in the case of the sorcerer startling his victim in the dark, swiftly exposing the charm to his gaze and then disappearing into the night before the victim has time to register consciously what is happening. Believing that he has merely slipped or stumbled in the dark, he pays no further attention to the incident. Presumably, however, the encounter has been registered subliminally. Though it is well known that conscious suggestion alone can have powerful psychological results, subliminal suggestion is particularly effective because it places the idea at a level of awareness below the threshold of rational, critical thought processes.

It should be made clear that I am not arguing that the suggestion itself is sufficient to strike down a victim or inspire a woman with passion; but rather that through such subtle means the sorcerer is able to activate unconscious processes in others, playing upon their hidden fears and desires in a way which gives powerful emotional support to his claims, and his belief, that he can control their souls.

The final point I wish to raise is the importance of body substance—literally 'body dirt' (*faga ofuga*)—in the rituals. While both medicines and spells are said to activate the soul, the bodily relics of the spirits (particularly the myth heroes and the water spirits) are considered the most potent and dangerous means to achieve this end. Any contact with these relics, or the mere sight of them, is said to jolt the soul out of the body. In the case of someone not suitably prepared, this is highly injurious but for the adept, who has properly prepared himself, this separation of body and soul is exactly what he desires. Why the relics have this effect is not explained—it is simply their nature to do so and the reality of their effect on the soul is demonstrated in the adept's dreams. After handling the powerful relics his dream consciousness *is* activated. Sometimes the myth heroes and water spirits are encountered in recognizable form in his dreams; at other times their presence is revealed symbolically. The relics thus both activate the dream-self of the sorcerer and attract the dream-images of the spirits to him.

Bodily substances, or personal leavings, of the victim (faeces, urine, sweat, blood, sexual secretions—also termed *faga ofuga*) are also used in various techniques of love magic and death-dealing magic. The intention is to attract the soul of the victim to the adept. This is explained by pointing out that the soul is able to leave the body during sleep but is eventually attracted back to it; it may also be attracted to some separated part of the substance of its body. The demonstrable proof of this, as far as the adept is concerned, is that possession of personal leavings brings the dream-image of the victim to him.

Why should the symbol of body dirt have such a potent effect on the dream consciousness of the sorcerer? In contrast to the symbolism of magic, Mekeo social symbolism places little emphasis on bodily substances—unlike the heavy cultural elaboration of such symbolic substances as semen, blood, milk and the like observed in many Highland cultures (Berndt 1962; Reay 1959; Strathern 1972; Wagner 1967; Gell 1975; Herdt 1981). This, of course, raises a multitude of complex issues and I can do no more here than make a few concluding comments.

Social anthropologists are properly suspicious of inter-pretations based on the assumption that there are 'universal' symbols. Cultural symbolism takes as its motifs whatever is at hand—in the natural world, in the existing cultural environment, in the structures of the human body—and each culture uses this material in its own way. The symbols

I am concerned with here, however, are of a different order. They are not public but esoteric symbols—culturally defined and transmitted it is true, but used by the individual to activate unconscious processes (and probably originally arising from the unconscious). Such symbols are likely to be less rooted in the specifically cultural constructions of the intellect, but grounded more in basic emotional and physiological processes. Body symbols are by no means confined to Mekeo or even Melanesian sorcery; they are characteristic of magic everywhere. Moreover, as we are aware from psychoanalytic studies, basic bodily processes—particularly those associated with sexuality and defecation—are recurring themes and motifs of the unconscious in our own culture.

Examined from these various perspectives, the psychological effects of spell and substance become apparent.[11] In addition to the more obvious use of sensory deprivation, the sorcerer, I have argued, employs autosuggestion and subliminal suggestion to effect other levels of awareness in himself and his victims. The spell, the substances and the relics constitute a mutually reinforcing series of symbols (verbal/cognitive; concrete/sensory/emotional) that provides the link of communication between conscious intent and other states of awareness for the adept.

Conclusion

The more the shaman and the sorcerer are compared, the more the differences in their roles appear to be primarily ones of emphasis. Both gain vivid experiential conviction of the reality of the spirit realm in ritually induced states of altered consciousness. Both believe that these states reveal knowledge of the unseen and the future, and enable the exercise of occult powers. The 'classic' shaman is a master of souls; he rescues the soul from the spirit world and returns it, thus curing his patient (Eliade 1972:215 ff). The Mekeo sorcerer injures his victim by attacking and imprisoning his soul. Yet, at the same time, the shaman may be suspected of black magic (Eliade 1972:184; Herdt 1977); and the Mekeo sorcerer, in those circumstances when he treats patients not injured by his own magic, acts exactly as the shaman does—he rescues the soul of the sick person through the journey of his own soul to the spirit world in a ritually induced dream. He no less than the shaman might be described as a 'master of souls'.

While the Mekeo sorcerer employs only quietistic states, in particular dreams, the shaman, too, may employ quietistic states (Peters and Price-Williams 1980, 1983). Herdt (1977) argues that the shaman's dreams have tended to be overlooked by anthropologists. The real difference seems to be not so much in the states employed, as in the communication of them. The shaman shares his experience with an audience (though the degree of dramatization varies greatly); the sorcerer carefully guards his privileged access to the other realm. It is this that makes the one so readily available to ethnographic observation and description, and the other so much more elusive.

The vocation of the shaman is characteristically revealed following some severe affliction or psychic trauma (Eliade 1972:33ff). The Mekeo sorcerer assumes his position on the basis of birth and inheritance. In some societies, however, as Herdt (1977) points out, shamanic training is stressed, and those who are the offspring of shamans will expect to follow their parents' calling. The emphasis is on instruction in esoteric knowledge rather than innate abilities in the case of the Mekeo adept; but once his training begins, he must demonstrate his capacity to handle the situation. Many are the cautionary tales of sorcerers who go mad or die of injuries they inflict on their own souls. If the shaman's role grows out of controlling a spontaneous psychosis, then the Mekeo sorcerer might be said to gain his by deliberately seeking to induce psychosis. Both shaman and sorcerer, however, require some training, and both must be able to keep control of their contacts with non-ordinary reality.[12]

The real divergence in the two roles seems to lie in the emphasis placed on the destructive or creative nature of the ritual powers invoked. The shaman may be suspected of controlling dangerous powers, but it is his restorative role as healer that is stressed by the community. The Mekeo sorcerer, for all his other magical knowledge, is regarded by his community primarily as the vehicle of punitive force. Why this should be so cannot be entered into here.

My intention has been to illustrate, with reference to the Mekeo, that the Melanesian sorcerer is not necessarily merely a mystical assassin (as he has so often been regarded in the literature) but is in some communities the pre-eminent ritual expert—a mediator of sacred power[13] whose experiences of an inner reality are directly comparable with the shaman. The ethnographic evidence, discussed in the final chapter of this volume, indicates that the sorcerer as a 'master of terrible power' (Nachman 1981) figures prominently in many other Melanesian societies. The variations in this role and the extent of its distribution across different societies are yet to be determined. How it relates to the Melanesian shamans reported by Herdt (1977), Wagner (1972) and others; to the division of powers between 'black' and 'white shamans' reported for the Kapauku of West Irian (Pospisil 1965); to Mitchell's (1977) 'shaman-witch'; to other ritual specializations found in Melanesia; to the geographical distribution of the shamanistic complex identified by Eliade—are some of the many questions which must await future field and comparative studies.

NOTES

[1] Occasionally sorcery and shamanism are treated as synonymous terms. I use the term 'sorcerer', as it has usually been used in the Melanesian literature, to mean specifically: one who is attributed with ritual (as distinct from intrinsic) powers to destroy other human beings by magical means.

[2] I would like to thank Professor Peter Lawrence for his detailed and insightful comments on an earlier version of this paper. The responsibility for the conclusions presented here is, of course, my own. Fieldwork among the Mekeo was supported by the Australian National University in 1969, and 1970-71; by the Humanities Research Grants Fund, La Trobe University, in 1978-79 and 1983; and by the Australian Research Grants Council in 1980-81 and 1981-82.

[3] This paper represents a departure from my previous writings on the Mekeo since it reflects an 'insider's' view of sorcery and magic. During my 1980-81 fieldwork I discovered that the information I had previously collected on the topic—even that provided by knowledgeable adepts—represented only what the layman

understood, or what was deemed suitable for him to understand. My previous statements thus should be qualified as representing a layman's view. The strictest secrecy and deliberate deception preserve the exclusiveness of the adept's knowledge. My responsibility, as my instructors always forcefully impressed upon me, is to protect that exclusiveness. Consequently, I have been careful not to include any specific information which could be actually put to use; though I outline general principles not known to the layman, the actual formulas, the 'real' knowledge (*ikifa gomega*— lit. the 'root of the knowledge') is not revealed—*onina mo la ifa*, I have said only the tip.

4 While Hau'ofa stresses the 'sacredness' of the central space of the village, I would rather stress the safeness and domesticity of this space—it is both womb and tomb and thus in essence 'female'.

5 A whole paper could be devoted to describing the range and complexity of magical knowledge. Each area of magic encompasses many (probably dozens) of discrete, unrelated units of knowledge which have in common only the circumstance that they are all concerned with the one area of activity—hunting, war, love, etc. There exists a vast body of esoteric knowledge, the full extent of which is impossible to determine; for no one individual, no matter how much he knows, can encompass it all. It consists not of a single body of knowledge to which all adepts are privy, but of innumerable separate traditions which are the personal property of particular individuals.

6 I follow Evans-Pritchard (1937) in using the term 'medicine' to refer to the substances used by the magician.

7 Malinowski's (1961:428–63) arguments about the primacy of the power of the magical word clearly needs some modification in this case. The significance of the use of medicine as the minimal effective magical act in Mekeo magic would also suggest a revision of the contrast between the relative importance of spell and medicine in African and Melanesian magic (Evans-Pritchard 1967).

8 The word *lalau(ga)* is usually translated into English as 'soul', but this is a far from satisfactory rendition of the concept. The *lalauga* is the entity that is activated in dreaming; it is thus more accurately referred to as the dream-self or dream consciousness. At the same time, the *lalauga* can also leave the body when it is not asleep. This suggests a level of consciousness which is coterminous with waking consciousness, but which is known to waking consciousness only through dreams and similar states. In this respect, it is close to the psychoanalytic concept of the 'unconscious'.

9 From the adept's point of view, of course, such states reveal not an 'inner' reality but manifestations of the normally unseen world of spirit forces.

[10] Cohen (1979:225-8) points out the many difficulties in establishing a clear correlation between dream content and external attempts to influence it. I cannot pretend to have overcome these problems in what was, in any case, not an experimental situation. I can say only that recall of dreaming was increased following the recitation of spells (and the handling of ritual objects) and that the adept was skilful in relating the remembered dream content to the aim of the ritual.

[11] In this paper I have confined myself to the psychological effects produced by the rituals. To my knowledge, no hallucinogenic substances are deliberately employed by the adept. Even betel nut, which is commonly used by all adults, is forbidden in the most rigorous ritual regime because it produces saliva, and thus is antithetical to the aim of achieving heat and dryness. It is possible that in the most extreme forms of ritual preparation, which I have not witnessed, the adept may consume mind-altering substances but if so, they are not described in these terms. Though there is much talk among laymen about the sorcerer's employment of poison, the adept dismisses poison as a physical means of attack which anyone can use. His potions require many possibly poisonous ingredients but they are never administered to the victim—they are used symbolically to injure the victim's soul. It is, however, true that the adept's interest in magical medicines gives him a wide knowledge of the properties of many different plants, many of which are used medicinally.

[12] It is not my intention to suggest that shamanism or sorcery should be explained in terms of psychopathology. I would agree with Peters and Price-Williams (1980:406-7) and others who argue that states regarded as pathological by Western standards are not necessarily to be so judged in other cultures. The shaman and the sorcerer encourage a dialogue with an inner reality, but they must control this interaction and be able to relate their experiences to external reality. The individual who loses control and is overwhelmed by his inner reality becomes, in the eyes of his own community, mad or sick.

[13] The view that the sorcerer is one who mediates sacred power—of the ancestors and spirits—is stressed in two reports prepared by Papua New Guinean lawyers for the Law Reform Commission (Narikobi 1978; Kaputin 1978).

REFERENCES

Berndt, R. M.
    1962   *Excess and Restraint: Social Control Among a New Guinea Mountain People*. Chicago: Chicago University Press.

Blacker, C.
  1975   *The Catalpa Bow: A Study of Shamanistic Practices in Japan*. London: George Allen & Unwin.

Cohen, D. B.
  1979   *Sleep and Dreaming: Origins, Nature and Functions*. Oxford: Pergamon Press.

Deikman, A. J.
  1972   'Deautomatization and the Mystic Experience'. In Tart (1972:25-46).

Eliade, M.
  1972   *Shamanism: Archaic Techniques of Ecstasy*. Princeton: Princeton University Press.

Elkin, A. P.
  1977   *Aboriginal Men of High Degree*. St Lucia: University of Queensland Press.

Evans-Pritchard, E. E.
  1937   *Witchcraft, Oracles and Magic Among the Azande*. Oxford: Clarendon Press.
  1967   'The Morphology and Function of Magic: A Comparative Study of Trobriand and Zande Ritual and Spells'. In J. Middleton (ed.): *Magic, Witchcraft and Curing*. New York: Natural History Press:1-22.

Fortune, R. F.
  1963   *Sorcerers of Dobu: The Social Anthropology of the Dobu Islanders of the Western Pacific*. New York: Dutton.

Fromm, E.
  1951   *The Forgotten Language: An Introduction to the Understanding of Dreams, Fairy Tales, and Myths*. New York: Rinehart.

Gell, A.
  1975   *Metamorphosis of the Cassowaries: Umeda Society, Language and Ritual*. London: The Athlone Press.
  1977   'Magic, Perfume, Dream'. In I. Lewis (ed.): *Symbolism and Sentiment*. London, New York: Academic Press: 25-38.

Hau'ofa, E.
  1981   *Mekeo: Inequality and Ambivalence in a Village Society*. Canberra: Australian National University Press.

Herdt, G. H.
  1977   'The Shaman's "Calling" among the Sambia of New Guinea'. *Journal de la Société des Océanistes* 33:153-67.
  1981   *Guardians of the Flutes: Idioms of Masculinity*. New York: McGraw-Hill.

Kaputin, W.
  1978   'Sorcery Among the Tolai People'. *Law Reform Com-*

mission of Papua New Guinea, Occasional Paper No. 8.
Port Moresby: Law Reform Commission.

Lawrence, P. and Meggitt, M. J.
1965 Introduction to P. Lawrence and M. Meggitt (eds): *Gods, Ghosts and Men in Melanesia: Some Religions of Australian New Guinea and the New Hebrides.* Melbourne: Oxford University Press:1-26.

Ludwig, A. M.
1972 'Altered States of Consciousness'. In Tart (1972:11–24).

Luthe, W.
1972 'Autogenic Training: Method, Research and Application in Medicine'. In Tart (1972:316-26).

Malinowski, B.
1961 *Argonauts of the Western Pacific: An Account of Native Enterprise and Adventure in the Archipelagoes of Melanesian New Guinea.* New York: Dutton.

1974 'Baloma: Spirits of the Dead'. In B. Malinowski: *Magic, Science and Religion and Other Essays.* London: Souvenir Press: 149-274.

Meares, A.
1982 *Relief Without Drugs: The Self-Management of Tension, Anxiety and Pain.* London: Fontana Books.

Mitchell, W. E.
1977 'Sorcellerie Chamanique: "Sanguma" Chez Les Lujere du Cours Supérior de Sépik.' *Journal de la Société des Océanistes* 33:179-89.

Nachman, S.
1981 '*Buai*: Expressions of Sorcery in the Dance'. *Social Analysis* 8:42-57.

Narikobi, B.
1978 'Sorcery among the East Sepiks'. *Law Reform Commission of Papua New Guinea, Occasional Paper No. 10.* Port Moresby: Government Printer.

Peters, L. G. and Price-Williams, D.
1980 'Towards an Experiential Analysis of Shamanism'. *American Ethnologist* 7: 397-418.

1983 'A Phenomenological Overview of Trance'. *Transcultural Psychiatric Research Review* 20:5-39.

Pospisil, L.
1965 *The Kapauku Papuans of West New Guinea.* New York: Holt, Rinehart and Winston.

Reay, M.
1959 *The Kuma: Freedom and Conformity in the New Guinea Highlands.* Carlton: Melbourne University Press.

Seligman, C. G.
1910 *The Melanesians of British New Guinea.* Cambridge: Cambridge University Press.

Singer, J. L.
1974   *Imagery and Daydream Methods in Psychotherapy and Behaviour Modification*. New York: Academic Press.
Stephen, M.
1974   Continuity and Change in Mekeo Society, 1890–1971. Ph.D. thesis, Australian National University.
1979   'Dreams of Change: The Innovative Role of Altered States of Consciousness in Traditional Melanesian Religion'. *Oceania* 50:3-22.
1982   "Dreaming is Another Power": The Social Significance of Dreams among the Mekeo of Papua New Guinea'. *Oceania* 53:106-22.
Strathern, A.
1972   *One Father, One Blood: Descent and Group Structure Among the Melpa People*. London: Tavistock.
Tart, C. T.
1972 (ed.) *Altered States of Consciousness*. New York: Doubleday.
1972(a) 'Toward the Experimental Control of Dreaming: A Review of the Literature'. In Tart (1972:134-46).
Wagner, R.
1967   *The Curse of Souw: Principles of Daribi Clan Definition and Alliance in New Guinea*. Chicago: University of Chicago Press.
1972   *Habu: The Innovation of Meaning in Daribi Religion*. Chicago: University of Chicago Press.
Weiner, A. B.
1977   *Women of Value, Men of Renown: New Perspectives in Trobriand Exchange*. St. Lucia: University of Queensland Press.
Williams, F. E.
1940   *Drama of Orokolo: The Social and Ceremonial life of the Elema*. Oxford: Clarendon Press.

PART TWO:

Sorcery, Witchcraft and Warfare

3

The Magico-Religious Foundations of New Guinea Highlands Warfare

MARIE REAY

The Kuma and their congeners live in the south-eastern part of the Mid-Wahgi area in the Jiwaka division of Western Highlands province, mostly on the ridges and in the foothills of the Kubor Range. The township of Minj is located in the heart of Kumaland. Every man belongs to a series of nesting segmentary groups to which women are attached as daughters and wives. Primary identification is with the named localized patriclan, which is the exogamous, ceremonial, land-holding and war-making unit and forms the local community. The traditional groups of widest span are the phratries. These were once phratry-tribes, territorially and politically unified, but irreconcilable enmities between various clans divided and scattered them, and all they shared when the white men arrived was a tradition of common descent.

Sorcery and Warfare

Kuma Warfare

The Kuma practised two kinds of organized warfare depending on who the enemy happened to be. The deadliest enemies were those I call 'traditional enemies'. Kuma themselves designated these by saying that they fought them wearing Raggiana plumes. The usual battle headdress was a modest fountain of cassowary plumes fixed to a netted skull cap which could be turned inside out to cover the feathers for storage or transport. But at certain points in warfare with traditional enemies, warriors donned the flamboyant Raggiana in anticipation of their triumph. A clan triumphed over its traditional enemies when it managed to displace them from their territory and out of the immediate area. There are groups in the Jimi, Gumine and elsewhere that were driven from Minj. The enmities were 'traditional' in the sense that they were irreconcilable over the generations. Up to 1965 there was strict avoidance between traditional enemies. But there was also warfare with temporary enemies, clans with which there had been and eventually would again be intermarriage. This kind of warfare accounted for few deaths, just enough to make even the score of dead, whereas in one war between traditional enemies there were more than a hundred dead on the winning side alone. A neutral clan arranged peace-making ceremonies between temporary enemies. These included importantly an exchange of pigs and culminated in an exchange of women. Various authors have contrasted Highlands societies like Kuma, in which marriage is with friendly clans, with those like Central Enga, in which men assert that they marry those they fight. But it is difficult to imagine marriages being arranged (except by capture) between clans that are currently at war, and the exchange of women as the ultimate transaction in Kuma peace-making between temporary enemies suggests that the contrast is a spurious one. There is also Brown's (1964:355) reminder that the collectivity of affines is not coterminous with the group that goes to war, so that affines are friends but the groups to which they belong are actual or potential enemies.

Sacred Guardianship and the Propitiation of Spirits
Meggitt's book on Enga warfare, *Blood is Their Argument* (1977), makes only two or three cursory references in passing to 'spirits'. This is consistent with the common designation of Papua New Guinea Highlanders as 'pragmatic'. That designation is apt but, as I hope to show in this essay,

to one people of the Papua New Guinea Highlands the pragmatic thing to do was to get the spirits on side, particularly in dealings with the clan's enemies. Durkheim would have found the Kuma to be a convincing illustration of some of his arguments. Living clansmen were the congregation that worshipped the group identity they shared with dead clansmen they had known and those agnatic ancestors who were no longer remembered as individuals. They were the congregation, too, that performed rites to secure the collaboration of the individual agnatic ghosts and the collective ancestral spirit. Simply being born into the clan did not automatically award the right to seek the co-operation of the spirits in matters affecting the entire clan. Persons who were credited with an inborn ability to 'see ghosts' (*kibe kanem*) communicated with particular ghosts on purely individual matters, not on behalf of the clan. Their talent was not prestigious and did not earn them high status. The war sorcerers, however, commanded respect. They continually demonstrated their determination to uphold the faith. They were solid citizens who obeyed the rules of social life laid down by the ancestors and had reason to hope that their actions would be pleasing to them. They always performed creditably as warriors.

If we follow the sixth edition of *Notes and Queries on Anthropology* (Royal Anthropological Institute 1951:187) in affirming that 'In magic no appeal is made to the spirits', then the Kuma had no war magic to speak of at all. But such a narrow view of magic makes it difficult to describe magico-religious practices in which magic and religion are inextricably intertwined.

Each subclan had a group war magic house known as the 'taboo house' (*nggar ma-bil*) or 'war magic house' (*obo-kundje nggar*). It was taboo to all but the war sorcerers, a very select body of men. The taboo house was used, however, towards the end of the pig festival for secret meetings of the men responsible for building the little house of the Red Spirit Bolim, not all of whom were war sorcerers. One of the sorcerers was the hereditary guardian or, as I prefer to say, curator of the taboo house. The positions of war sorcerers were not explicitly hereditary: each could teach his skills to any close agnate who seemed to be suitable. But, almost without exception, they taught their skills to their own sons. An eminent war sorcerer, generally one in each subclan, had in addition his own personal taboo house, which he shared with another (often the only other) sorcerer in his subclan.

The overt purpose of the taboo houses was the storage of weapons. Young men, who were greatly oppressed by their elders, had no hope of rebelling against their authority so long as the control of the weapons of war lay firmly in the hands of the older men, as the older men themselves explicitly recognized (Reay, in press). To help themselves to the weapons that were stored in the taboo houses invited death at the hands of the agnatic ghosts. These weapons included not only those in contemporary use but also some with distinctive historical significance: perhaps a spear captured from a fallen enemy or one that had accounted for many enemy lives in ancient battles. Other trophies might include a feather from the headdress or shield of an enemy warrior; a cartridge or scrap of manufactured material as relic of a former cargo cult; or human bones which Nopnop Tol, president of the Minj Native Local Government Council, was to insist that the missionaries should be led to believe were cassowary bones. There were also relics of clansmen whose death in warfare had not yet been avenged.

Both individual and group taboo houses contained at least one prehistoric mortar in which to mix potions containing the blood of pigs or fowls, and other prehistoric artefacts such as mortars, pestles, clubs and figurines. These were all *kibe yap*, 'things of the spirits'. Prehistorians are of the opinion that the ancestors of the present-day Highlanders must have created these objects, but the Kuma admit only that the ancestors may well have created them once they themselves were spirits. The figurines, in particular, were conceived to be the guardians of particular places— the central meeting places, ceremonial grounds, or burial grounds of the clan. The guardian or curator of the group taboo house had an especial duty to preserve these figurines, for so long as these artefacts survived intact clansmen felt that their group was safe from its enemies; if they were accidentally lost or smashed, the clan might be doomed to extinction.

Aufenanger's (1959) otherwise excellent account of 'war-magic' gives a misleading impression of the naïvety of the men concerned. He states that in addressing various objects as ancestors they actually believed the objects to be the ancestors. This is a distortion: they believed the objects to be connected with the various spirits and connected so closely that it was possible to address the spirits through them. Confusingly for an observer, when the clan was at war and sometimes at other times the sorcerers addressed objects associated with recent ghosts as ancestral spirits. To avenge the ghosts was pleasing to the collective ancestral spirits, so the sorcerers could address them, they said, through the objects associated with the ghosts. But, further, this practice accentuated the secrecy of the rites. The transposition generated an atmosphere of secrecy and occurred in other contexts besides war sorcery. Towards the end of the pig festival there was a rite to nullify the evil brought inadvertently inside the clan's territory by visitors with their gifts of firewood and sweet potato and greens. During this rite the actors referred to the evil of bush spirits, *kibe kangi*, but this substituted for the evil of the spirits of the dead. Further, when a select band of men were erecting the prefabricated dwelling of the Red Spirit they addressed each other only by their fathers' names. This practice gave the men's secret activity a solemnity it might not otherwise have sustained: the role of building the spirit house was hereditary and the builders were truly re-enacting what they (i.e., their fathers) had done before.

In addition to practising war sorcery inside the taboo houses with the aim of extinguishing the enemy and avenging every unavenged death, the war sorcerers had the duty of setting up and maintaining objects they and everyone else called 'wooden bones' or 'bones of the tree', *ont embĕgĕm*. I have referred to these somewhat loosely as 'sorcery traps' (Reay 1967). War sorcerers placed them upright in holes into which they had poured sacrificial pigs' blood and added special bark and other materials credited with magical power. Bones were in this context conceived of as the long bones of the human body, the spine and the bones of the arms and legs, and bone was agnation as contrasted with blood, which came from the mother. Thus the *ont embĕgĕm* were a line of agnation represented in wood (*ont*). The war sorcerers stood an *ont embĕgĕm* on either side of every entrance to the clan territory through which friendly visitors would pass. The 'bones' were tree-fern stumps of the kind used for decorating the roofs of taboo houses.[1] The 'bones' constituted a protection for the clan (the 'tree'). A traditional enemy entering to finally defeat and scatter the group avoided the entrances guarded by them. And when the defeated group had abandoned its territory, no other group could occupy land protected in this way, for all who passed between the 'bones', apart from members of the local community and their invited guests, were in danger of being struck dead by the agnatic ghosts. The protection remained until the 'bones' rotted through inattention and an absent clan's failure to renew them. After that any clan that needed land could treat the abandoned territory as waste and vacant and settle there. But the new settlers still had to risk the fatal consequences of ritual performed not only by the war sorcerers but also by ordinary warriors who might plant certain trees in a compost of pigs' or fowls' blood with a curse upon particular enemy groups. These were men whose close agnates (often actual brothers) had been killed by those groups. A tree here would repel the advances of one clan, and a tree there an intrusion by another. Only a clan that had never warred with the original group could settle with complete confidence upon its abandoned land even after the 'bones' had rotted.

The Kuma purchased war magic from particular clans in the North Wahgi area living close to the Jimi River region. Perhaps surprisingly—among a people whose greatest aesthetic achievement, apart from the art of bodily decoration, was oratory—the spells were the least important elements of war magic. A simple command to the ghosts or to the materials informed by the ghosts or ancestral spirits sufficed. The distinctive part of the war magic, the part men thought they paid for, was the magical technique itself, confirmed by the sacrifice of pigs or fowls that accompanied every rite. One valued technique was to smoke a cigar backwards, inhaling the smoke directly from the lighted end; another was to coat the entire face and body with charcoal instead of, for example, allowing the closest agnates of an unavenged clansman to cover themselves with mourning clay and dab blotches of charcoal about their persons. War magic was dearly bought. One technique was known as *Kobun amp*, 'Jimi River woman', because the clan had to yield nubile brides in addition to the usual complement of pigs and other valuables. But the purchase of war magic exceeded the resources of the official war sorcerers; and other men who were wealthy or had useful relatives and trading partners in the relevant groups contributed to the purchase and became practitioners of the war magic outside the group taboo houses. They could participate, for example, in smearing the bodies of warriors going into battle with charcoal and other preparations, but they did this in the yard surrounding the taboo house and were not admitted to the house itself. Thus war magic became the business of the war sorcerers and also a few other men who were specialists in particular forms of war magic. Similarly the close agnates of men who had been killed in war and not yet avenged, might specialize in the war magic directed against the murderers of their fathers or brothers, again outside the group taboo houses.

In 1979 slain warriors became fresh ghosts demanding vengeance and their mortuary rites now entailed the sacrifice of pigs—on the battlefield itself when this was feasible—to their ghosts. Each man who killed an enemy had to sacrifice a fowl to gain the protection of the spirits from the wrathful interference of his victim's ghost. *Tol yĕbĕ* is the generic term for all the rites of revenge and protection from revenge. *Tol* is an abbreviation of *tolmon*, 'paint'. Unless another colour is specified, or is indicated by the context, it usually signifies 'red paint'. Red ochre and reddish clay are daubed on the actors or on objects in some of the rites. But 'red paint' is also a metaphor for human blood, for example in joking converse about menstrual blood. Kuma admit no conscious derivation for *yĕbĕ*, but it seems to me to derive from *yibe* meaning 'nowadays', giving *tol yĕbĕ* the sense of 'blood nowadays' or perhaps 'blood in consideration of what has gone before'. The Kuma to whom I offered this as a possible interpretation told me that this was what the term meant but that it also referred to blood that was spilt right now. That is, *tol yĕbĕ* are rites concerning blood that has been spilt in a current war; and in fact the rites of *tol yĕbĕ* only take place while the clan is actively engaged in war. The most spectacular rite takes place on a hillside, within sight of the enemy, with the aim of intimidating by a splendid exhibition of shields and vocal messages projected so that the enemy will hear.

An unritualized precaution against damage from the ghost of the slain was to dismember him, reducing an incipient ghost to a scatteration of minor bush demons. This was to protect the killer from the ghost of his victim. It also deprived the victim's clan of one of its aggressive ghosts and, later, one element of its benevolent and protective ancestral spirit. This rationale for chopping up the bodies of fallen enemies justifies, in modern warfare, the demonstration of what seems to an observer to be an unrestrained excess of violence. A practice not unique to the Highlands, but revived in 1980 by the Kuma's eastern neighbours, was to decapitate an important man well known in the neighbourhood and display his head on a pole within sight of the enemy as a challenge to try to recapture it and risk decimation.

Deaths in warfare against temporary enemies accounted for most of the fire taboos that prohibited the use of the same fire for any purpose other than keeping warm. Two men who were *dop ma-bil* (fire taboo) could eat portions of the same raw food cooked on different fires. They could sleep around the same fire but neither could light a smoke or torch from it in case the other should also do so. The sons and brothers of a war victim were *dop ma-bil* to any men who had taken wives from the killer's clan, and the killer himself was *dop ma-bil* to men who had taken wives from the victim's clan. Women were allegedly the passive carriers of the sorcery practised by their natal clans to satisfy a vengeful ghost or claim more victims for him. War sorcerers observed an even more demanding fire taboo: they could share a fire only with each other. A wife of such a man could cook his food for him but had to cook her own food on a different fire. A war sorcerer could only kill pigs for himself and other war sorcerers to eat, so other men had to kill his pigs for him at the end of the pig festival.

War Magic and War Sorcery
Some opaqueness has entered the literature on sorcery and witchcraft through a tendency to lump the two together,

often under the head of either sorcery or witchcraft. Middleton and Winter (1963:3), recognizing the dilemma posed by the absence of a term that embraces the two, suggest 'wizardry', but this word has inappropriate connotations for many people ranging from the performance of minor miracles to a male witch.[2] A difficulty in classifying sorcery and witchcraft as sub-types of something more general is that what they have in common—being supernatural means of bringing about death or sickness in human beings—does not apply to the full range of sorcery reported from Melanesia, which includes bringing about crop failure or damage to other property. Death-dealing sorcery in Papua New Guinea takes at least four different forms: 'A', the use of materials associated with the victim (e.g., the widely reported personal leavings); 'B', the use of magical or magico-religious objects (e.g., the Huli's Toro sorcery, Glasse 1965:41–2); 'C', sympathetic magic (the Huli's Hambu sorcery, ibid.:42); and 'D', cursing (widely reported). Anthropologists do not usually class cursing as a form of sorcery; yet as a ritual procedure invoking ghosts or deities, often with an invariant spell, it is certainly a supernatural means of bringing about death in human beings. Cursing in Kuma is only marginally relevant to warfare and I shall not be discussing it here.

What I have termed (Reay 1959:145–51 and later writings) 'war sorcery' and 'war magic' belong respectively in the first and second categories of death-dealing sorcery distinguished above.[3] The definitive difference between the two is that a 'war sorcerer' manipulated objects associated with his intended victim ('A' sorcery), whereas the 'war magician' manipulated objects associated with the supernatural powers he was invoking to do his work ('B' sorcery). Another difference lies in the identity of the persons against whom the magic was directed. 'B' sorcerers sought to destroy the enemy collectively and also to kill any one enemy warrior in revenge for each war death, since one clansman was equivalent to any other for this purpose. 'A' sorcerers also sought to destroy the enemy collectively; but they directed their sorcery at the enemy individually. They sent their sons surreptitiously into the enemy territory at night to steal articles in some way associated with men of the enemy clan. They also gave the lads sharpened slivers of bamboo and other traps treated with snake venom to set up on paths where the enemy would walk.

The 'A' sorcerer also directed his skills against the few men in the enemy clan who were personally known to him, namely eminent fight leaders and 'A' sorcerers. But bigmen never resided on the fringes of a clan settlement. The sorcerer would not risk the extreme threat to the lives of his sons by sending them to search for appropriate sorcery materials about the bigman's own house, even if they had any means of locating it without detection. He had to rely on other sources for these materials.

Warfare and Witchcraft

Witchcraft and the Death of a Bigman

A bigman was impervious to the war magic his enemies directed against his clan collectively: he could only be destroyed by powerful sorcery directed specifically against himself. And yet the only persons who had access to objects associated with him which the enemy could use as sorcery materials were the members of his own clan-community. 'Real' (normal) people would not conceivably collaborate with the enemy; therefore any persons who did so must necessarily be *agamp kum*, 'witchcraft people'. I define witchcraft as an innate psychic or supernatural power and propensity to harm others. This definition follows Evans-Pritchard's (1937:387) distinction between sorcery and witchcraft. It accommodates Azande witchcraft but omits elements that are specific to Azande. People describe *kum* (witchcraft) as a creature which, if it were visible, would look like the foetus of a tree kangaroo. Allegedly it lodges in a person's abdomen and takes over the host's will, impelling him or her to harbour unnatural thoughts and perform unnatural actions. When a bigman died the hunt was on for the witches in his own community who had stolen sorcery materials and passed them on to the enemy.

It seems to me to be most unlikely that witches would have an opportunity to deliver sorcery materials into the hands of the enemy. Up to mid-1965 there was a strict prohibition on any association with the traditional enemy apart from specifically hostile encounters. It would have been difficult, if not impossible, for a witch to seek out a member of the enemy clan without his own clansmen observing and apprehending him. Further, with no communication between the two clans, it is mysterious that the enemy could identify him as a collaborator, instead of simply recognizing him as a member of a hostile clan to be killed on sight. And yet many witches, when challenged, gladly confessed to delivering sorcery materials to the enemy.

It is necessary to distinguish between individual witches, who were tried singly, and the covens of witches found to be associated with the death of bigmen. An individual witch was not ordinarily convicted of having caused a particular death. He was convicted of being a witch and then recent deaths were attributed to him. Accusations of witchcraft were commonplace in the course of heated disputes, particularly when domestic quarrels were aired publicly, but many of these were promptly dismissed. The Kuma found certain African peoples I told them about naïve in acting upon accusations made by persons who had some kind of grudge against the accused. In Kumaland dislike prompted observable and often institutionalized avoidance; grudges were impossible to conceal; and people placed no credence on accusations that were obviously based on ill will. But sometimes things people said during a dispute or at any other public gathering suggested that they, or some persons they referred to, were behaving in a witch-like manner. Witch-like behaviour included going off for solitary walks, eating voraciously on public occasions, eating meat without sharing it, staring wildly, neglecting personal attire, and appearing in company with an unidentified cat or dog. A man or woman exhibiting any of these symptoms was apt to be accused of witchcraft. The person who made the accusation, however, was usually a disinterested bystander drawing an inference from the evidence as it mounted.

An accused person who denied being a witch, and did not falter in this denial throughout a strenuous cross-examination, might be given the benefit of the doubt for the time being but be kept under observation, and perhaps be tried again later on the basis of more recent evidence. But many witches readily confessed the first time they were

publicly accused. They appeared to welcome being recognized as witches and they boasted of their unnatural
deeds. These deeds were culturally standardized: robbing
graveyards to satisfy the cannibalistic appetites of their *kum*;
stealing piglets to provide the *kum* with more meat; inducing
illness in animals and humans; sending their animal
familiars into other people's houses to steal food; and
turning themselves into cats or dogs for this purpose. Any
witch whose confession omitted some of these items was
cross-examined and he or she readily admitted to these as
well, giving an elaborate and detailed account of one or
more.

'Real people' (*agamp wei*, here non-witches) were wary
of those suspected of witchcraft and desperately afraid of
convicted and confessed witches. They believed that a witch
could kill simply by staring at a person. They believed, too,
that the *kum* inhabiting the body of a witch could arbitrarily
leave and leap into the body of a bystander, forcing him or
her to perform the actions attributed to witches. Some of
the persons accused of witchcraft admitted that they had
indeed harboured a *kum* but that it had left them, and this
led to an urgent investigation to determine who the new
host might be. When a person was publicly accused the
people standing near by drew away from him and when a
witch confessed they jumped aside. He stood alone, the
object of spectators' undivided attention and seemingly
revelling in his power to make people afraid. The confession
was the witch's finest hour.

Identifying the witches responsible for the death of a
bigman was the task of his clansmen, but responsibility for
searching them out lay with his matrikin or other extra-
clan relatives. It was their duty to consult with the eminent
war sorcerers of the enemy clan and obtain from them the
sorcery materials they had used together with a list or description of the witches who had allegedly handed them
over. After the death of a bigman in 1955 I was present at
the deliberations of his matrikin. The sorcery materials
were not objectively identifiable as belonging to the dead
man, but they were clearly identifiable with activities that
had been engaging him (and many of his clansmen as well)
at the time he became ill. The matrikin associated the sorcery

materials with the dead bigman on the say-so of his enemies. The descriptions the enemies had given of the alleged witches were vague and the matrikin had to decide to whom they applied. Thus a dead bigman's extra-clan relatives could wield considerable power over his clansmen at this time.

A dead bigman's traditional enemies were eager to reduce his clan further by the death and exile of many witches. His extra-clan relatives, too, saw the need for numerous witches as a measure of the importance of the bigman and proof of their assiduousness. During the mourning rites they watched for any unusual behaviour on the part of the dead man's clanspeople and kept their ears open for any mention of such deviations. The list of suspects they reported to the prominent men of the dead man's clan comprised up to twenty names, including those that fitted the enemies' description and some the extra-clan relatives had added. The extra-clan relatives did not attend the witchcraft inquiry at which the suspects were examined: they simply delivered the sorcery materials and the accompanying information. Witchcraft inquiries, and also the trials of individual persons suspected of witchcraft, were open to all clanspeople but private to the community. I was not able to attend the 1955 inquiry because the men who would have accompanied me were prohibited from witnessing such an event in a different community. I would certainly have observed an inquiry held in 1961 if I had been in Minj at the time. My most detailed information on witchcraft inquiries concerns these events of 1955 and 1961. A few of the many witchcraft trials I witnessed in 1963–65 were of persons who had been investigated but neither convicted nor exonerated in 1961. People were assuming that if it could be proved that these persons were witches, they had certainly been implicated in the bigman's death, as well as subsequent deaths. What I am calling an 'inquiry' appears to have been conducted as a series of witchcraft trials.

It is possible to reconstruct from several retrospective accounts much of what happened in the witchcraft inquiry held in 1961 after the death of the bigman El at the end of the preceding year.[4] El's community was small for this area numbering just over three hundred, but the clan had a formidable reputation through having routed its much more numerous traditional enemy a few years before the suppression of warfare with the help of powerful allies secured largely by El himself. He was the orator of his subclan, ceremonial leader of his clan, and an astute marriage broker. He was a renowned war sorcerer and fight leader with a reputation for devising unusual and successful military tactics. His clansmen attributed their success to a freshly acquired complex of war magic, but many people outside the clan said that El was responsible. His counterpart in the enemy clan was Pi, who was also an eminent war sorcerer and fight leader. In December 1960 some young people who had attended a courting ceremony in the homeland of a mutually related group reported that Pi had composed a song which had been sung during this ceremony. The song was a thinly veiled statement that El was about to die. He was suffering from a cold at this time but, after hearing the song attributed to Pi, he became very ill and depressed, his stomach swelled up, and he died within two or three weeks.

It was inconceivable to El's clansmen that Pi could have brought about his death without the co-operation of witches in their own clan-community. Immediately after the death, suspicion fell upon one of El's widows but she was soon exonerated, probably on account of her assiduous and convincing demonstrations of sorrow. This sequence of events is customary after the death of a polygynist. El's matrikin came to mourn but lived some distance away and did not have a detailed knowledge of the dead man's community. The persons who took responsibility for finding the witches were the sons of El's close female agnates living near by. They produced a scrap of netted material allegedly taken from the pubic apron El had been wearing and bearing his semen. They gave this to some of the remaining leaders of El's clan (I am not certain which ones), named sixteen alleged witches, and departed. The public inquiry then began.

One of the first witches to be positively identified was Pende, a woman who resided by marriage with a different subclan from that of the dead leader. She readily confessed to being a witch. She described orgies of feasting on human flesh in company with others, whom she named, and nightly dances in company with yet others during which her body was illumined with coloured lights. The persons she named as fellow witches, with one exception, belonged to subclans other than that of her husband, and this was a recurring pattern in the accounts of a medley of accusations and counter-accusations. Pende boasted that she had stolen the scrap of cloth from El's pubic apron when she had visited him the day before he died and one of his wives, who had been looking after him, had left her alone with him for a moment. She had given it, she said, to a member of Pi's clan she had met at Minj. It would have been practically impossible in 1960 for a woman to meet one of her husband's enemies at Minj without other women observing her and reporting her movements to their menfolk. There is also an anomaly in respect of time. El had heard Pi's song and gone into a decline some weeks before Pende's alleged theft; and he was already dying before she was supposed to have stolen the materials to cause his death. My informants, however, found her confession credible and placed importance on the testimony of the bigman's close agnates that they had seen her visit him the day before he died. The widow—who had initially been suspected of witchcraft— confirmed that she had been looking after El that day and she had indeed gone outside leaving Pende alone very briefly with the sick man.

Accusations flew backwards and forwards between the different subclans until more than half the men, women and children of the clan-community had been accused. No children were convicted: individual children had been executed as witches, but they were not usually included in the covens held responsible for the deaths of bigmen. Some of the adults were immediately exonerated when the accusations seemed irresponsible or spiteful. Many who denied being witches were cross-examined closely concerning their activities during the time leading up to El's death. Three men and the wife of one of them remained under suspicion despite their denials, but were not actually convicted. Five men and five women were found to be witches. Only one of these, a man, persistently denied being a witch and having anything to do with El's death. Two men and three women began by protesting their innocence but confessed under duress. Two men and two women confessed freely and boasted of being implicated in El's death. As well as the woman Pende, these included a man in a different sub-subclan of El's own subclan, his wife, and a man, Yap, in the subclan of Pende's husband.

Pende named Yap as the leader (*yi kumna*, 'first man') and bigman (*yi og-ma*) of the coven (*dugum*, a corporate group) of witches responsible for the death. The other confessed witches, including Yap himself, confirmed this. He boasted of having convened mass meetings of the coven in a particular public place where they were invisible to ordinary people. Here he gave the witches their instructions, celebrated the death of El with a distribution of human meat, and demonstrated his power in various ways. He proclaimed that he was king (*sic*) of the witches and that his followers included many whom ordinary people could not see: these were people, bush demons, domestic animals, and creatures of the wild. All obeyed when he told them to dance, lie down on the ground, perform impossible athletic feats, and call their names as if for a census. Pende said that she had stolen the scrap of material at Yap's instigation. The other confessed witches confirmed that he had ordered the grave robbing and feasting and dancing.

It was too late in 1961 for El's clansmen to chase the convicted witches to a high bank and topple them into the rushing river with spears and arrows sticking in them, as they once used to dispose of witches (cf. Bergmann 1971, 4:18,24,27). The man who had refused to confess and the men and women who had confessed under duress went to stay with relatives elsewhere but eventually returned, their *kum* having allegedly left them. Three of the witches who confessed freely and boastingly were permanently exiled, but clansmen have made periodic attempts to induce the son of the married pair, now a grown man, to return. The man Yap, however, was not exiled but died soon after he had confessed. I have no evidence that he was surreptitiously killed but I strongly suspect that that may have happened. In 1980, after missionary activity had put a stop to public witchcraft trials and inquiries, two men whom most people judged to be witches coincidentally died. In the rural Highlands no inquest is performed on a village death.

Witchcraft belief bestowed blame upon persons who flouted the norms of everyday social living—upon, for example, persons who craved solitude or were inordinately greedy. But it was also an elaborate metaphor for revolutionary sentiment, for betrayal of the clan. Witches were expendable in the clan's fight for survival. A mystery to which I have so far found no solution is why the death of an important man from enemy sorcery should involve the work of so many witches when the clan would need as many warriors as it could muster for further engagements with the enemy. Individual witches were more often men than women; those convicted of complicity in the death of a bigman usually included two or three females and a majority of males. The inquiry after El's death was unusual in convicting as many as five females and unusual, also, in convicting as many females as males. At that time a militantly evangelical mission was trying to raise the status of women. The missionaries' propaganda (e.g., that the wife-mother was the most important person in the home, and that a man who was married to a Christian woman could not take a second wife) gave many women the confidence to be more assertive. The men, to whom this message was extremely threatening, would have been in a mood to find many female witches and there would have been women whose behaviour they judged to be aberrant.

A witchcraft inquiry not only deprived the clan of some potential warriors. Identifying an individual witch was an occasion for the clan to unite in getting rid of a non-conformist and boost the solidarity of its members. But a witchcraft inquiry after the death of a bigman divided the community into unstable factions, and must have undermined the corporate solidarity it required to fight the enemy successfully. It took some time to identify the witches with certainty. Weeks and even months could go by when the clan was paralysed by its inability to differentiate witches from non-witches. People must have gone about their everyday tasks with profound unease. All suspects had to be investigated, including all persons the confessed witches named as members of their coven. It would seem that such an inquiry would only be possible at times when the clan was relatively safe from its enemies, who might otherwise strike when it was in disarray. But the enemy was evidently content to wait for the clan to reduce its own strength by executing and perhaps banishing its witches, balancing the chance of a few deaths in battle against the certainty of some executions. Further, the death of a bigman important enough to warrant a witchcraft inquiry was a rare occurrence in any particular group. In thirty-one years (1953–83) El's was the only such death in his clan, though four minor bigmen died during that time.

The Problem of Witch Confessions

Africanists have assumed that because some of the actions attributed to witches (such as flying or changing into animals) are objectively impossible, the proper study of witchcraft is the accuser and his motives for imputing witchcraft to persons who are actually innocent of it. Thus anthropology has portrayed the witch as the victim of witchcraft accusations, reversing indigenous perceptions of the sick and the dead as victims of witchcraft. As Douglas (1970b:xxxiv) remarks, 'This has made it hard for us to interpret witchcraft confessions'.

Kuma witchcraft was not entirely imaginary. Rather, it was a blend of fact, culturally standardized fantasy, and ambiguity between the two. The *kum* creature that was supposed to inhabit the bodies of witches was, of course, an artefact of imagination and comes within the scope of supernatural belief. It is my own belief that this fantasy was empirically based, since individual witches were often persons who had the least legitimate access to pork and were desperately hungry for it (cf. Steadman 1975). The behaviour that identified people as witches was consistent with their being chronically under-nourished (Reay 1976: 14). There is a certain ambiguity, however, in people's reports that they have disturbed witches feasting on cuts of human flesh. On the one hand they could easily have observed them consuming the flesh of a stolen pig; on the other hand a few have been caught disturbing graves. Witches did exhibit behaviour that was asocial and suffi- ciently deviant to be judged anti-social. Reported sightings of spirit familiars, always at night, could easily be optical illusions. But reported sightings of the witch in the form of such an animal must have been motivated by a desire to identify the person concerned as a witch. Personal malice could conceivably prompt such a report; but it always concerned someone who was already accused or at least generally suspected of being a witch. In the atmosphere of a witchcraft inquiry or an individual trial, people were eager to discover the witches and put an end to the anxiety and suspicion that clouded their lives. And people who had no intention of confessing to be witches were particularly anxious for others to identify them as witch-finders rather than as witches.

I have suggested elsewhere (Reay 1976) that the ideology of witchcraft may sometimes cloak the surreptitious practice of poisoning. Snake venom found an honoured place in war magic delivered where it could affect the enemy, but men deliberately suppressed the idea of poisoning within the clan-community for fear women should find it attractive and kill off their menfolk in an effort to gain control of the clan's resources. But in recent years Kuma have had increasing contact with the people of Mt Hagen, among whom the practice of poisoning is overt. Kuma men have turned now to overt allegations of poisoning, always against women married into their own subclan. Men cooking meat are under close observation, they say, whereas women cooking vegetable foods have ample opportunity to slip in an extra ingredient, particularly when the use of pungent herbs can hide the smell of poison. When a man accuses a woman of using poison to make him ill, however, he does not also accuse her of witchcraft: witches have no need to use poison.

By 1970 public witchcraft trials and accusations had ceased but people still suspected others of being witches. One man attracted the suspicion of many members of his community on account of his fiercely burning stare and most people avoided him. Seeing him often alone confirmed their suspicions but no one accused him. Ten years later a band of close agnates in another subclan alleged in gossip that they had found him standing against a house one night and that he had run away and changed into a dog. In 1982 a minor bigman died and his son recalled this story but told me that the remaining leaders were intimidated by the mission and refused his request to hold a public meeting to investigate. When a clansman was killed in the war of 1979–80 there was no suggestion that this suspected witch might have been responsible for the death, for all his extra-clan relatives were in allied groups. Instead, two men, who were related through women to the current enemy, fell under suspicion of being witches and of having betrayed the young warrior.

Structural considerations play a part, though not necessarily a decisive one, in identifying the witches responsible for enabling a bigman to succumb to enemy sorcery. I have mentioned the propensity of confessed witches to name persons in other subclans as their collaborators. Among the convicted witches at any witchcraft inquiry there was likely to be a man whose mother's clan was a traditional enemy of the dead bigman's mother's clan; there was also likely to be a woman who had herself come from such a clan.

In a community where nearly all of the men have spent their entire lives personal history is common knowledge. Further, Kuma make no distinction between confidentiality, privacy and secrecy. To seek privacy is to be secretive. It was the duty of the older men and of some individuals among them to meet in private and keep secrets they could not share with others, but what they were doing was for the good of the clan as they themselves determined. The only motives people recognized for wandering off alone for longer than it took to defecate were adultery and witchcraft, so it was in a person's interests to have a companion wherever he or she went. Thus information was available concerning the precise movements of everybody in the community. Witches were supposed to operate by night but Pende, a confessed witch, visited El in daylight when several witnesses saw her. I surmise that her purpose in doing so was to advertise her contact with the dying leader, be convicted of witchcraft, and get sent home to her brothers. She had never become reconciled to an uncongenial marriage which forced her to live among strangers far from her own kinsfolk. Witchcraft offered a way out now, though she would have been speedily executed as a confessed witch before the banning of homicide. I am suggesting that Pende's confession (and perhaps that of some others) was a dramatic performance. But the life of the Kuma entailed many dramatic performances and it is sometimes impossible to distinguish polished method acting from the spontaneous expression of emotion (Reay 1982:167–8). Certainly confessed witches were playing set roles already scripted by the culture: they all confessed to the same improbable and impossible activities. They did so with burning conviction and appeared to revel in the power they had over their audience. In a case I have described elsewhere (Reay 1968:199–200) a self-confessed female witch took advantage of the Australian administration's disbelief in witchcraft to terrorize her whole community.

Kuma Witchcraft in Comparative Perspective

Lawrence and Meggitt (1965) seem not to include witchcraft in Melanesian religion, since they do not mention it. Glasse's (1965:36) brief account of female witches in Huli is the only systematic description of witchcraft beliefs in their volume. Salisbury (1965:58) and Bulmer (1965:156) carelessly dub simple forms of sorcery 'simple witchcraft' and 'a mild form of witchcraft' respectively. According to Burridge (1965:230ff), the Tangu term *ranguma* covers witch, sorcerer, and a host of other unusual and non-conforming men; but he discusses the *ranguma* as a composite of them all and it is impossible to distinguish what he interprets as witchcraft belief and behaviour. With such vagueness in the literature it is impossible to generalize about the distribution of witchcraft beliefs in Papua New Guinea.

Douglas's (1970b:xxvi-xxvii) classification of witch beliefs is ambiguous since she does not use 'sorcery' and 'witchcraft' as technical terms but lumps them together under 'witchcraft', as in lay English usage. Thus she is able, confusingly, to ignore the witchcraft beliefs Forge reports for Eastern Abelam in the same volume and discuss Eastern Abelam sorcery as 'witchcraft' instead.[5] But it may be illuminating to apply Douglas's classification, or parts of it, to witch beliefs actually reported as such from Papua New Guinea. The witch as a person outside the community appears in Hewa (Steadman 1975:116) and Kaluli (Schieffelin 1977:16,41) and sometimes among the Etoro

(Kelly 1977:79). But Etoro witches and their victims are residents of the same community in 72 per cent of the recorded cases (ibid.:79). Kelly (ibid.:85) says explicitly that the Etoro witch is 'normally' a co-resident but does not examine whether the remaining 28 per cent of cases may have been exceptional in some other way. Schieffelin (1977:41) reports that accusations between longhouse communities in Kaluli are 'not infrequent' but does not explicitly rule out the possibility of accusers and accused being co-resident. Douglas's judgement that one would associate the belief in the witch as an outsider with a very small-scale and simple form of organization fits the Hewa very well, though her other proposed correlates of this belief do not apply.

According to Douglas (1970b:xxvii), the witch as an internal enemy appears with 'a slightly more complex form of social organization in which two or more factions are embraced within the community'. Of course there are often factions, led by rival bigmen or would-be bigmen, in a Papua New Guinea community and these may be relevant to accusations of witchcraft (Reay 1976). But it may be useful to consider more formal divisions—different clans in the multi-carpellary parishes of the Sepik, and parallel segments in Highlands segmentary systems—as equivalents of Douglas's 'factions'. Eastern Abelam believe that the witches operate within the village (Forge 1970:268). Both Central Chimbu (Bergmann 1971,4:18; Brown 1977:27) and Kuma witches are supposed to afflict only members of their own community. 'To do harm the *kumo* must live in their midst' (Bergmann 1971,4:32). In Kuma witchcraft accusations are bandied backwards and forwards between subclans during the inquiry into the death of a bigman, giving the subclans (and in 1961 even some of the sub-subclans) the appearance of factions. The examples Douglas gives of sub-types of 'the witch as internal enemy' are mutually exclusive but the sub-types themselves (the witch as a member of a rival faction, as a dangerous deviant, and as an internal enemy with outside liaisons) are not incompatible with each other and may occur in the same belief system, as the Kuma material demonstrates.

Chimbu presents a variant on the third 'sub-type'. Instead of the witch collaborating with outsiders, the witch-finders hire outsiders to kill the witch on their behalf (Bergmann 1971,4:29. See also Aufenanger 1965). This could not happen among the Kuma: an outsider who killed any clansman invited retaliation against his own group, and the clan had to rid itself of its own impediment. There were many similarities between the two systems and also some important differences. According to Bergmann (1971,1:207) the Chimbu accepted that some deaths came about naturally without any supernatural intervention and there was a kind of divination procedure to discover whether or not a witch was involved. For the Kuma only aged persons died naturally when their time (*kunum*) was ended. When Chimbu diagnosed witchcraft they surreptitiously set out to identify the witch. Among the Kuma there was only a witchcraft inquiry after the death of a bigman. When an ordinary clansman died the ghost responsible for his death had to be identified and placated; later the death was attributed also to anyone who was found to be a witch. A curious difference between the two systems is that the Chimbu did not accuse the witch to his face and he only knew, if he knew at all, that he was suspected when it became obvious that he was going to be killed. Kuma witchcraft accusations were part of the ordinary converse of disputation, and suspicions that had any element of credibility led to public accusation and trial.

Kuma have adopted and adapted from Chimbu many elements including a massive religious complex. I have found no tradition that they imported witchcraft belief from Chimbu, but if they did the substitution of open accusation and public trial for secret plotting and surprise killing would be plausible. This could also explain why the Kuma diagnosed multiple causes of death (Reay 1975:155). The action of ghosts may well have been sufficient to account for the death of an ordinary clansman in the absence of witch belief. Assuming that witchcraft was imported from Chimbu, war sorcery that depended upon the belief that witches stole the sorcery materials would not have been possible previously, and the deaths of bigmen may have been simply attributed to war magic. This could explain why the one term, *obo-kundje*, serves for war magic and both kinds of war sorcery. The failure to co-ordinate the timing of Pi's courting song, El's death, and Pende's theft could be symptomatic of an imported witch belief not fully adapted to indigenous beliefs. But the timing of these events could not be co-ordinated without a recognition that El was already dying when Pende visited him. In Kuma ideology to reveal foreknowledge of a death is tantamount to admitting that one has done something to cause it. The suggestion that the Kuma may have adopted and adapted Chimbu witchcraft is based largely on speculation. But the Chimbu and Kuma terms for witchcraft, *kumo* and *kum* respectively, are plainly variants of the one word. And when Kuma adopt cultural items from Chimbu they usually abbreviate the Chimbu terms for them, so that *kanana* becomes *kanant* and *gerua* becomes *geru*.[6]

Witchcraft and Group Structure

Several Africanist scholars have suggested that witchcraft belief occurs in societies that are relatively small as tribal societies go; but it is something that the greatly fragmented Hewa have in common with the populous, highly organized corporate groups of Chimbu and Kuma, so the correlates of witchcraft belief should be present in all three societies. They all have a dispersed pattern of residence, rather than living in nucleated villages. But elsewhere in Papua New Guinea there are people living in nucleated villages who also believe in witchcraft, though they rarely make accusations. And in the Highlands there are people living in scattered farmsteads who do not seem to harbour a belief in witchcraft. Nevertheless it may be possible to correlate witchcraft belief with certain aspects of social structure of their entailments.

Chimbu, Kuma, Melpa, and Central Enga are organized in very similar systems of segmentary groups, but the societies with witches (Chimbu and Kuma) have what Strathern (1969) has called 'systems of production' as distinct from 'systems of finance', the cyclical *moka/tee* exchange systems found in Melpa and Central Enga in the absence of witches. The Chimbu or Kuma clan, producing its own pigs to kill at the climax of its pig festival, engages in preparatory rituals that are private to it for a year or more beforehand, whereas Melpa and Enga bigmen are engaged mostly in dealings with men of other clans. The isolation of the Kuma clan-communities, even when their territories were adjoining or only a couple of kilometres apart, was so intense before the introduction of locally owned and operated motor vehicles in 1964, that they might have been living in islands separated by many nautical miles. Each community was inward-looking and outward-fearing to an extent that would not have been possible in Melpa and Enga. In this respect the Kuma community (and perhaps also that of Chimbu), though it could comprise many hundreds of people, had more in common with the Etoro longhouse and the isolated household of the Hewa. It would appear, then, that a community that is inward-looking and outward-fearing is apt to espouse witchcraft beliefs.[7] (I am not certain, however, how we might define the degree of social isolation that makes a community 'inward-looking'.) Whether the witch is identified as an outsider or as an enemy within may then be a question of scale, the Hewa community being a handful of close kinsfolk who cannot be spared, and the Kuma community consisting of at least a hundred, and more often some hundreds of men, including many who are only assumed to be agnatically related, together with their wives and children. Molima witchcraft appears to support this proposition. Molima attribute witch attacks to outsiders, not to the witches of the victims' own community. The community here is very small, perhaps no more than twenty-two persons. Chowning (personal communication) cautions that Molima communities were much larger in the period before European contact; but it seems improbable that they would have been comparable in size to the sharply segmentary societies of the Highlands. The association I am suggesting between inside or outside witches and relative scale applies only where the identification of witches as outsiders or co-residents is clear-cut and invariable. Where there is a mix, as in Etoro, I assume that other factors are operating.

A contradiction in Kuma between the ideology of witchcraft and the fate of exiled witches identifies it emphatically as an internal concern of the local community. When a person convicted as a witch went to live with his extra-clan relatives or her own agnates they did not expect him or her to continue to behave as a witch. (For a similar belief in Central Chimbu, see Brown 1977:27–8). When the clansmen of an exiled male witch needed to swell their numbers—for their pig festival or a military engagement or, in 1964–65, in an attempt to get independent representation on the council—they might decide that his *kum* would have left him by then and take him back, if necessary by force. Resident male non-agnates were not usually found to be witches, and I never heard one accused. In 1982 I met a man who had been exiled as a witch about three years earlier and was now residing with extra-clan relatives. He impressed me as being somewhat unbalanced in the particular sense of being over-elated, foolish, and irresponsible. This man did continue some of his witch-like behaviour. He wandered about aimlessly and was sometimes observed standing up against the outside of people's houses in the listening attitude of a witch. But his relatives assured me that he was harmless and they treated him as something of a joke. They said that these witch-like traits were habits he had picked up when he had harboured a *kum*.[8] They also commented that although he was not very intelligent, he was a daring and fearless bowman. At that time they were expecting to resume a war that had been interrupted by a truce to accommodate the national election. Thus one clan's witch could be another clan's warrior. But if his own clan became involved in the war it is certain that his agnates would have taken him back and required him to demonstrate his fearlessness on their behalf.

Epstein's (1967:153) insightful observation concerning witches in Mysore is relevant here: 'By blaming misfortune on the supernatural powers of a certain woman the victim is not really accusing the person of the witch, but rather the evil spirit which operates within her' and this enables victim and accused to continue their relationship. Similarly, by blaming the *kum* rather than the person who harboured it, and by positing that it could leave him, Kuma were able to take back exiled witches when they had need of them. Up to the 1940s, however, they executed those witches whose acquisition of *kum* they judged to be the onset of an incurable impairment.

Deviants and Scapegoats

In 1534 the Holy Maid of Kent, a 'strange dreamer' and prophet, said that the Devil had flown about her chamber in the likeness of a bird (Maple 1962:36–7). Anne Armstrong of Northumberland hallucinated that she went to a witches' Sabbath in the form of a horse and underwent extraordinary adventures there (ibid.:103–4). Some of the persons executed as witches in England were eccentric and delusional. There were eccentrics, too, among those the Kuma found to be witches. Those who freely confessed during the witchcraft trials of the 1960s seemed to genuinely believe that they harboured *kum* and had done all the things that witches are supposed to do. They appeared to be dissociated and it was not possible to communicate with them satisfactorily after they had confessed. Assuming the identity of a witch was not, of course, the only form of dissociation available. But it was sometimes possible to predict accurately that certain persons would be found to be witches. These were people who were beginning to reject the sociable, extroverted, and energetic Kuma lifestyle. Lethargy, gloomy dispositions, carelessness of dress, chronic absentmindedness, and breaches of social conventions marked them off from others. A few seemed to me to be behaving somewhat ostentatiously as witches were supposed to behave, and I believe they may easily have been 'psyching' themselves into becoming witches. If that impression is correct it raises the question, which is implicit in the free and boastful confessions, of what such persons had to gain from being identified as witches when the penalty for witchcraft was often death. If they wished for death there were other ways of attaining it. It is clear that severe depression preceded the euphoria of the confession and it is possible that they wished for death but were not able to inflict it on themselves.[9]

I suggest that what people had to gain from being identified as witches was social recognition, brief and unfavourable though it might be. Confessed male witches were usually either rubbishmen or men who just escaped this label. They were the non-achievers, the rubbishmen not bothering to compete and the marginal men trying hard against situational and personal odds but having little success. Women who were still childless after several years of marriage were sitting ducks for witchcraft accusations but were not necessarily convicted. Few women received adequate social recognition, so it may seem strange that more men than women were convicted as witches. But men considered other men to be more dangerous than women. They held such a low opinion of women that, recognizing that their wives as outsiders might wish to do them harm, they tended to dismiss the possibility that women would be generally capable of doing so. A man, on the other hand, had to be dedicated to serving the clan and if he slackened in this purpose he could easily be suspected of betrayal, which was so unnatural that it identified him as a witch. These comments are not, of course, intended to explain why male witches predominate in so much of the high country of Papua New Guinea, in contrast to the predominantly female witches of the Gururumba, and the exclusively female witches of the Massim area.

When I left Minj in 1955 I could not have predicted that Yap, Pende, Pu and Poro would confess to being witches six years later. Yap was only marginally a 'real man' but not quite a rubbishman. He had a nervous manner but led a conventional life. Pende became an obvious target for witchcraft accusations as a woman who had been married for ten years without having children; but she had not seemed a likely person to be convicted, let alone to confess. Pu was a 'real man' and had distinguished himself as a warrior but by 1955, aged about fifty, he was frail with a chronic chest ailment. Poro, his wife, was a very quiet woman, a good worker and a dutiful wife and mother. She had come from Pu's mother's clan, which was a long-standing enemy of El's mother's clan. Pu and Poro had been suspected of witchcraft in 1957–58 but had been exonerated.

Suspicion of witchcraft can lead to witch-like behaviour and eventually to a witchcraft trial and confession. When a person suspects someone of being a witch he avoids him to guard against the *kum* jumping into his own body. When many people suspect a person of being a witch there is wholesale avoidance and he is ostracized. He is then forced to exhibit a solitary habit, a certain indication that he is a witch. Aware that he is being treated as a witch, he may well wonder whether he may be one.

Tsi and his wife, who were interrogated as suspected witches in the inquiry after El's death, maintained throughout that they were not witches and they were neither definitely convicted nor cleared of suspicion. When I spoke to Tsi two years later he was very confused about what had happened during the inquiry but volunteered the opinion (which he did not elaborate) that either he or his wife must be a witch: he did not think they both were.

In 1980 Kidzi, a 'real man' who had always been somewhat eccentric, became recognized as a witch. He had been unusually individualistic, often putting his own interests before those of his group. Now his clan was at war with a group in which he had non-agnatic relatives and, instead of avoiding them as he should have done, he met them constantly. Kidzi's clansmen saw a real danger of his betraying them so they ostracized him. Essentially a sociable man, he took to wandering about aimlessly. Soon he was going into the bush and emerging wild-eyed and muttering. Witch trials were no longer held, but there were rumours that he had been dancing *dad* (the witches' dance)[10] and changed himself into animals at night. No one seemed surprised when he died suddenly of an unexplained illness, allegedly killed by the ghost of a clansman who had been a victim of the present enemy thirty-three years earlier.

Lewis (1970:293–309) compares the victim of witchcraft with the victim of spirit possession but does not compare the latter with the witch her/himself. Witchcraft in Kuma, however, appears to be a kind of spirit possession. The *kum* itself is not known as a spirit (*kibe*), for this term refers only to the spirits of once living humans and creatures that are supposed to be humanoid. The most prominent of these, the *kibe kangi*, bush demons, are transparent and Lilliputian and are often described as having gross deformities but are basically human in outline. Cartoon figures in newspapers were always immediately identified as representations of *kibe kangi*.[11] Possession by various kinds of *kibe* (including now the Holy Spirit) does occur, though hit-and-run attacks by ghosts and bush demons are more frequent.[12]

The *kum*, though only a thing (*yap*), is described as an invisible creature with appetites, volition, and the ability to issue compelling and easily understood commands in the host's own language. Creatures of the wild are *kamp*, and

the tree kangaroo whose foetus the *kum* allegedly resembles
is *kamp tinya*. Since the *kum* is located in the witch's abdomen
a clear inference, unacknowledged by most of the Kuma,
is that the man or woman who confesses to being a witch is
pregnant with (and perhaps to) a creature of the wild. It is,
however, a static pregnancy which cannot be terminated
without killing the witch and never reaches full term. The
association with wildlife makes the witch appear to have
regressed to the long time past, when men had allegedly
not yet settled in stable communities and adopted rules for
living together, but were themselves uncontrollable
creatures of the wild. The few children I have heard of
being convicted and executed as witches had shown themselves to be incapable of being socialized; for example, a
boy of nine or ten, who should have been training as a
warrior and loyal group member in battles between subclan
gangs, had not learned to distinguish between the subclans
and arbitrarily attacked his own close agnates. The
association with wildlife also accentuates the unnaturalness
of the witch's proclivities. The Kuma ideology of witchcraft
gathers all the varieties of what is considered unnatural into
a single concept: a man suspected of being a traitor has to
be a witch and a person of solitary habit invites rumours of
cannibalism, coloured lights, and changing into animals.[13]

Occasionally a confessed witch would boast that he or
she was going to breed a whole clan of witches and wipe out
the clan of the accusers (the male witch's own clan). I heard
this threat uttered by two female witches in 1963–65 and
it was attributed to the man Yap, acknowledged and self-
styled leader of the coven held responsible for El's death.
The two women had been childless long enough to be certain
that some kind of supernatural intervention would be
needed for them to reproduce themselves. The threat could
conceivably be connected with the idea of pregnancy suggested above. Breeding a whole clan of witches mirrors the
ambition of successful men to establish in their own lifetimes
lineages which their descendants will form into independent clans. But Kuma witchcraft, unlike that of Azande
and even Central Chimbu (Bergmann 1971,4:27), was not
supposed to be hereditary, though occasionally a confessed
witch was the child of a confessed witch.

It is difficult to make a general statement that Kuma witches are or are not scapegoats, *pace* Patterson (1974–75:145) who asserts that they are. Some of the witches of the coven have a clear motive for injuring the bigman: they are jealous of his power, wealth, and renown, as others recognize, and they rejoice in his death. Some have a further motive in that their extra-clan relatives are hostile to his. These are not scapegoats in Patterson's sense. But the Kuma's own model of the witch is the freely confessed individual witch motivated only by his *kum*. He is jealous of all ordinary men and not necessarily of anybody in particular. He has a motive for *killing* objectified and located in his abdomen, but the selection of particular victims is not purposive. Persons discovered to be witches after the death of a bigman are linked directly with his death; and when a warrior is killed a man who has relatives in the clan that is the temporary enemy is likely to be suspected of betraying his group and found to be a witch, since he is assumed to have reason for helping the enemy. But an individual found to be a witch at other times has blame for recent deaths tacked on to his guilt as an afterthought. The deaths may have occurred months or several years beforehand and there need not even be firm consensus on precisely which deaths. We might call that a kind of retrospective scapegoating both in Patterson's sense and also in the more usual sense of allocating blame arbitrarily or for reasons unconnected with the offence. But the connection between witch and victim, so clear in the witchcraft inquiry and assumed by Patterson and many of the Africanists to be an indispensable part of witchcraft accusations, was quite tenuous and rarely even mentioned in the individual witchcraft trial. The Kuma witch did not necessarily have to have a victim at all. What was important was the threat the witch represented to the whole community. The conviction of a witch was meant to guard against future deaths, not simply to allocate blame for deaths that had already occurred.

Conclusion

When Marwick (1967:125) identified sorcery as a means of formulating tense relationships, he was referring to dyadic relationships between individuals, as most writers on African witchcraft and sorcery have done. But in the New Guinea Highlands the group is a most important character in any social drama. Kuma sorcery is enacted between groups. And within the community the witch is ranged not against any individual but against the group. Up to the onslaught of the missionaries the Kuma clan acted as one; men obeyed their leaders and women were required to obey their husbands. Such unity was essential for the survival of the group before the suppression of warfare. The practice of war sorcery, together with the distinctive taboo houses and *ont embĕgĕm*, contributed to that unity. And witchcraft belief helped to preserve it by removing persons who appeared in their several ways to be capable of injuring the group.

When a warrior was killed his clansmen had an extensive repertoire of supernatural forces to blame for the spears and arrows finding their mark. He had been in continual danger from the ghosts of unavenged clansmen, enemy 'B' sorcery, and, if he lived on the outer edges of the clan settlement, 'A' sorcery too. He might inadvertently offend the ghost of a close agnate, and an angry ghost could direct the enemy's missiles towards him. There was the ever-present danger of witches. I found no deaths attributed to the witch's evil eye, which was allegedly lethal; but many people displayed fear of suspected witches who fixed others with a burning stare. Another source of supernatural danger was the invisible host of bush demons (*kibe kangi*), who made their presence known by striking a person and causing him or her to fall ill or die. Warfare exacerbated the danger of bush demons since dismembering a foe was believed to release a bevy of these instead of a ghost.

Mair (1969:180) suggests that witchcraft belief 'was not as terrible in its consequences as is often supposed'. She stresses the '*everyday* quality' (her emphasis) of witchcraft to the African and says that when people are 'going about their daily affairs, they are not obsessed with fears of something monstrous; they simply recognize that they have enemies and had better look out for them. So do we'. This is a salutary reminder that an account of witchcraft or sorcery can easily give an impression, which may be completely false, that the people who hold these beliefs are in perpetual dread of what may befall them. The idea of witchcraft occurred to the Kuma when a bigman died and also when they saw someone behaving strangely. Otherwise the topic did not arise except for an occasional mention of it in story or in gossip. It assumed overriding prominence for the duration of a witchcraft trial, but this was over in a few days at the most and was often concluded in a single day. The witchcraft inquiry after the death of a bigman could drag on for months, but it appears to have been conducted for only a few days at a time as more witches came seriously under suspicion. In the intervals between, people trod cautiously but were certainly not disabled by terror.

From 1964 onward, Highlanders and their national politicians gained a reputation for being conservative. They wanted to delay political independence until their grandsons were grown men. There was a valid reason for the men of Minj to take this view. They saw a recurrence of tribal warfare as inevitable unless independence could be delayed until no one remained who had known a slain warrior as a living person and was therefore obliged to avenge his death. This obligation was not simply an urge to exact retaliation: it was a sacred duty to which men felt themselves driven by their clansmen's ghosts. Thus Kuma warfare is not the secular affair that warfare in Enga appears to be from Meggitt's account. It is the ultimate expression of a ghost religion in which fear of the ghosts enforces the values for which the ancestral spirits, as collective spirit, stand. And it is embedded in a belief system in which magic, sorcerers, witches and bush demons help and hinder the clan and its enemies.

NOTES

[1] O'Hanlon (1983:325) mentions a related but certainly not identical institution in North Wahgi known by the same name in its Banz dialect form. The North Wahgi version uses a single stake of durable wood instead of the paired treefern stumps. At Minj these objects, themselves perishable as individual clansmen are, nevertheless stood for the clan conceived as a hardwood tree, its lastingness assured by continual renewal and ritual attention.

[2] Parrinder (1963:139) considers that the wizard 'is best regarded as the practitioner of conscious magic, whether through spells or known poison'.

[3] Patterson (1974-75:229) has suggested that what I described as sorcery might be more accurately termed war magic. She refers to pp. 149-51 of my 1959 book but has evidently not noticed the passages on pp. 145-6 describing the use of enemy property as sorcery materials.

[4] The names used here are fictitious and are words that are not likely to occur as personal names.

[5] Forge's distinction between sorcery and witchcraft (1970:267-8) is emically sound and agrees with that drawn by Evans-Pritchard.

[6] The Chimbu term *kumo* appears further east among the Siane, who use it to designate both a simple form of sorcery and also some beneficial magic including a cure for disease caused by foreign *kumo* (Salisbury 1965:58). The Gururumba, much further east, use a very similar term, *gwumu*, for witches and witch-substance (Newman 1964:259; 1965:86). According to Rappaport (1967:121) *kum yu* is a sorcerer, not a witch, in Tsembaga and a witch is *koimp*. It is not clear from his account whether there are actually people who identify themselves as witches and by what means they are supposed to harm others. *Koimp* in Kuma is a belief that a person can cause illness or death by implanting a stone in someone's body by magical means. The *koimp* men (*koimp yi*) are unidentified and thought to be far away to the east, whereas the Tsembaga *koimp* are supposed to harm members of their own communities. The term *kum koimp* occurs in North Wahgi, but I am not certain whether it designates witchcraft or the imaginary implanting of stones. O'Hanlon (1983:324, 331), who worked with the Kombulno (Komblo in his orthography) in North Wahgi, does not explicitly say that they have no witchcraft, but he translates *kum* as 'betrayal', which is strongly identified with witchcraft at Minj. According to oral traditions collected by myself, the ancestors of the Kombulno came from Chimbu, the witchcraft country of Brown and Bergmann. The distribution of the term *kum* and its cognates to signify not simply betrayal, but witchcraft of a kind at least as developed as the *mangu* Evans-Pritchard reported, suggests that *kum*, in the sense of 'witchcraft', is prior to *kum* in the sense of 'betrayal'. If the ancestors of the Kombulno took witchcraft with them when they left Chimbu, they and their descendants may have discarded it in the course of their migrations. Their unusually stormy history of military defeats and enforced migrations would have given betrayal a remarkable prominence.

[7] Cf. Douglas's comment (1970a:140) on the Exclusive Brethren 'erecting . . . a high wall between themselves and the rest of the

world', which occurs in her discussion of the kind of community that may be conducive to witch belief.

8 The belief that a former witch may retain some particular characteristic of witches appears also in Chimbu. Brown (1977:27) reports that a woman who was a former *kumo* retained the ability, attributed to witches, to recognize other witches and was sought as a witch-finder. Kuma witches were also credited with this ability but this belief was tempered by a conviction (which seemed to me well founded) that when confessed witches named others they often did so arbitrarily or from malice.

9 Cf. Bergmann (1971,4:19): 'I was quite surprised to learn that some people quite openly said that they had *kumo*, yes, even boasted to have killed so and so many people. Did the others not believe them? Or did such people want to die?'

10 A dance is known as *dad* (*ndadl*) when it duplicates the style of dancing in the religious pig festival out of context. Thus it signifies the dance performed by women in trance during the 'shivering madness' associated with mushrooms and also the condition of those women (Reay 1977). It also signifies the dance of the witches, which various people have seen in visions. The participants are again mainly women and usually include only one man, thus reversing the sex ratio among persons actually found to be witches. The vision of *dad* is cited as evidence against the man.

11 The *kumo kanggi* of Central Chimbu (Bergmann 1971,4:7), which are otherwise very similar to the Kuma *kibe kangi*, are curiously connected with witchcraft. The name labels them '*kanggi* witches' in contrast to the Kuma's '*kangi* spirits'. They were thought to eat the bodies of humans, as witches were supposed to do, but the bodies they found floating down the river would have been the bodies of witches. Thus the ultimate fate of cannibal witches was to be consumed by demon witches.

12 I disagree with Salisbury's (1966:103-7) interpretation of the collective 'shivering madness' of the Kuma as spirit possession. The afflicted men said that bush demons boxed their ears, causing a temporary disturbance of their auditory and visual perception. But the demons did not stay with them or take control of them, as the term 'possession' implies (Reay 1977).

13 Many peoples view incest as unnatural and it has sometimes been associated with witchcraft in both Europe and Africa. Kuma considered incest to be natural but highly undesirable in the interests of orderly social life. In 1965 a man had sexual intercourse with his own mother. Neither of them was accused of witchcraft, but as soon as their deed was discovered the man fled to the coast and stayed away for several years.

REFERENCES

Aufenanger, H.
  1959   'The War-magic Houses in the Wahgi Valley and Adjacent Areas (New Guinea)'. *Anthropos* 54:1-26.
  1965   'Kumo, the Deadly Witchcraft in the Central Highlands of New Guinea'. *Asian Folklore Studies* 24:103-15.

Bergmann, W.
  1971   '*The Kamanuku*'. 4 vols, mimeo.

Brown, P.
  1964   'Enemies and Affines'. *Ethnology* 3:335-56.
  1977   'Kumo Witchcraft at Mintima, Chimbu Province, Papua New Guinea'. *Oceania* 48:26-9.

Bulmer, R. N. H.
  1965   'The Kyaka of the Western Highlands'. In Lawrence and Meggitt (1965:132-61).

Burridge, K. O. L.
  1965   'Tangu, Northern Madang District'. In Lawrence and Meggitt (1965:224-49).

Douglas, M.
  1970a *Natural Symbols: Explorations in Cosmology*. London: Barrie and Rockliff.
  1970b (ed.) *Witchcraft Confessions and Accusations*. London: Tavistock.

Epstein, S.
  1967   'A Sociological Analysis of Witch Beliefs in a Mysore Village'. In Middleton (1967:135-54).

Evans-Pritchard, E. E.
  1937   *Witchcraft, Oracles, and Magic among the Azande*. Oxford: Clarendon Press.

Forge, A.
  1970   'Prestige, Influence, and Sorcery: A New Guinea Example'. In Douglas (1970b:257-75).

Glasse, R. M.
  1965   'The Huli of the Southern Highlands'. In Lawrence and Meggitt (1965:27-49).

Kelly, R. C.
  1977   *Etoro Social Structure: a Study in Structural Contradiction*. Ann Arbor: University of Michigan Press.

Lawrence, P. and Meggitt, M. J.
  1965   (eds) *Gods, Ghosts and Men in Melanesia: Some Religions of Australian New Guinea and the New Hebrides*. Melbourne: Oxford University Press.

Lewis, I. M.
  1970   'A Structural Approach to Witchcraft and Spirit-pos-
          session'. In Douglas (1970b: 293-309).
Mair, L.
  1969   *Witchcraft*. London: World University Library, Wei-
          denfeld and Nicholson.
Maple, E.
  1962   *The Dark World of Witches*. London: Robert Hale Ltd.
Marshall, M.
  1982   (ed.) *Through a Glass Darkly: Beer and Modernization in
          Papua New Guinea*. Boroko: Institute of Applied Social
          and Economic Research.
Marwick, M. G.
  1965   *Sorcery in Its Social Setting: a Study of the Northern Rho-
          desian Ceŵa*. Manchester: Manchester University
          Press.
  1967   'The Sociology of Sorcery in a Central African Tribe'.
          In Middleton (1967: 101-26).
Meggitt, M. J.
  1977   *Blood is Their Argument: Warfare Among the Mae Enga
          Tribesmen of the New Guinea Highlands*. Palo Alto, Cal-
          ifornia: Mayfield Publishing Co.
Middleton, J. and Winter, E. H.
  1963   *Witchcraft and Sorcery in East Africa*. London: Rou-
          tledge & Kegan Paul.
Middleton, J.
  1967   (ed.) *Magic, Witchcraft, and Curing*. New York: The
          Natural History Press.
Newman, P. L.
  1964   'Religious Belief and Ritual in a New Guinea Society'.
          American Anthropologist (Special publication) 66 (4),
          Part 2: 257-72.
  1965   *Knowing the Gururumba*. New York: Holt, Rinehart
          & Winston.
O'Hanlon, M.
  1983   'Handsome is as Handsome Does: Display and
          Betrayal in the Wahgi', *Oceania* 53:317-33.
Parrinder, G.
  1963   *Witchcraft: European and African* (first published 1958).
          London: Faber and Faber.
Patterson, M.
  1974-75 'Sorcery and Witchcraft in Melanesia'. *Oceania* 45:
          132-60, 212-34.
Rappaport, R. A.
  1967   *Pigs For the Ancestors: Ritual in the Ecology of a New
          Guinea People*. New Haven and London: Yale Uni-
          versity Press.

Reay, M.
>1959 *The Kuma: Freedom and Conformity in the New Guinea Highlands.* Carlton: Melbourne University Press.

>1967 'Structural Co-variants of Land Shortage Among Patrilineal Peoples'. *Anthropological Forum* 2:4-19.

>1968 Review of Marwick 1965, *The Journal of the Polynesian Society* 77:198-201.

>1975 Letter to the editor, *Oceania* 46:154-6.

>1976 'The Politics of a Witch-killing'. *Oceania* 47:1-20.

>1977 'Ritual Madness Observed: a Discarded Pattern of Fate in Papua New Guinea'. *Journal of Pacific History* 12:55-79.

>1982 'Abstinence, Excess and Opportunity: Minj 1963-1980'. In Marshall (1982:163-74).

(in press)
>'Of Ghosts and Gargoyles: the Pragmatic 'Architecture' of Kuma Ritual'. In D. Barwick, J. R. Beckett, and M. Reay (eds): *Metaphors of Interpretation.* Canberra: Australian National University Press.

Royal Anthropological Institute of Great Britain and Ireland
>1951 *Notes and Queries on Anthropology.* London: Routledge & Kegan Paul.

Salisbury, R. F.
>1965 'The Siane of the Eastern Highlands'. In Lawrence and Meggitt (1965:50-77).

>1966 'Possession on the New Guinea Highlands: Review of Literature'. *Transcultural Psychiatric Research* 3:103-8.

Schieffelin, E. L.
>1977 *The Sorrow of the Lonely and the Burning of the Dancers.* St Lucia: Queensland University Press.

Steadman, L.
>1975 'Cannibal Witches in the Hewa'. *Oceania* 46:114-21.

Strathern, A.
>1969 'Finance and Production: Two Strategies in New Guinea Highlands Exchange Systems'. *Oceania* 40:42-67.

Winter, E. H.
>1963 'The Enemy Within: Amba Witchcraft and Sociological Theory'. In Middleton and Winter (1963:277-99).

4

Sorcery Divination among the Wola

PAUL SILLITOE

Revenge is the foremost motive given by people throughout Melanesia for engaging in armed conflict. When they lose a relative through others' physical or supernatural death-dealing actions, they are morally obliged to balance the account by uniting and despatching the killer or one of his kinsmen.

This 'man for a man, life for a life' precept is potentially an injunction for never-ending hostility because the deaths on both sides are unlikely ever to tally. This is improbable because it is not a matter of simple arithmetic. Both sides will interpret and account differently for deaths that occur: one corpse does not equal another regardless of age, sex, status and so on. Eventually they may forget the exact score of deaths and the original cause of their fighting, their hostile relationship becoming a permanent one of the kind commonly labelled a feud.

The above sequence pertains to some parts of the world. For the Bedouin, Peters (1967:262) puts the situation crisply: their 'hostilities are of a sort which cannot be terminated . . . [they] know no beginning and are insoluble'. But this applies to few places in Melanesia.[1] Here people are able to stop the revenge juggernaut when it hurtles into action; they can brake its remorseless progress. The question is: how do they stop revengeful conflict when it threatens or starts without emasculating and turning into a sham the revenge principle in which they all believe?[2]

The Wola and their Revenge Conundrum

Those speaking the Wola tongue live in the Southern Highlands of Papua New Guinea where they occupy five valleys, from the Ak River in the west to the Mendi in the east. They are typical Highlanders. Shifting cultivators whose staple crop is sweet potato, they live in houses, which like their gardens, are dotted along the sides of their valleys. They keep numbers of pigs, which together with other valuables such as sea shells, cosmetic oil, birds' feathers, and today money, they exchange with one another in an interminable series of transactions. These ceremonial exchanges feature in many of the important events of their lives; their social and political order is founded upon them. This acephalous order also depends on a tenet of revenge, which gives rise to frequent outbreaks of fighting.

The motive force rallying the Wola to take up arms and fight is, like elsewhere in Melanesia, the moral obligation they observe to wreak vengeance on those who lethally harm a kinsman. Yet the structural logic that prompts their inculcation with this ethic, leading them to engage in armed combat against others, does not require the interminable hostilities threatened by a literal application of the revenge injunction. It only demands a show of concerted force to keep political power labile and beyond the reach of individuals, to stymie the emergence of enduring political corporations led by the holders of instituted offices (Sillitoe 1979a:77–8).

Yet the revenge rationale enunciated by the Wola is to secure a balance of deaths on either side; until this occurs fighting cannot theoretically cease. This poses a potential problem for those who become embroiled in aggressive encounters, or wish to avoid them because of the intolerable disruption they bring to social life: how can they balance the death account to the satisfaction of all concerned and terminate hostilities? In terms of physical casualties this will be difficult, probably impossible: those on top, for instance, may aggravate the imbalance by killing again in protecting themselves against the revenge efforts of the other side, or sustain a death which they consider redresses the balance too far in their enemy's favour, prompting them to persecute hostilities further to avenge it, and so on. If they followed their revenge commitments to the letter, hostilities would drag on without end, which they do not.[3] Instead the Wola stop fighting after a few months, agreeing to an unstable truce which, if it holds, passes into a state of peace that grows stronger as time passes (Sillitoe 1979a:81–2).

They are able to cease fighting without making a mockery of their revenge beliefs by shifting hostilities from a physical to an occult plane, settling outstanding scores through poison, sorcery and ultimately retributory divination. This allows the Wola to circumvent the impasse of expecting people to agree to a cease-fire when they have blood-debts outstanding which they should first square.[4] Furthermore, hyperphysical revenge can eventually achieve a balance of deaths that both sides consider equitable, so long as no overt fighting erupts again and leads to further violent deaths.[5]

Sorcery and Poison

The Wola distinguish between two kinds of sorcery, one a local indigenous variety, which they call *woktoiz*, and the other of foreign origin, coming they say from the neighbouring Huli, which they call *hul tort*.[6] Similar procedures feature in both, although they vary in details. Practitioners perform their nefarious rites at night, activating the sorcery force to attack and kill the roaming *wezow* life force of victims (which the Wola believe leaves the body in sleep). They slaughter a pig and mutilate certain of its organs to the accompaniment of muttered incantations which, mimicking the destruction of the victim, they believe releases the sorcery force.

In addition to sorcery, and closely allied to it in the Wola mind, there is poison, which they call *mogtomb*. This is a substance, believed to be toxic, which is furtively introduced into a victim's body, usually in his food. Although all are aware of poison, those I have spoken to on the subject have always expressed ignorance of its composition, some surmising that it must include menstrual blood in its ingredients (which is understandable given men's fear of this substance—Sillitoe 1979b). They all denied having ever handled any. Similarly, men are reluctant to discuss sorcery openly, maintaining that they have only sketchy hearsay knowledge of the kind given here. This is expectable, for to admit to dealing in sorcery or poison is tantamount in the Wola mind, as this paper recounts, to confessing to killing someone: such an open declaration would nullify the outcome of these practices as interpreted here. Secrecy is of the essence, which makes the collection of reliable information on the subject by an outsider difficult.[7]

Neither sorcery nor poison are directed at relatives. The Wola use them against enemies to revenge those killed by them, without having recourse to open violence: a crucial point from this article's perspective. But there is another killer force; and its unconscious possessors may use it unwittingly to strike down relatives. This is akin to witchcraft. It is a new phenomenon according to the Wola, brought into their region by outsiders accompanying government patrols, during the last two decades or so. They call those possessed by it *ten sokol*. These people, usually women, have no conscious control over it. Jealousy, usually of food delicacies, activates it. No open accusations are made, nor action taken against suspected witches.

Retributory Divination: the *Komay*

It is in a payback frame that the Wola apprehend and solve their revenge conundrum, once it has moved to a supernatural level. They ask themselves, when convinced that someone has clandestinely resorted to some nefarious practice to murder a relative, how they can prove it and secure redress, given the absence of conclusive evidence, which is a crucial feature of these crimes. And their solution, retributory divination, short-circuits their relentless drive for physical revenge, preventing an outbreak of fighting, and finally nullifying between those concerned any outstanding scores from previous hostilities.

They resort to a retributory divination, which they call a *komay*, when they believe that a man, woman or child has died from sorcery or poisoning and those thought responsible deny culpability. Either side may initiate the ritual and supply the pig necessary: relatives of the victim who wish to prove the veracity of their accusations, or those defamed who wish to demonstrate their innocence by sponsoring and taking part in a *komay* divination.

The following case is typical of those which lead to *komay* rituals. It concerns a man called Komep, whose death prompted a divination in the Was valley at a place called Hombila on 15 June 1981. It illustrates the issues considered significant by those involved and features throughout this account to illustrate various points relevant to Wola clandestine homicide divinatory practices; the genealogy gives the *dramatis personae* and the parts they played.

Komep was aged about forty years when he died. Initially his relatives thought that he had fallen victim to the *hul tort* sorcery of a man living at Keshmal, but they later revised their ideas and attributed his death to poisoning when it came to light that he had told three relatives (Pes, Kuwnhaema and Bon) that he feared that two men, Kogiyt and Paenuw, had poisoned him. They were members of a *sem* called Gaip, located at Hombila and related to Komep's *sem* called Gez (see genealogy).[8]

When sick Komep, trying to reason out the cause of his illness, had apparently come to suspect them of slipping poison into some pumpkin he ate, which they had all cooked together in an earth oven and shared. When his relatives heard of his suspicions, they concluded that this was the probable cause of his demise because those accused had a motive for wishing to kill him. They did so, they surmised, to revenge the death of Komabay, one of their relatives, whom they had long suspected unidentified persons related to Komep of poisoning some six years or so previously. The Gaip pair accused of poisoning Komep and their relatives, persistently denied culpability, to the anger of the Gez men who became convinced of their guilt. Relations between them deteriorated until they reached the point where they decided on a *komay* divination to settle the issue (the details and outcome of which are summarized in the genealogy).

About a week prior to his death in 1977 Komep's relatives carried him to my house for medicine. He had a large tumour on his neck and was in some pain. Medical persons to whom

I've described his condition, doubting the efficacy of substances which the Wola believe to be poison, have thought that in all probability, according to their clinical beliefs, he was suffering from cancer.

Before the ritual, tension between those concerned slowly builds up, one side accusing and the other denying in an interminable series of arguments. These may continue for a year or more before the suppurating sore of their differences bursts with a *komay* ritual, if it does not erupt in a fight beforehand. Tempers become frayed, on one side

Wola genealogy of participants in a *komay* sorcery divination ritual

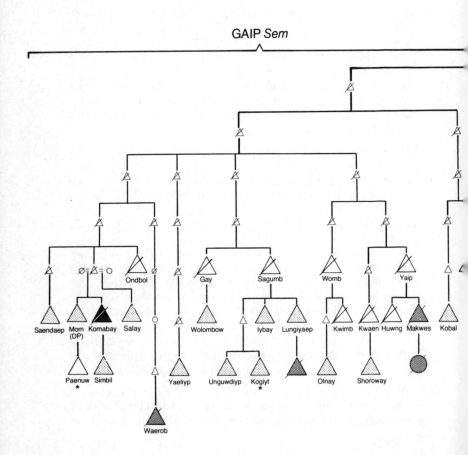

by the other's presumed intransigence and on the opposite by the supposedly unjust accusations levelled at it, and exasperated, those concerned sometimes come to blows: a violent death at this time will abhort any plans for a divination that may be afoot and activate revenge obligations, which the ritual would have circumvented if it had proceeded.

So long as open hostilities do not break out, a *komay* or jaw-rubbing ritual is probable. During the heated disputes, it is common for some of those present to call for one to

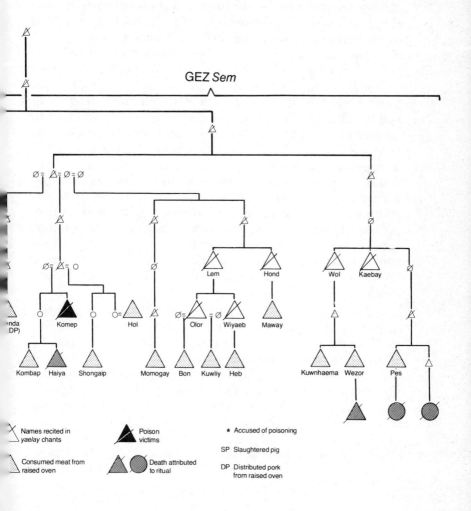

settle the issue once and for all. Gradually the opinion of the majority crystallizes, over several months of recurring disputation, in favour of a retributory divination, until finally someone comes forward with a pig and those concerned fix a definite date to stage it (usually within the week). All those concerned are prepared for, and ready to participate in, the coming ritual.

The Chants

Just as the pressure slowly builds up in the months preceding a ritual so for two or three days before the divination those involved work themselves up gradually to a high pitch of excitement by shouting stylized chants at one another: one side accusing and the other denying the sorcery or poisoning charge. These chants the Wola call *yael piyp kay* or *wor kay*. They consist of a series of phrases shouted out by one man, at the end of each of which all those present yell the chorus '*Wor*'. Those present may take it in turns to shout the chant to ease the strain on their throats, or one man with a particularly loud and resonant voice may yell it repeatedly. There is no stipulation that individuals standing in a certain relationship to the victim or those accused of the nefarious act should be responsible for shouting the *yaelay* chant. For the two or three days preceding the jaw-rubbing, during which they yell the chants, those on either side congregate four or five times daily on some prominent spot on either their own or a neighbouring territory, from which their yelling may be heard by the other party, and bawl out the chant.

The Wola maintain that these chants serve a number of purposes. They declare the shouters' predicament and case. They announce to all those within earshot (and by word of mouth, those living further afield), who are not directly concerned in the dispute, that those participating intend to put the matter to the test of a *komay* divination, thus serving to make the matter clearly public and invite all those interested to attend and witness the event. And they attract the attention of the spirits or *towmow* of the chanters' dead relatives, which is their most important purpose to the Wola mind. They believe that at death an individual's life force leaves the body and becomes a *towmow* spirit, haunting familiar places on the territory where he or she resided, sometimes attacking relatives and descendants, causing sickness and occasionally death. They are believed to play an important role in meting out punishment to the party in the wrong: to those accused of having worked sorcery or administered poison, or to their accusers if their assertions are wrong.

The chants are clearly framed as invitations. Those yelled by the accusers and the accused are similar in form and content, except that one contains accusatory and denunciatory phrases and the other refutative and negatory ones. The following two chants, yelled prior to the Hombila *komay* divination, illustrate the nature of these refrains.

Each chant opens by calling out some of the names of places within the shouters' territory, where they have houses and gardens. They follow each place name with the word *haelaiba* which is the standard call used by the Wola when shouting out a message to a place some distance away and may freely be translated as: 'is anyone there?' So the chants open by calling out: 'is there anyone at Hombila, anyone at Hiyt? . . . ' and so on. But in these chants they are not calling out to the living, they are hailing the *towmow* spirits of deceased relatives believed to haunt these places.

This is clear in the phrases that follow on from the recitation of place names: they consist of a list of the shouters' deceased relatives, giving their individual names prefixed by the name of the *sem* to which they belonged at the place where they resided.[9] Normally, in everyday conversation, the Wola avoid saying the names of dead relatives for fear of attracting the attention of their *towmow* and provoking an attack upon themselves or others, giving rise to illness and maybe even death. But in the jaw-rubbing ritual they set out explicitly not only to attract their attention but to invite them to assemble amidst the living who will gather for the divination. This is made explicit in the phrase *lusimbaebtuw*, with which the recited list of deceased persons' names closes, which freely translates as 'come and gather over here'. In the chants each name ends in '-a', as do the words at the end of later phrases too, to couple in rhythmically with the '*Wor*' chorus.

The chants shouted by participants in the *komay* divination ritual

The accusing *yaelay* (chant)

Hombila Place name	*haelaiba* anyone there?	[*Wor*]*,	Hiyt Place name	*haelaiba* anyone there?	[*Wor*],	Shomak Place name	

haelaiba anyone there?	[*Wor*],	Haenda *Sem* name	Hond-a deceased's name	[*Wor*],	Haenda *Sem* name	Lem-a deceased's name [*Wor*],

Luwimb *Sem* name	Wol-a deceased's name	[*Wor*],	Luwimb *Sem* name	Kaembay-a deceased's name	[*Wor*],	Haenda *Sem* name

Wiyab-a deceased's name	[*Wor*],	Hiyt Place name	Olor-a deceased's name	[*Wor*],	Lusimb-a Come and gather here [*Wor*],

niy me	*lay* struck	*hendelba* look	[*Wor*],	Haenda *Sem* name	Komep-a victim's name [*Wor*],

lubtuw struck	*kay-a* say	[*Wor*],	*nobtuw* ate	*kay-a* say	[*Wor*],	*bubtuw* did for	*kay-a* say [*Wor*],

Uwt-waeb Black palm bow	*shuwai* chant word (no meaning)	*buruk* sit	*iyb-a* come	[*Wor*],	*kongliyp*† decorative bush	*buruk* sit

iyba-a   [*Wor*],
come

* *Wor* = chorus
† *Graptophyllum pictum*

The denying *yaelay* (chant)

Yuw	Haenda	*haelaiba*	[*Wor*],	Goi	*haelaiba*	[*Wor*],	Baelol
Up there	place name	anyone there?		place name	anyone there?		place name

haelaiba	[*Wor*],	Tel	*haelaiba*	[*Wor*],	Haenda	Huwng-a	[*Wor*],
anyone there?		place name	anyone there?		*Sem* name	deceased's name	

Haenda	Kwaen-a	[*Wor*],	Haenda	Gay-a	[*Wor*],	Haenda
Sem name	deceased's name		*Sem* name	deceased's name		*Sem* name

Sagumb-a	[*Wor*],	Haenda	Yaip-a	[*Wor*],	Haenda	Komabay-a	[*Wor*],
deceased's name		*Sem* name	deceased's name		*Sem* name	deceased's name	

Haenda	Kwimb-a	[*Wor*],	Haenda	Womb-a	[*Wor*],	Haenda
Sem name	deceased's name		*Sem* name	deceased's name		*Sem* name

Ondbol-a	[*Wor*],	*Lusimb-a*	[*Wor*],	Haenda	Komep-a	[*Wor*],
deceased's name		Come & gather here		*Sem* name	victim's name	

niy	*na*	*hondowa*	[*Wor*],	*niy*	*na*	*luwa*	[*Wor*],	*nim*	*na*	*buwa*	[*Wor*],
I	not	know		I	not	struck		I	not	did	

niy	*kelobtuw*	*kay-a*	[*Wor*],	*niy*	*showmay-a*	[*Wor*],	*Uwt-waeb*
Me	falsely accuse	say		me	falsely accuse		Black palm bow

shuwai	*buruk*	*iyb-a*	[*Wor*],	*kongliyp*	*buruk*	*iyb-a*	[*Wor*],
chant word (no meaning)	sit	come		decorative bush	sit	come	

The Wola maintain that there are no prescriptions stipulating that the names of certain deceased relatives should
be included in the chant (for instance, that the names of
dead individuals standing in a certain relationship to the
victim, or the person accused of killing him or her, should
be included or listed in a certain order). The genealogy of
those involved in the *komay* divination at Hombila supports
their assertions regarding the random choice of names. It
also reveals two significant points regarding the names
selected. They tend to be of those who have died within
living memory, by and large those who have died recently.
There are, the Wola point out, two reasons for this: firstly,
these are the names they readily recall (for their genealogical knowledge is very shallow—individuals can rarely
remember names or precise relationships beyond their
great-grandparents' generation), and secondly, and more
importantly, the *towmow* spirits of the recently dead are
stronger and more virulent than those of the long deceased,
whose power to cause illness and kill wanes with the passage
of time. The second significant point is the marked male
bias of the genealogy; only the names of deceased men are
included in the chant, which correlates with the exclusion
of females from the entire jaw-rubbing event. When asked
why they only include the names of deceased men in the
chant, informants initially replied that it was because male
towmow are the strongest, mirroring the physical strength
of men over women among the living. When told that this
explanation was inconsistent because they believe the *towmow*
of females are as lethal as those of males, causing sickness
and death, they fell back on their standard reply when
faced with a perplexing question to which they have no
ready answer, and said that as their ancestors only called
out the names of deceased male relatives so do they.

The chants go on, after listing places and deceased
men's names, either to accuse or deny complicity in the
disputed death. The accusers appeal to their *towmow* spirits
to look at how those they accuse have nefariously struck
down one of their number, Haenda Komep: that they have
'done for' him, 'eaten' him.[10] Those accused, on the other
hand, declare their innocence in their chants: that they
know nothing about Komep's death, that they were not

responsible for his death and never struck him down. They maintain that they are falsely accused, using for emphasis the phrase '*niy showmay*' which men only utter to swear their innocence when very angry.

Both chants conclude in the same way, again urging the participants' *towmow* spirits to be present at the coming jaw-rubbing ritual, to come and 'sit' amongst them as they put it. They request them to come and sit near the *kongliyp* bushes, which are shrubs men cultivate for decoration around homesteads. Normally the living would not make such a suggestion, wishing to keep *towmow* at a distance because they fear attack and sickness. But at a *komay* divination both sides invite them to be present to 'see', as the Wola put it, the truth and attack not them, but their lying opponents.

The reference to a black palm bow in the chants has a double meaning. It alludes to the attack that the shouters' *towmow* will make on the other side because they are in the wrong. It also invites them to come and 'sit' on their bows, that is infuse them with their deadly presence. When both sides meet to participate in the ritual, they are understandably worked up to a high pitch of excitement by the preceding days' chanting of *yaelay* and violence is possible, each dwelling on the injustice done to it by the other. They invite these ghostly powers to haunt their bows so that if a fight erupts, their arrows will fly true and inflict many lethal wounds on the other side.

On the day of the ritual each side yells its respective chant several times. They start as they set out for the event's venue, stopping several times *en route* to shout it out. They continue until they meet at the clearing where they will perform the divination, when they stand clustered facing each other on either side and yell their chants at each other in turns.

Preparing for the Ritual

They usually meet on neutral ground somewhere between their territories, although they may stage the ritual on a clearing that belongs to one of the parties involved. Here, the day before the *komay* ritual, men erect a leaf-faced wall

of saplings at the base of a large tree (any species is suitable—
it was a hoop-pine *Araucaria cunninghamii* at the Hombila
divination). This fence-like erection, extending for perhaps
two metres, is of a particular construction. The builders
drive any species of leafy sapling into the ground to give
the foundation, standing two metres or so high. Across
them they lash pieces of wood horizontally, and behind
these they poke *bat* (*Bubbia* spp.) and *shiyp* (*Chisocheton cer-
amicum*) tree leaves with their pale (whitish-green and light-
brown) undersides facing outwards. The completed effect
is a wall of pale leaves topped by the saplings' waving green
fronds.

When asked why they build this particular erection
faced with pale leaves, men were unable to expand upon
their standard 'our ancestors did it that way, and so we do
too' explanation. But they could explain one feature at the
Hombila divination. This was a small boy's bow which Mom,
whose son was one of those accused of poisoning Komep,
placed on the leaf wall. They related it to the coming ghostly
attack on the guilty ones, and their allusion to black palm
bows in the chants: it symbolized, they said, the calling up
of the *towmow* spirits, 'arming' them as they passed the wall
during the ritual to attack the lying party.

Just in front of the leaf wall the participants build a
raised oven in which to cook with hot stones the pieces of
meat that they will eat to put to the test the truthfulness of
their assertions. They construct this from the crown of a
tree-fern (*Cyathea* spp.), driving the trunk into the ground
to give a leafy platform at about waist height. They trim off
the fronds, leaving their tough stalks radiating out like the
trunkated spokes of an enormous umbrella. Around the
edge of these they lash a sheet of bark in a hoop to give a
receptacle in which to cook the pork and greens. This giant
mushroom-like structure with its bark rim the Wola call the
shor tor (lit: raised structure); both it and the leaf wall
together they refer to as the *komay*, from which the divination ritual's name derives. In front, at the foot of the
raised oven, they dig a standard circular earth oven pit in
which to cook with hot stones the pork not steamed on the
tree-fern crown. This is nearly all of the pig, for they cook
only a few pieces in the raised *shor tor* oven.

Those taking part in the ritual, notably those intending to partake of the pork cooked in the raised oven, put on their second-best decorations: what the Wola call their *serep yort*. They blacken their faces with powdered charcoal, on which they paint designs in white clay (principally lines on the cheeks and down the nose), and rub their torsos with glistening *tigaso* oil. On their heads they wear knitted string caps rubbed over with white clay, topped with cassowary feather pompons, mounted birds' wings or feather circlets. They don their best knitted aprons and wear over their buttocks leaves from the palm lily cultivar *ago*, which turn yellow and maroon when mature. This, men maintain, is the proper dress for those participating in a jaw-rubbing divination because it is fearsome, which is only appropriate when you are about to have dealings with dangerous and malevolent *towmow* spirits.

The entire event is one fraught with danger as malignant ancestral spirits are being invoked. To protect them, neither women nor children are allowed to be present at any stage.[11] It is enigmatic that women are forbidden to attend the jaw-rubbing ritual for their life force not only become *towmow* as potent and dangerous as any male's, but the avenging *towmow* spirits are as likely to strike them and their children as they are any man who turns out to be on the lying side. Women and children may fall helpless victims to the supernatural machinations of their menfolk; their absence from the ritual is actually no defence.

The Divination

The participants punctuate their bouts of competitive chanting when they meet at the venue with impromptu shuffle dances called *hor korbobtuw*, in which the two parties stand facing each other across the clearing and stamp their feet while standing on the spot, making cries in unison of Brrrr . . . and Uw-uw-uw . . . They continue on and off in this fashion chanting and dancing, until the pig is killed whose pork they will eat as part of the divination sequence.

When the time comes to kill the pig, both parties turn towards the short wall of saplings driven into the ground in front of the large tree, and performing the shuffle dance,

advance towards it as two hooting bodies. This final performance, following which the chanting and dancing ceases,
the Wola call *komay iysh ma maebtuw* (lit: jaw-rubbing-ritual
tree cause to climb). All those taking part carry a bow and
arrows, as they would at any event that has the potential to
erupt into a fight, and they rattle these in a threatening
manner as they advance, some of them also waving leafy
branches to increase the noise made and give their advance
a more formidable aspect. This shuffling dance is a feature
of any tense situation, such as a deadlocked dispute at which
tempers are running high, that could flare up into a violent
confrontation, possibly resulting in a death and months of
revengeful fighting. It epitomizes the event's instability,
teetering between violent confrontation and peaceful co-
existence.

In this advance, as its name suggests, the participants
drive their summoned *towmow* spirits up the large tree at
the base of which they have prepared the leaf wall and
ovens. They believe that they will haunt the tree's crown
and from there judge between the two sides taking part in
the divination. On other occasions when their *towmow* spirits
come to their aid to redress some injustice done to them
(primarily in the event of some ceremonial exchange der-
eliction) the Wola say that they ride on their shoulders, and
one imaginative young man speculated that the leaf wall
served as a path up the tree for the summoned *towmow*
riding on the shoulders of the participants, that they hop
off as they converge on it and run along the top and up the
tree. Other men scoffed at this intriguing suggestion, saying
that no one knows the behaviour of *towmow*. According to
them the purpose of the leaf wall is to act as a sort of chimney
deflecting the smoke of the fire lit to cook the pork, together
with the smell of the singeing bristles and steaming meat,
up the tree in which the *towmow* sit. The spirits 'eat' these
smells; they are their share of the slaughtered pig and,
pleased with them, they are drawn into the divination
sequence to play their part.

As the two hooting parties converge on the leaf wall,
two men, one from either side, slaughter the pig between
them. Any of the participants on either side may supply the
pig; there are no stipulations that a specified relative of the

victim, or those accused of perpetrating the deed, should provide it. At Hombila a man on the accused side provided the animal, whose FBS and FFFBSSS stood accused of killing Komep. Neither are there any rules prescribing who should club the pig: at Hombila, it was Komep's FF½BSS for Gez and the accuseds' FFFFFBSSS for Gaip. Each carries a club and they vie with one another to land the first blow on the pig, showering blows on the creature's snout and head simultaneously. Their competition is watched with interest, for it is taken to signal the likely outcome of the divination: the side landing the first blow is probably the one telling the truth.

The clubbers at a ritual staged at Porsera in 1976 climbed two trees standing close together on the clearing and four men lifted the pig above their heads for them to club. No one could explain this variation, but they elaborated on the significance of the clubs used. They had put the sorcery victim in a raised coffin standing on four posts some two metres above the ground, and they had fashioned the clubs from two of these posts. This effected, they said, the transference of some of the deceased's essence to the pig. Putrid juices from the decomposing corpse had run down and soaked into these poles, so they contained something of his person which was passed on to the pig in clubbing.

This transference of the victim's essence to the pork to be eaten in the divination is an important feature of the ritual. Besides using the poles of the raised coffin to effect this, those staging the Porsera *komay* also used pieces of wood from the coffin for the fire over which they singed off the dead pig's bristles before butchering it. At Hombila, where they had buried the victim in the ground, they used for the bristle-singeing fire the pole to which his corpse had been lashed for the four or five days of keening prior to burial and his knitted apron, both of which were infused with his person. Thus the smoke that climbs up the tree in which the *towmow* are sitting contains the victim's presence and is thought to enervate and prompt them to strike down the killers or their relatives in revenge. But, more importantly, the victim's essence permeates the pork to be cooked in the raised oven and acts, it is believed, like poison, infecting the meat such that when eaten by those lying, they or their relatives will die as a result.

The participants take the pieces of meat that they will eat to test their assertions and cook them in the tree-fern crown oven first. These vary from one divination to another; in keeping with Wola rituals in general, which display considerable variety in details, although having the same overall structure. At Hombila they cooked the pig's heart, lungs, liver, head and a strip of pork from the belly. They put them to cook together with *omok* Acanth greens (*Dicliptera papuana*), *henk* edible tree-fern fronds (*Cyathea* spp.) and *shombiy* ginger (*Zingiber officinale*), all seasoned with a sprinkling of *eb* or salt. These pieces were more or less ready to eat by the time the remainder of the pig was butchered and put to cook in the earth oven at the foot of the raised one.

The climax comes with the opening of the tree-fern crown oven. Each piece of meat cooked in it, including the head, is cut exactly into half: one piece for the accusers to share and eat, the other for the accused. One man from each side cuts up the meat that his relatives taking part in the ritual will eat, and gives it to them. Again, there are no rules stipulating that specified relatives should be responsible for this; at Hombila the two who shared out the meat were Komep's FF½BSS for Gez and the accuseds' F and FFFFBSSS for Gaip.

Before eating the piece of meat they receive, those subjecting themselves to the test of the *komay* increase its infection with the victim's essence. They rub it on his jawbone to imbue it further with his presence and heighten its toxic effect on the liars and their relatives.

At Hombila, where Komep's relatives had interred him in the ground, they modified this step because it was not only more difficult to retrieve his jawbone than it would have been from a raised coffin, but also because they feared contracting some illness by digging up his grave and meddling with his decomposed corpse (following the dire warnings of the administration about what happens to those who do not dispose of their dead properly). When keening over Komep's corpse lashed to a pole in his houseyard, they had placed a stone on the ground beneath him. On to this the putrid juices leaking from his body dripped, thus imbuing it with his essence. They left this stone buried where it stood under the corpse until the day of the ritual, when they dug it up and included it with the others heated for cooking the head and so on in the raised *shor tor* oven. They said that this stone acted on the meat like rubbing it on the deceased's jawbone, filling it with his essence and giving it lethal properties when eaten by those lying about the cause of his death.

Jawbone or stone, the lethal effect, the Wola believe, is the same: both are equally efficacious at punishing the wrongdoers. This inventiveness in the face of changed circumstances characterizes the general flexibility of their rituals. This informality parallels their (so far as an outsider can understand it) unsystematic and variable belief system.[12] It also bears significantly on the issue of revenge obligation obfuscation through divination. A degree of laxness promotes the ambiguity and disaccord necessary for this outcome, where consistency would undermine it.

Just before they put the potentially lethal piece of meat in their mouths, the participants swear an oath declaring the truth of either their assertions of guilt or protestations of innocence. At Hombila, the accused Gaip men said '*niy menja na buwol, nak*' (lit: 'I something not did, [I] eat'), while the Gez accusers charged them '*lisindis kalol, nak*' (lit: killed [you did I] tell, [I] eat), and the three men (Pes, Kuwnhaema and Bon) who maintained that the victim had told them that the accused had poisoned him said '*niy kornjisol, nak*' (lit: 'I [he] told, [I] eat').[13]

The jaw-rubbing and oaths that accompany the eating of meat from the tree-fern stump oven mark the high point of the ritual. Those participating thus expose themselves and their relatives to the judgement of the *komay*. The tense atmosphere eases when they have eaten; they have abrogated their revenge responsibilities to non-human powers, they are out of their hands and they can forbear knowing that justice will be done on their behalf. They share out the remainder of the pig cooked in the ground oven when they have consumed the charged pork from the raised one. It is not believed to have the same lethal properties. Many of those who have come to witness the event, some of whom will not be related to either of the disputing parties, will receive and consume it at no risk (though the entire pig imbued some of the victim's essence when slaughtered and singed, it will not harm anyone unrelated to the guilty party, and those related to it are at risk whether or not they consume any).

The Deaths: Retribution and Obfuscation

The lethal powers of the *komay* are twofold. Firstly, the essence of the sorcery or poison victim imbued by the meat makes it lethal to his or her killers or those falsely accusing others of the death. It is lethal to both those who eat it and by some process of transference, that people are unable to articulate beyond saying that it is the consequence of the *komay* ritual, to their relatives and dependants who do not partake of it. Secondly, the *towmow* spirits assembled at the event and sent up the large tree 'see' the case under dispute and sit in judgement, and attack those on the lying side and their relatives, causing sickness and killing in revenge. The *towmow* spirits of the guilty side are impotent to attack back. The *komay* ritual is one of the few occasions when people are able to turn their *towmow* on persons unrelated to them; ghosts normally only have the power to launch their malevolent death-dealing assaults on their relatives, who perform the majority of their rituals to keep them at bay, not to invite their attacks.

Who eats the meat from the raised tree-fern oven, so putting themselves and their relatives to the test of the *komay*? According to the Wola anyone related to the principal figures in the clandestine murder dispute may elect to do so. The participants at the Hombila *komay* support their assertions that any kin, both residing on the same *sem* territory as the principal actors and those living elsewhere, may take part.

Although several persons will share the meat, it only needs one of them to eat it to put at risk all those eligible. Some may decline to take part out of fear, thinking that by not partaking of the *komay* charged pork they reduce to some extent the danger to themselves and their close kin, but they are mistaken in this assumption because all those related to the guilty side are equally at risk. The deaths attributed to the Hombila *komay* demonstrate this clearly. None of those who ate pork died, and only four of the eight whose deaths have been attributed to the divination were close relatives of these men: two losing baby sons, one a baby daughter and one his brother. Persons of all ages and either sex are equally at risk: three of the eight dying were females. While it is men who incite these revengeful supernatural forces, they are not placing themselves alone in danger but their womenfolk and children too; indeed judging from the number of child deaths attributed to the Hombila *komay* (six out of eight—which is probably typical given the high rate of infant mortality among the Wola) it would seem that men are putting their dependants more at risk than themselves when they engage with such supernatural forces.

When challenged on this point, men disagreed that it was unfair that their actions should result in the deaths of women and children, saying that this was the way of the *komay*, that they only have the ability to invoke, not the power to control, its vengeful forces. If this is so, it only seems fair that women and children should be present and share the pork, but men disagree, believing that they would not be strong enough to deal with the lethal supernatural forces invoked, that they would be in extreme danger. When related to their obligations to fight in wars which, concerning revenge killing, are closely connected to men's actions in staging a *komay*, their viewpoint is easier to appreciate. Revenge is men's business: that women and minors sometimes fall victim to these forces is regretful, but men do their best to shield them and face the dangers alone. They are largely successful in this endeavour in times of war: far more men fall as casualties than women or children. In fourteen recent wars 87 per cent of the 144 people killed were men, 10 per cent women and 3 per cent children.

There is more to the random occurrence among the participants' kin of deaths attributed to the *komay*, to its indiscriminate slaying of women and children, than the Wola apparently are consciously aware of. If the divination ritual is believed to be responsible for the deaths attributed to it, it seems rough justice indeed, but looked at callously and coldly, the more fatalities people can attribute to it the more potential there is for obscuring outstanding revenge scores on either side, which is a significant outcome of this ritual.

Several points corroborate this interpretation. There are no prescriptions stipulating the range of kin liable to supernatural attack, the deaths of distant relatives may be counted as *komay* strikes. Neither is there any way of deciding to which side's score should be added the deaths of persons related to both. This woolliness increases considerably the scope for putting varying interpretations on the ritual's outcome. Also importantly, people cannot prove conclusively that the *komay* caused the deaths some attribute to it. In short, there is considerable room for disagreement: both sides can reach different conclusions about deaths that occur after the divination and both think that it has dispensed retribution in their favour. Furthermore, those on each side will disagree among themselves over the outcome, and so become paralysed and unable to take any concerted revenge action, even if some are dissatisfied.

The interpretations put on the deaths that followed the Hombila *komay* illustrate this clouding process. Those involved disagreed over which deaths they could legitimately attribute to the ritual, but, in their accounting, the fatalities they countenanced either balanced or were fewer on their side, they discounted some among them attributed to the *komay* by their opponents as occurring for other reasons. The maximum number of deaths ascribed to the divination was eight, four on either side. Several agreed with these figures, which do not restrict the deaths to one side, as expected for a ritual that purports to punish those in the wrong, but spread them equally over both. Some disagreed with these balanced figures, arguing that to believe them is tantamount to saying the ritual went wrong somewhere. But there is an answer for everything in this lethal game. Others explained that the tally demonstrated that both parties were guilty: Gez for poisoning Komabay in the first instance, and Gaip for poisoning Komep in revenge. They argued that justice had been done, for the resulting deaths balance at five each, which is as it should be according to Wola conceptions of revenge, such a balance calling for no further revengeful action. Whatever interpretation they put on the deaths, both sides, while they remain wary of one another, have solved their revenge obligations and are living in peace.

Similar considerations apply to sorcery and poisoning accusations, the originators of retributory divination. Given the nature of their crime, those believed responsible for clandestine homicides cannot be positively identified without an improbable confession, unlike those answerable for physical assaults, who are painfully obvious and demand combative revengeful action against them. Deaths imputed to nefarious acts are ambiguous and invite conflicting constructions: some will be convinced of the cause of death and others doubt it, and those sure of it will differ in their explanations of the precise cause and motive, and in their identification of the culprit. Again, they fog the issue. And divided opinion militates against direct revenge, which would lead to further open hostilities. The upshot is a stand-off.

Some may resort to sorcery or poison to exact revenge on those they believe responsible, and privately gloat over a subsequent death, which their 'enemies' may put down to another cause, even blaming others of supernatural murder. After some years and several deaths on either side, the significance and cause of which those involved disagree over, the antagonists will think the score either favours them or balances—either way their revenge obligations are satisfied. The contrary interpretations these deaths invite are crucial, making them apt circuit-breakers of the otherwise remorseless current of revenge.

It is somewhat ironical that deaths attributed to clandestine manipulations, which damp down and terminate the revenge cycle, can spark off physical violence and activate it. Backfires are uncommon and people do what they can to prevent them. It is in this context that retributory divination can be seen as the ultimate arbiter of the system, with its power to settle revenge scores fairly once and for all by passing responsibility for dealing out revenge to higher powers. It can prevent both the resurgence of open fighting in a conflict that has passed on to hole-and-corner combat, and the flaring up of hostilities between those living in peace. While warfare, a significant force in maintaining the egalitarian acephalous political environment of the Wola, is unavoidable, their sortilegious removal of the revenge sting refutes the applicability to their polity of Milton's lament 'For what can war but endless war still breed?'

NOTES

[1] A handful of writers have reported societies where groups engage in never-ending hostilities, referring to them as wars that are total, permanent or major, rarely as feuds (Sillitoe 1978:263-5). While it is difficult, as Radcliffe-Brown (1940:xx) noted some time ago, to distinguish between war and feud, this terminological contrariety is disconcerting. Although it may indicate some fundamental difference, not clearly stated, between organized aggression here and that called feud elsewhere, this discordance is also symptomatic of the lamentable confusion and disagreement over the precise meaning of the labels applied to the markedly different aggressive encounters that occur between the varyingly constituted socio-political groups of the stateless world (for attempts at definition see Berndt 1962:232, Malinowski 1941:523, and Newcomb 1960:318-20).

[2] A comment on an earlier draft of this paper by Professor R. N. H. Bulmer, for which I am grateful, prompted me to recast it in terms of this problem. I also acknowledge discussions on feuding with Professor E. L. Peters which helped me to see differences between it and Wola hostilities, and consequently the significance of the ritual described here.

[3] A possibility, not discussed in this paper, is that following the first fatal fracas the killer and his kin will offer wergild wealth to prevent hostilities going further (Sillitoe 1979a:222,235), but these payments are only likely to be offered and accepted between relatives, who are unlikely to kill one another.

[4] They may also, while setting aside current attempts at revenge, maintain a stance, at least to themselves, of seeking revenge at some time in the future, which can be important to those emotionally involved and desiring immediate physical vengeance: their attitude changing gradually to one where they turn to sorcery to exact revenge.

[5] It is not implied that the Wola engage in retributory divinations, nor sorcery and poisoning, to subvert feuding. This is *one* of the

consequences of their behaviour. There are, of course, several other social, psychological and intellectual sides to these activities, many of which are difficult for an outsider to comprehend, let alone communicate to others (such as their efficacy, the 'truth' regarding their supposedly lethal import).

6 There is a third variety, which they call *waisem tok* or *hayow tok*. This is the terrifyingly potent sorcery they believe the Foi people who live around Lake Kutubu practise. The Wola claim they are ignorant of the procedures that feature in it, unlike the above two forms of sorcery, of which they believe some of their number have knowledge, and occasionally use to kill others.

7 See also Ryan 1961:288-91 and Lederman 1981 for accounts of sorcery and poisoning in the Mendi valley.

8 A *sem* is a variably sized grouping of relatives, consisting of cognatically and affinally related persons (see Sillitoe 1979a:30-46). This case was somewhat atypical in that the two sides centred on two *semgenk* (Gez and Gaip) that belonged to the same *semonda* (called Haenda); that is, they occupied the same territory—it is more usual for the two sides to centre on *sem* occupying separate territories.

9 The Wola customarily prefix individual names with those of one of the *sem* with which they are associated, in a manner reminiscent of our surnames (Sillitoe 1979a:32).

10 The Wola commonly refer to sickness caused by a spirit attack or female pollution (see Sillitoe 1979b) as being 'eaten', that is having their vital organs gnawed away by malignant forces.

11 This prohibition is not unique to the *komay* divination but characterizes all rituals concerning *towmow* spirits.

12 The question of exegetical dissent and the variability that is inherent in Melanesian religious practices and beliefs has recently come to the fore; see Lewis 1980, Juillerat 1980 and Brunton 1980 (plus subsequent correspondence in the journal *Man*).

13 If someone unrelated to either side in the sorcery case is embroiled in some other intractable dispute with someone who is, he may attend the *komay* ritual and demand to eat a piece of the meat from the tree-fern oven shared by those on the opposite side to the person with whom he is in dispute. By partaking of this meat he will demonstrate his innocence or the veracity of his accusations, for his opponent or one of his relatives will be struck down and die as a result of his lying (this way of resolving a dispute resembles the *showbez* pork slapping contest, which has obscurant aspects similar to the jaw-rubbing divination, although it does not involve the intervention of any supernatural forces—Sillitoe 1981).

REFERENCES

Berndt, R. M.
1962   *Excess and Restraint: Social Control among a New Guinea Mountain People*. Chicago: Chicago University Press.

Brunton, R.
1980   'Misconstrued Order in Melanesian Religion'. *Man* 15: ll2-28.

Juillerat, B.
1980   'À Propos de L'initiation Gnau', *Journal de la Société des Océanistes* 68: 227-30 (plus Lewis's response :230-2).

Lederman, R.
1981   'Sorcery and Social Change in Mendi'. *Social Analysis* 8: 15-27.

Lewis, G.
1980   *Day of Shining Red: an Essay on Understanding Ritual*. Cambridge: Cambridge University Press.

Malinowski, B.
1941   'An Anthropological Analysis of War'. *American Journal of Sociology* 46: 521-50.

Newcombe, W. W.
1960   'Toward an Understanding of War'. In G. E. Dole and R. Carneiro (eds): *Essays in the Science of Culture: in Honor of Leslie A. White*. New York: Crowell: 317-36.

Peters, E. L.
1967   'Some Structural Aspects of the Feud Among the Camel-herding Bedouin of Cyrenaica'. *Africa* 37: 261-82.

Radcliffe-Brown, A. R.
1940   Preface to M. Fortes and E. E. Evans-Pritchard (eds): *African Political Systems*. London: Oxford University Press: xi-xxiii.

Ryan, D'A.
1961   Gift Exchange in the Mendi Valley. Ph.D. thesis, Sydney University.

Sillitoe, P.
1978   'Big Men and War in New Guinea'. *Man* 13: 252-71.
1979a   *Give and Take: Exchange in Wola Society*. Canberra: Australian National University Press.
1979b   'Man-eating Women: Fears of Sexual Pollution in the Papua New Guinea Highlands'. *Journal of the Polynesian Society* 88: 77-97.
1981   'Pigs in Disputes'. *Oceania* 51: 256-65.

PART THREE:

*Sorcery,
Legitimacy and
Social Order*

5

Sorcery and the Social Order in Kove

ANN CHOWNING

Ever since Malinowski, in *Crime and Custom*, described the Trobriand sorcerers who openly punish those who offend the chiefs and infringe their privileges, anthropologists have tended to note the positive side of sorcery beliefs and practices, even though few have gone so far as to endorse Malinowski's (1926:94) characterization of sorcery as 'on the whole a beneficent agency, of enormous value for early culture'. So Epstein, in *Contention and Dispute* (1974:18), says that 'in certain circumstances sorcery beliefs may be put to work in the service of damping down conflict and strengthening group solidarity', while Lawrence (1973:218) speaks of sorcery—by which he seems to mean, following Marwick (1965), sorcery accusations—as functioning 'in the socio-political system as a strain gauge and safety valve'. I shall return later to the question of the functions of such beliefs and accusations; here I only wish to indicate that there is nothing new in suggesting that sorcery beliefs can act as powerful conservative forces in maintaining a social system. Indeed, Patterson (1974–75:137) points out that their usefulness has been somewhat overemphasized by many structural-functionalists. It is nevertheless noteworthy that few societies have been described in which leaders maintain power by openly threatening to sorcerize

149

their subordinates. In Melanesia the best known such
societies are those in which hereditary leaders are expected
to employ official sorcerers to help maintain their privileges: the Trobriands, the Mekeo (Hau'ofa 1981), and the
Roro (Monsell-Davis 1973) (see also Tonkinson 1981).
Judging from the available descriptions, rarely was the
leader himself thought to use sorcery within his own community. In her survey of sorcery and witchcraft in Melanesia,
Patterson (1974–75:149) concludes that 'accusations following a death are made almost exclusively against . . .
members of an out-group', and Forge (1970:258) states that
throughout New Guinea, 'at least the overt accusations are
directed outside the [local] group'. These generalizations
so contrast with what I found in one of the societies in which
I have worked, Kove of West New Britain, that I have chosen
to describe it in some detail before contrasting the situation
there with that in other parts of Melanesia.

I must begin by defining my terms. Unlike a number
of other anthropologists (Royal Anthropological Institute
1951:189), I prefer not to lump together all forms of
harmful magic. Instead, I normally follow Seligman
(1910:281) in defining sorcery as 'magical practices directed
towards the production of disease and death'. Magic
designed to attract wild pigs to a garden, bring bad luck to
a trader, make a woman promiscuous, or produce rain
when a rival is giving a feast, is certainly malevolent, but its
consequences are typically of a different order from those
produced by sorcery.[1] Still less would I include love magic.
Furthermore, I fully agree with Patterson (1974–75:141)
that protective spells placed on property, which she calls
tabu, should be distinguished from acts motivated by 'the
desire to cause harm to a specific individual'. The Kove do
not normally equate such protective spells, and the ailments
caused by them, with sorcery (though I have heard this
done in Pidgin, in which categories kept separate in Kove
may be lumped together). They do, however, equate magical
procedures used to harm others with the use of foreign
chemical poisons which are thought to require no ritual to
be effective. In this paper I shall be following Kove usage,
and so extend 'sorcery' to embrace one non-magical
technique.[2]

The Kove (Kombe) occupy the Kombe Census Division, just to the west of the Willaumez Peninsula on the north coast of New Britain, except for two offshoot settlements, Tamoniai and Arumigi, located far to the west. The Kove had been brought under partial government control prior to World War I, and mission stations were established within the census division in 1930 by the Roman Catholics and in 1953 by the Seventh Day Adventists. My fieldwork was carried out between 1966 and 1983.[3] I was originally attracted to Kove, the fourth Papua New Guinea society in which I had worked, by reports from both government officers and missionaries of strong resistance to European influence. I was interested in the possible reasons for this reputed conservatism, and although it turned out to be more apparent than real (Chowning 1972), ceremonial life and the assertion of traditional privileges by adult men and semi-hereditary leaders were much less weakened than in many nearby societies with an equally long history of contact. Sorcery threats and fears were obviously a major force in maintaining this situation, and the constant mention of in-group sorcery contrasted notably with what I had observed elsewhere.

The pertinent aspects of Kove social organization are as follows. Each village usually contains members of several patrilineages, who trace descent from named ancestors who dispersed from the same single ancestral village a few generations earlier (four to five for middle-aged men). Descendants of the first man to settle in a particular village claim authority over other lineages. Associated with each lineage are rights to names, ornaments, other property, and one or more men's houses, each of which contains distinctive ritual paraphernalia such as masks and noise-makers. Women are either completely forbidden to enter the men's house or, under special circumstances, admitted only to a front room, with the paraphernalia hidden elsewhere. Some men's houses contain two lineages or 'sides', the result of the incorporation of a non-agnate (see below), and marriage between the sides is permitted. Otherwise, because lineages are exogamous, so are men's houses. Heading each men's house is a senior male member of the lineage, called a *mahoni*, whose position is partly hereditary and partly achieved. Men desiring to become *mahoni* often set up their own men's houses, and internal quarrels also lead to fissioning, but the men's houses associated with a single lineage are usually built side by side and bear the same name.

Because a village typically contains several lineages, it contains more than one hamlet. Ideally, the residences of hamlet members are contiguous, facing the men's house across a plaza, but the extreme crowding of the tiny offshore islets on which many Kove villages are built may prevent this ideal pattern from being followed. The men of a single hamlet speak of each other as brothers, although sometimes family quarrels or divorce may lead to a man's joining the men's house of his mother's brother or wife's brother. If a hamlet contains more than one men's house, considerable rivalry may exist between them, though they present a united front *vis-à-vis* other hamlets. The men of a single hamlet fish together and often eat together, and in the past usually slept under the same roof, but nowadays married men normally sleep in the family house. Women do not wholly lose lineage and hamlet affiliation on marriage; they are often buried in the hamlets (formerly, actually inside the men's house) of their fathers and brothers rather than in those of their husbands. Divorced women usually go home to their brothers, and sometimes their sons grow up and remain in the mother's natal hamlet, though the woman's brother is likely to press her to marry again so that he can receive the affinal payments.

The Kove express a preference for marrying cross-cousins, with whom there is a joking relationship and who, in theory, can be trusted not to sorcerize each other.[4] In addition to the prohibition on marriage within the lineage, marriage to any close parallel cousin is strongly disapproved. Rivalry and hostility between villages lead to a high rate of community endogamy, and consequently other men's houses of the same village may contain a man's mother's brother (with whom he has a close lifelong relationship) and his affines. Marriages are sometimes arranged between children, but most result from premarital affairs, thought to be inspired by love magic performed by either partner. The stability of the marriage, however, depends largely on the ability of the husband to satisfy the demands of his wife's kin, led by her eldest brother, for payments of shell money on various occasions honouring the children, especially the first-born, of the marriage. I have described the complex marital exchanges elsewhere (Chowning 1978). Here I shall only note that a married man obtains the money he needs by making loans to his agnates, to be repaid at one hundred per cent interest, and by making 'gifts' to his sisters, real or classificatory, for which he eventually demands a repayment in shell money. Attempts to collect debts involve much intervillage travel. When a ceremony honouring a child is imminent, whole families spend periods of weeks or even months in the village of the sponsor. Only those who work for the sponsor during this period, including helping him collect his debts, can hope for adequate amounts of shell money, regardless of how closely they are related to his wife. The desire to obtain shell money leads many Kove of both sexes to live for lengthy periods outside their natal communities. Sometimes the host community contains consanguineal kin of the visitors: members of the mother's family, a married daughter, or even an offshoot of one's own men's house, founded after some quarrel in the past. All of these can be expected to offer hospitality and some support in the quarrels that tend to break out during these long visits. Nevertheless, residence in a foreign community may be regarded as dangerous, especially if the community is reputed to contain prominent sorcerers, but it is also inescapable if one is to accumulate wealth and prestige.

In general, except for the individual whose parents are from different villages (described by the Kove in Pidgin as *hapkas* 'half-caste'), each village presents a united front both in dealing with outsiders and in arranging and scheduling ceremonies. Fights with other villages over insults and property rights are still common, and only the *hapkas* are not expected to join in. (For major battles, consent should be given by the assembled *mahoni* of all the men's houses.) Within the village, although one men's house is identified as the sponsor of a ceremony, the others co-operate in attending and in not scheduling their own ceremonies at the same time. All village men are expected to attend a feast

held in any men's house of the village, even though fac-
tionalism may make a man nervous about eating in any
other men's house than his own or that of his mother's
brother. As will be seen, the group within which a Kove
feels secure from sorcery is very small.

Sorcery is usually designated by the word *muso*, which
means 'dirt' and 'dirty', as well as designating personal
leavings (Pidgin *doti* or *dati*) used in sorcery. The term for
'sorcerize' is always *kea muso*, 'take *muso*', even when the
technique involves putting a substance into a victim's food
or on to his body, though on very rare occasions I have
heard *karo muso*, 'perform *muso*'. I do not intend to dwell
on the techniques, about which I have relatively little information, being primarily concerned here with the social
implications of sorcery beliefs. A few points need to be mentioned, however. Traditional types of sorcery can usually
be undone by the practitioner and occasionally by other
curers, but some types recently acquired from outside Kove
have no counter-magic. If an illness is long drawn out, it is
assumed that the sorcerer wants to be bought off; if he has
an implacable desire to kill, he disposes of the victim quickly.
Sorcerers are often thought to act in concert, either dividing
up the leavings of one victim or passing them around. Consequently a man paid to undo sorcery can legitimately claim
to have fulfilled his bargain even if the victim dies; he simply
blames colleagues. Indeed, sometimes the ghost of a victim
reproaches his kin for having paid the wrong man. It can
be financially profitable to be regarded as a sorcerer; not
only do victims attempt to ransom themselves, but notorious
sorcerers may be hired. These men are also most successful
in collecting debts in shell money, threatening implicitly or
explicitly to kill a defaulter.

Almost all major sorcery is in the hands of men.[5]
Occasionally the first-born daughter of a *mahoni* is treated
by her father like a man, including admission to the secrets
of the men's house and even instruction in sorcery and
other major magic, such as weather control (Chowning
1978:210). It is widely believed that at least one grand-
daughter of a famed female sorcerer now practises both
sorcery and rain magic. But most women are thought to
know either no malevolent magic or only minor forms, such

as that designed to make a man reject a rival such as a co-wife or to make a woman bear twins. I have heard women accused of sorcery, as when one was blamed for the death of a co-wife and another was tried in a village court because she was seen collecting earth where someone had urinated, but I suspect that further enquiry would have indicated that these women were thought either to be delivering food or drink sorcerized by a man or supplying material to male sorcerers.[6] The real power possessed by women is of a different sort, and considered non-magical by the Kove: a woman can harm a man by introducing menstrual blood or sexual secretions (obtained from boiling her genital covering) into his food, or by stepping over his cooked food. Harm of this sort, which is not equated with sorcery, cannot be undone, but a woman can be begged to stop before the respiratory disease so induced becomes fatal. The reason a woman would attempt to kill her husband is either because he has ill-treated her or because she wants to marry someone else. In addition, a wife may be asked to help her brother by stealing some of her husband's personal leavings so that the brother can dispose of a man who fails to give adequate affinal payments.

Sorcery can be detected by the nature of the disease or death, by divination or revelation, or by knowledge of a quarrel or cause for offence involving a known sorcerer. Sorcerers do not undergo any sort of public apprenticeship or wear special insignia, but in the past it was taken for granted that any son of a noted sorcerer who was adult before his father died was taught the techniques. In recent years rumours often circulate that particular men have acquired powerful sorcery (or poison) abroad, and perhaps have allowed certain others a share. Open boasting about practising sorcery, possession of materials, or attempts to buy spells or materials, may lead to gaol sentences, so that men both allow rumours to circulate and deny direct accusations. (Those who get a sorcerer gaoled, however, fear his vengeance when he is released.)

All disease and death are not attributed to sorcery. Some ailments have very specific, well known causes, such as the respiratory disease just mentioned; sores on the face (the result of eating fish taboo to one's patriline); and other specific afflictions, such as fits and a kind of sore called 'fish-eye', both the result of contact by oneself or one's kin with protective spells placed on property. Occasionally serious ailments in adults are attributed to spirits of non-human origin (Pidgin *masalai*), though these creatures more often attack children. Children may suffer from ailments, sometimes fatal, which rarely or never afflict adults, such as soul loss or the consequences of a parent's eating some food that should be avoided while a child is small. Ghosts of dead kin are often blamed for the deaths of small children, but usually for only hastening the deaths of adults. Minor illnesses in adults are sometimes said to become serious because ghosts, especially those of dead kin, are attracted to the sick person and try to get him to join them, and they are also said to encourage potential suicides. By contrast, ghosts kill small children because they are angry with the child's parent. Although many adults of both sexes fear to sleep alone because of danger from ghosts, and some report encounters or nightmares in which a ghost cuts off one's breath, very rarely is an adult death generally agreed to be the result of a ghostly attack or persuasion, though I have heard this explanation put forward (as an alternative) by the kin of a sorcerer accused of responsibility for the same death.

Minor ailments are often said to have no known cause; in Pidgin, they are said to *kamap nating*. Epidemics which do not kill are not usually blamed on any particular agent, human or non-human, though some suggest that earth-quakes, frequent in this region, bring disease. Death by violence, in warfare or a fight, is 'natural', and so are deaths, usually those of children (as from drowning or burns), that result from simple human carelessness. A few individuals are thought to die of old age. But any sudden death, other than that of an infant or the very old, and any fatal or serious accident to an adult, will be attributed by at least some observers to sorcery. Falls from trees, attacks by a wild pig, shark, or crocodile, being struck by lightning or cutting oneself with an axe, are taken to indicate that the victim 'had sorcery on his skin', both because such happenings are unusual, and because nothing that so harms a human being can be truly accidental (cf. Evans-Pritchard 1937:63 ff).

There is disagreement about deaths resulting from eating shellfish contaminated by the red tide,[7] but since some victims recover, deaths do tend to be attributed to sorcery. In contrast to the Azande, the Kove believe that minor injuries may be truly accidental, but those that develop into bad sores, cripple, or kill, demand further explanation. Sorcery is not always blamed; for example, one fatal fall from a tree was said by some to be the result of the man's climbing it on a Roman Catholic holy day (while others did say sorcery was involved). A man who cut himself badly told me that while he was unconscious, the ghost of his recently dead cousin appeared and told him that he did not have 'sorcery on his skin', leaving him baffled as to the real cause of the accident.

As is evident, different people give different explanations for the same event. Nevertheless, almost all deaths of adults, and most deaths of children, are attributed to sorcery by at least some adults. Sorcery is also blamed for many illnesses, especially those that develop rapidly or become chronic, and frequently for such afflictions as blindness, deafness and insanity, whether temporary or permanent, when these are not congenital. (Sorcery can kill a child in the womb or make the mother die in childbirth, but congenital deformities and mental defects tend to be attributed to contact of a parent with a non-human spirit (Pidgin *masalai*).

The reasons given for the sorcerer's act are various, but the most common are envy and anger. The former is considered natural but not approved, whereas neither anger nor actions arising from it are condemned, though the victim may be blamed for arousing the anger. Like many other present-day Melanesians, the Kove report that they often employ sorcery nowadays to punish offences, such as an intrusion on the secrets of the men's house, seduction of the daughter of a *mahoni*, or letting a fire get out of control and burn down houses, for which in the past the offender would simply have been speared (Chowning 1974:188–9). The use of sorcery as a substitute for force that might more easily lead to a gaol sentence is widely regarded as entirely legitimate. Common, but more to be deplored, is envy of those richer and more successful than oneself, though the boastful are considered to be inviting trouble. *Mahoni* and their families are inevitably targets of sorcery, and so may be those who excel in school or earn large salaries. This phenomenon is widely reported in Melanesia, but more distinctively Kove is the frequency with which deaths of beautiful young women are attributed to men who admired or coveted them and were unable to obtain them; it is sufficient explanation of such a death to say that a woman died because men desired her. (If, as often happens, she rejects a suitor insultingly, anger may be a factor as well.) A married woman may also be killed because a rejected suitor wants to avenge himself or to grieve his successful rival; on the other hand, widows have told me that their husbands were killed by men who wanted to marry them. One woman attributed elephantiasis of a leg to men she rejected after her husband's death. A 'real man' should know love magic that will attract women regardless of their conscious desires or marital status, but those who do not possess such magic will try other means, and avenge themselves if they fail. A woman may be suspected, because of jealousy of a rival or resentment of another woman's success, of collaborating with a man to kill another woman (women are not harmed by female secretions).

If male relatives help her it may be because they feel that she is neglected or mistreated. One of the most common justifications for sorcerizing an important man is his behaviour with women. It is characteristic of *mahoni* to have many affairs and to take many wives; indeed, polygyny is supposed to be practised only by *mahoni*. *Mahoni*, real or potential (the son or nephew of one) tend to marry the daughters of other *mahoni*, since only these can be expected to produce adequate affinal payments, but few men manage to keep multiple wives content, or to refrain from neglecting a legitimate wife while having affairs. The kin of the offended wives and seduced women try to avenge the women and themselves; consequently, many illnesses and deaths of *mahoni* and their closest kin (parents and children) are openly attributed to righteous wrath on the part of fathers and brothers (and outraged husbands, if a wife was stolen). When a *mahoni* suspects sorcery, he first approaches the powerful kin of women he has mistreated. With women from lesser families, he may feel more secure; the first-born son of one *mahoni* explained to me that he had managed to have so many affairs because people were afraid of the sorcery that his family controlled. Ordinary men and their kin may also be sorcerized for the mistreatment of a woman. In 1983 the death of an unimportant though respected old man was blamed by a kinswoman on his son's rejection of a wife.

Maltreatment of one's female kin is one of many stimuli to righteous anger. The practice of sorcery is justified by the following offences, among others: failure to pay debts or fines; infringement of property rights, as by carving a design belonging to another lineage; refusal to obey a *mahoni*; acting like a *mahoni* (as by building a separate men's house) if a man is not the son or nephew of one; revealing or openly discussing the secrets of the men's house; improper behaviour on ritual occasions; and, of course, sorcerizing or otherwise being responsible for the death of someone else. The most frequent reason given for the practice of sorcery is dissatisfaction with payments of shell money—default on debts, or failure to give adequate amounts at a ceremonial distribution. Quarrels about shell money involve the closest kin, consanguineal and affinal. I have seen great violence used or threatened between father and son, full brothers, brother and sister, and spouses, and although I have not heard of sorcery killings between father and son or full brothers,[8] they are assumed to occur within the lineage. One man told me that sorcerers could include 'another father'—a senior man of one's lineage other than a true father—as well as other close kin. In particular, women say that their full brothers will sorcerize them if they do not get adequate payments from the woman's husband, and men confirm that they would do this because it offends them so to see a married sister 'walking around not paid for'. What is universally agreed to be a recent dramatic increase in the number of men trying to make a reputation by dispensing large amounts of shell money has undoubtedly led to an increase in quarrels centring on debt (Chowning 1978). With the weakening of traditional leadership, of which this increased competitiveness is one manifestation, *mahoni* are less often thought to defend their privileges by sorcerizing upstarts; I have not heard this reason given for any recent deaths. Neither do men any longer sorcerize children for making noise near a men's house. Another change, according to a number of men, is that women now know a great deal about such 'secret' matters as how masks are manufactured and how the supposed voices of spirits are produced. Nevertheless, women still fear to talk openly about these things or to behave disrespectfully, as by refusing to cook for the 'spirits', and men are also afraid to be overheard discussing the secrets with their wives or to flout any of the strict observances surrounding one particular kind of ritual performance called *tuvura*.

In Pidgin, the Kove usually render *mahoni* as 'rich man' rather than 'bigman'. Balancing the fact that it is financially profitable to be regarded as a sorcerer is the risk of being killed in revenge; non-sorcerers are thought to live longer, even if they too run the risk of being sorcerized by the envious. *Mahoni* who do not know sorcery are usually wealthy enough to hire others to act for them. Unless the *mahoni* himself administers a substance provided by another, the actual sorcerer is often blamed (and always divined as the one responsible) rather than the man who hired him. Consequently an acknowledged sorcerer known to be angry with a prospective victim may hire someone else to attack him, hoping to escape detection. True wealth is needed both for hiring and for buying off a sorcerer. The most valuable form of shell money, finer and rarer than the ordinary kind, is reserved for these purposes, in addition to providing the initial marriage payment. I was told that a sorcerer given lower value currency would only pretend to undo his work, but it is immoral to accept high-value currency and not fulfil the contract. The ideal way to hire a sorcerer is to present him with some of the victim's leavings along with a strand of this currency. When the sorcerer and his kin are attacked, as they almost inevitably will be, they can use the same currency to buy off those responsible. A man who allows himself to be known as a sorcerer, usually by openly threatening vengeance on those who cross him (though without specifying the means), and who accepts payments either to sorcerize someone or to stop doing so, gains both wealth and power. A number of older men are prepared to run the risk of identification as sorcerers, and many younger ones boast of the sorcery controlled by their lineages and so easily available to them. Several men and women have freely told me that their fathers are or were sorcerers. On the other hand, particularly in view of the seriousness with which sorcery is regarded by the Papua New Guinea government, it is necessary to be careful in capitalizing on such a reputation. Payments to sorcerers, either to perform or to neutralize a spell, are always made with great secrecy. When a young man whose mother's brother is a renowned sorcerer openly threatened recourse to his uncle to punish boys who had hurt his son, he successfully pleaded in the village court that he was only trying to frighten them; if he had really meant to harm them, he would have done so surreptitiously. (If any of the boys had sickened, however, his position would have been precarious.)

It is too early for me to know whether the knowledge of the elders will automatically be assumed to have been passed on, as would have been the case in the past. At present, it is sometimes suggested that old-style sorcery is not always transmitted, and that the sanctions it particularly supported, having to do with the men's houses and rituals, are weakening for this reason. The Kove say that they worry less about food leavings than they did in the past. If indeed younger men are not learning from their elders, they are reputed constantly to acquire new and particularly deadly forms of sorcery, as well as increased knowledge of chemical poisons, during their travels and employment abroad. People suggest not that the actual use of sorcery is decreasing, but that it is employed for somewhat different purposes than in the traditional society, and perhaps by a different range of individuals, who are not dependent on learning the techniques from a father or uncle.[9] At the same time, it must be noted that the men who were elders at the time of my stays in Kove had travelled widely in the period before World War II, many of them having been employed in the New Guinea Constabulary, and most having worked in regions, such as the Gazelle Peninsula, believed to be inhabited by particularly powerful magicians, whose techniques and materials they had an opportunity to acquire.

In contrast to some other peoples of Papua New Guinea (Lawrence,this volume), the Kove do not believe that sorcery has to come from the ancestors in order to be effective. On the contrary, they often esteem and fear foreign magicians above local ones. The use of sorcery may have deep roots in Kove culture, but the actual techniques used have long been subject to constant revision. It is interesting that the Kove seem to be regarded as a source of sorcery by their neighbours to the west (Counts 1974:140).

When disaster strikes and sorcery is suspected, the victim and his kin have at least two problems to solve: the actual cause, and the identity of the sorcerer. Concurrently, if the victim survives long enough, they may also seek for cures other than neutralization of the sorcery. If death is quick, the only reason to ascertain the cause is vengeance, but if a cure seems possible, various techniques are called into play. Judging from reported cases, it seems rare for the Kove to conclude in the first instance that a case is incurable, although encounters with aid posts and hospitals frequently lead not only to this conclusion, but also to confirmation of suspicion that the cause of the ailment is sorcery. I agree with Lawrence (this volume) that aid post orderlies often share sorcery beliefs with the people they are treating (or refusing to treat), but the Kove, like other Papua New Guineans I know, also frequently report that nuns and European doctors informed them that a particular ailment was caused by sorcery; I assume that this was their interpretation of being told that a condition could not be treated (or diagnosed). I have most often heard such accounts from women; many men are aware that at least some Europeans do not believe in sorcery, though some think that all human beings practise it.

It would be easy to conclude that for some there is a simple dichotomy between diseases that are caused by sorcery or spirits and so can be cured, if at all, only by indigenous techniques, and others that can be cured by European methods and so have a different cause, but matters are not so simple. Although some would agree that a cure based on a particular diagnosis confirms the diagnosis, people do not often abstain from trying any available remedy because of a fixed idea about the origin of the ailment. One woman told me that her stomach trouble, caused by sorcery, was cured by a combination of a hospital operation and prayer, but European remedies are not the only alternatives. A man suffering from respiratory distress for which he constantly blamed his wife, nevertheless talked of visiting a curer (from the Gazelle Peninsula) reputed to be skilled in dealing with such ailments. Another man said he had been cured, when virtually on his deathbed, by a Tolai whose potion made him vomit up the material administered (via a woman) by a sorcerer who had threatened to 'devour' him after being knocked unconscious during a drunken fight. Local curers may also claim to be able to cure minor afflictions caused by sorcery, such as an infected foot attributed to a sorcerer's having speared the victim's footprint. If sorcery is suspected or certain, the ideal is certainly to try to persuade the sorcerer to undo his work, but if he cannot be identified or will not yield, other cures may at least be tried, and they are also used to restore a sorcery victim to full health after the affliction has been neutralized.

Curers, *valuvalu*, do not necessarily know or practise harmful magic. They may have learned their cures from kin, bought the knowledge while away at work, or had a revelation as the result of an extraordinary experience such as 'dying' and returning to life, or being possessed by a ghost. They charge non-kin for their services, but not their close kin. Claiming to be skilled in diagnosis, they may recognize the cause of a sore from its appearance, or of an illness from the look in the victim's eyes.[10] Their methods typically but not invariably involve the use of spells; they may be as simple as washing in hot water or administering a suppository of soap, but still contrast with cures known to everyone, such as eating uncharmed ginger for a stomachache. Particularly with children, whose illnesses are likely to be caused by spirits, the ideal curer is a diviner who can send his soul in dreams to locate, identify and deal with these spirits by pleading, offering payment or, with the aid of the ghosts of the kin, actually attacking them. Sorcerers are not spirits, however, and it is not usually considered possible for them to be identified by any soul other than that of a victim who has actually, in Kove theory, died. If he 'returns to life', he may have seen, in another world, the soul of the sorcerer, and one man gave me a detailed account of how he was cured at once when a man so identified was summoned to him (the man claimed that he had obtained from other sorcerers the bundle of leavings he brought). In most cases, identification by the soul of the victim comes only after he is really dead (see below), and is of no use in saving him. If he is to be saved, the sick person must rely on his recollection of past offences committed by himself or one of his close kin, and his knowledge of which men are willing and able to practise sorcery. The actual victim of a sorcerer may not be the offender, but his wife, child, or aged parent, any of whom seems to be considered more vulnerable than a strong man. (Children are also too ignorant or unsuspicious to reject poisoned food.) The death of a young mother, because it affects the children as well as the husband, is also considered a particularly devastating blow.

Often the sorcerer is identified simply by gossip; men who have kin in the village of a suspect are sent to ask the suspect's co-residents, and frequently return with a positive answer. If he is available, a known sorcerer may act as a go-between, being thought to possess special knowledge even when he is not implicated. Occasionally suspicious behaviour has been observed, such as a man entering a house when he knew the residents were out or asleep. The daughter of a man famous as a sorcerer told me that sorcerers must abstain from bathing until the spell takes effect and so can sometimes be identified by this aberrant behaviour. A sorcerer may also identify himself by sending word to the victim that he can be bought off for a certain sum (as one victim told me had happened to him). Failing such identification, the kin of the sick person are reduced to simply offering money to all known sorcerers they might have offended, usually spreading the payments through several villages. A man with many enemies may almost impoverish himself by these means. In a recent case, a *mahoni* paid so much to ransom himself from other *mahoni* offended by his many affairs that a major ceremony he was undertaking, and that planned by a sister who lent him some money, were delayed for several years. Furthermore, when his elder brother got sick, the *mahoni* could not afford to ransom him. It was generally assumed that the older brother had been attacked either by a man with whom he had just had a violent quarrel over a debt, or by a man whose daughter had been taken as a second wife by the old man's son and then rejected. Both men would have been motivated by anger. Sorcerers inspired by envy are more difficult to identify, and it is these who may only be detected after a death.

In such cases, the ghost of the dead person is the informant. He may appear to his kin in dreams, or possess a mourner at his funeral. Such appearances are not fully trusted because of the possibility of trickery by the living, and occasionally the ghost is reported to have made different accusations to different people. Sometimes the kin of the deceased deliberately try to attract the ghost, though they have abandoned as too frightening a technique in which it is supposed to appear directly to the questioner—a terrifying experience. One method of divination requires a cross-cousin, who summons the ghost with jokes and insults, thrusts a pole into his house, and asks questions about the death which are answered by the movements of the pole.[11] Some are sceptical about the efficacy of this method, and others consider it dangerous to the holder of the pole, so that it is rarely used. Regarded as superior is a method recently introduced from the Sepik in which a bamboo pole is placed on the grave, the ghost of the dead person and other ghosts enter it, and the pole leads the men or boys who hold it to the sorcerer—ideally to his house, but at least to his village. Use of this technique on one occasion in 1969 led to a major quarrel in which the accused man refused to admit guilt, and no satisfaction was obtained.

In 1983 the sudden death of a young woman in childbirth led to the use of both these methods, although a substantial number of people held that she had died of natural causes (she had had serious complications with preceding pregnancies and reportedly had been warned by foreign medical personnel to have no more children).[12] But not only had she and her husband recently outdone many of their elders in the ceremony they had sponsored, they had greatly offended both her first cross-cousins and her half-brother by giving more shell money to distant kin than to them. In addition, the husband, especially when drunk, boasted of his prowess, and I gathered that the wife also openly gloried in their accomplishments. The first two seances used the pole-in-house technique, and the ghost was asked whether the death was natural or whether someone 'took your *muso*' or 'heard talk' (the boasting). In repeated questioning by different cross-cousins, including those with whom she had quarrelled, both villages and their separate men's houses were named in the questions, but only in the victim's own village were individual men named—all of them, including the questioner. When the pole failed to move strongly and repeatedly in answer to a specific question, as it should,[13] this method was abandoned, at least temporarily, and the husband broke his mourning seclusion to accuse the cross-cousins who had been so incensed by the low payments. Another man then fetched from a different village a specialist in the Sepik technique. This time the ghosts were asked only whether certain hamlets in the victim's village were responsible, and directed to lead the pole to the houses of the sorcerers. The first ones whose houses were struck by the pole were residents of a hamlet adjoining the widower's, closely related to him. With the expert constantly asking, 'Who else?', several houses in other parts of the village were also struck. On the second night, when the technique was repeated for confirmation, the occupants of a house being approached by the holders of the pole erupted shouting abuse and throwing missiles, eliciting hilarity in the hamlet when the diviners dropped the pole and fled in terror. Although the indignant expert threatened to hold another seance on the next night (the last before my departure), he did not, but there were many discussions of recent events. The interesting point about the second lot of accusations was that those indicated by the pole did not include any of the very close kin known to have quarrelled so bitterly with the dead woman and her husband, but were men supposed to have been involved in other sorcery deaths in the village, as well as other lineage-mates of one of them. Two of them had also been tenta-

Polilipa, a Garia sorcerer and bigman of Wailagime patrilineage, Yaniba village, at a peace ceremony, 1950

Auwobu: Garia traditional healing, 1950

A Mekeo 'man of knowledge' bespelling the bone he uses in divination

Mekeo sorcerers at a ceremony to install a new chief: they are clearly identifiable by their black (or dark blue) garments, black armbands (containing magical 'medicines') and black face paint. The effect of their ritual fasting is evident here.

Wola warriors dressed in their second-best decorations for the *komay* 'jaw-rubbing' ritual

The jawbone of a sorcery victim used in the Wola 'jaw-rubbing' divination ritual intended to bring supernatural punishment to those responsible for the death

Kove women are not usually thought to practise sorcery, though they are often the motive for it. Any woman is thought capable of revenge against an unsatisfactory husband by feeding him ritually contaminated food. The seated woman in this picture is the wife and the daughter of bigmen; the woman dressed in rags with her hair in matted ringlets is in mourning for a husband who died of a respiratory illness which he attributed to her 'poison'.

The eldest son of a Kove bigman, who is a renowned artist and sorcerer. The son, here trying to emulate his father by carving a walking stick, boasts that he can engage with impunity in socially disapproved extra-marital affairs because of the community's fears of his father's sorcery prowess.

Notable bigmen among the Kwoma are also often reputed sorcerers, such as the man pictured here holding two spears and leading a dance performed during the yam harvest ceremonies.

A Kwoma bigman and reputed sorcerer holding a ceremonial sculpture
of the type displayed during the yam harvest ceremonies.

tively identified (by slight movements of the pole) in the first set of seances. One of the men was the first cousin of the dead woman's father, and was said to have been annoyed at not receiving more shell money at the ceremony, but the other was one of the husband's kin and had received nothing. Though I did not hear this said after the seances, the two men had been identified by the dead woman as those who had made the largest distributions at their own ceremonies until she and her husband had far outdone them. It seems safe to conclude that envy would be assumed to have motivated both men.

The hamlet of the widower had once been joined to that in which three of the accused sorcerers lived, and one of them was married to the full sister of the widower. The director of the pole in the last seance, a second cross-cousin to the dead woman, was leading it to the house of his full sister and her husband when they were chased away. The accused first cousin of the dead woman's father was also the person with whom the latter stayed whenever he quarrelled with his sister or daughter. It is clear that accusations were indeed made within the in-group. The widower's brother announced publicly that he believed all the accusations, and the father's sister of the dead woman (undoubtedly relieved that her sons had been absolved) said the same to me, adding however that those really guilty were the widower and his father-in-law (her own brother) for not giving enough wealth to the right people.[14] In the hamlet that contained three of the accused men, public discussion held that this type of seance was untrustworthy, among other reasons because the pole was initially directed towards certain hamlets and also because a ridiculously large number of people were implicated. Privately, however, the members of the other men's house in the hamlet of the three accused said that the men were indeed sorcerers: 'Their ancestors killed our ancestors'. Clearly, suspected sorcerers are likely to be the focus of accusations, even when their personal motives seem slight, but it is necessary to remember that they are also the ones likely to be hired by those who are truly aggrieved. Given that sorcery cases are now outside the adjudication of the village courts, I cannot predict the outcome of these accusations, but it seems safe to say that the widower and his brothers would enlist the aid of their mother's brother, now the most renowned sorcerer in the region, to avenge the death. (I am discounting the widower's statement to me that such vengeance, normal in the past, is no longer practised.)

On earlier field trips men had told me that instead of trusting seances they prefer to draw their own conclusions as to who is guilty, or learn his identity from gossip; bide their time without having an open quarrel; and then kill the sorcerer or one of his kin when they were off their guard. In the meantime, relations may appear perfectly friendly. Only occasionally, when several deaths occur in rapid succession, will a group of leaders unite to expel a notorious sorcerer from the community (in the past, he might have been speared if all the *mahoni* agreed). Such cases are rare, however; most sorcerers are respected as well as feared, and are too useful to their lineage-mates for these to abandon them to their enemies.

The lineage is, for men at least, generally considered to be secure from sorcery, despite presumed exceptions mentioned earlier. Men expect to be safe within the men's house, and because food brought there is shared around, the woman who cooks it is also not considered to be a threat to her husband, as she may be when he eats in the family house. By contrast, a woman is not safe eating with her own brother if he is cross with her or her husband, but she is safe under her own roof—except from surreptitious intruders—because she does not expect her husband to sorcerize her. Admittedly her co-wife may try harmful magic against her, but co-wives rarely share a single house. Paradoxically, then, a woman is safer from sorcery (though not from physical abuse) in her husband's hamlet than in her own, with the single exception of the situation in which the men band together against someone who betrays the secrets or violates the taboos of the men's house. A man is not, however, as safe in his own household as in his men's house.

The Kove would agree that the dangers described do exist, but it should not be concluded that they live in great fear and suspicion of each other, except when already weakened by illness.[15] Instead, the threat of the possible consequences is a spur to proper behaviour towards all those who might otherwise take their revenge; the statement that it takes a 'real man' to be married to a Kove woman, and to keep her and his affines content, is made as an affirmation of self-confidence by those who do not noticeably fear others. But such self-confident men are also the ones who give offence by arrogant behaviour, and lose their tempers if they do not receive the payments they think they deserve. Insulting or cursing someone else—or, worse, striking him—is very likely to lead to retaliatory sorcery, and it is precisely the men who are able to accumulate enough wealth to satisfy their creditors who also behave in this way. Boasting about one's personal achievements is said to anger everyone, and yet all *mahoni* seem to do it, and to encourage their children to emphasize their special position. Similarly, beautiful girls, endlessly and openly admired, are encouraged to place such a high value on themselves that they insult, rather than simply evade, suitors who then may reasonably be expected to avenge themselves. If the Kove were more afraid of sorcery, they might not so often behave as to provoke what is considered justified retaliation. Real fear manifests itself only when several of one's close kin die in rapid succession. I knew one man whose ambitions to become a *mahoni* were completely undermined by his dread of eating outside his own hamlet (as his wife explained to me).

Even though the Kove do not strike an observer as fear-ridden, it is still safe to say that dread of sorcery keeps all women subservient to all men when the latter are engaged in ceremonial activity, and it also makes young people of both sexes feel that they must devote their energies to acquiring shell money and paying debts, no matter how onerous and time wasting they find the tasks. The most difficult position in the society is that of the married woman who is supposed to identify with the interests of both her husband and her brother, and who may be asked either to divorce or help kill a husband who displeases her brother, or herself risk being killed. As long as one lives in a village, or even in an urban centre containing many Kove, there is no escape from these obligations. The young men who so deplore the endless exchange cycles end by having to participate in them, and then often show themselves as

ambitious to make a name as the elders whose preoccu-
pations they once denigrated. Not having acquired a
reputation, young men cannot use their knowledge to extort
payment from debtors—or even non-debtors, as a few
prominent sorcerers can—but the danger that they might
punish those who offend them (by using new forms of
sorcery or chemical poison obtained outside Kove) prevents
them from being thoroughly exploited by the older men.

As this balance of power indicates, sorcery can be used
by the weak man to bring down those he envies or to punish
those who mistreat him. It is nevertheless regarded by the
Kove as primarily an instrument of power, a complement
to the spear when not a substitute for it, and it is used to
enforce the edicts of those who should be in command and
to keep the society running along what the Kove consider
to be traditional lines.[16] On the whole, the situation is the
opposite of that described by Lindenbaum (1979:145) for
New Guinea societies in general, in which 'individuals fear
the retaliation of those they dominate'. Kove fear those who
dominate them; evoking fear is what produces domination.

Kove Sorcery in Comparative Perspective

Patterns of Accusations

The difficulties of classifying Melanesian societies as regards
sorcery fears and accusations are illustrated by the typologies
proposed by Berndt (1972) and Patterson (1974–75). Berndt
(1972:1050) puts all societies with matrilineal descent,
including the Lakalai of north-west New Britain, into a different type from any with patrilineal descent, and Patterson
(1974–75:153) makes a similar distinction. Berndt
(1972:1059) suggests that only in his Type II societies, which
all practise matrilineal descent and include the Lakalai (and
the Trobriands), is sorcery 'generally regarded as legitimate
procedure . . . [with] more positive recognition of the social
control aspect', although in some societies with patrilineal
descent, his Type IV, 'sorcery is an element of social control'
but 'penalties for illicit use are severe'. Patterson's typology
is more complex than Berndt's, giving more attention to
residence patterns and the nature of the political unit or
parish. She misrepresents the Lakalai, confusing the various
levels of residential grouping so that she thinks that people

move between parishes, but notes that she has trouble fitting them into her system along with other matrilineal societies (1974–75:217). In fact, despite the differences in descent systems, the Lakalai have much in common with the Kove. Prior to European contact, in both societies a coalition of older men used sorcery threats to maintain secrecy about masks and other male rituals, and some prominent leaders not only intimidated co-residents with their reputed knowledge of sorcery, but added to their personal wealth by accepting payments for undoing spells (Chowning and Goodenough 1971:156, 165, 170). The main difference seems to have been that the Lakalai sorcerer was considerably more secretive about his activities, even when he accepted payment; the openness of Kove sorcerers is more distinctive than the way they use their reputations both to gain individual power and to maintain institutions generally accepted by other members of the society (Berndt 1972:1059, 1063). Boasting about one's use of sorcery is also reported for the Kaliai, immediately to the west of the Kove (Counts 1974:138). An even more important difference between Kove and Lakalai was the Lakalai assumption that one was usually safe from sorcery within not only the matrilineal descent group, which was dispersed throughout Lakalai, but the hamlet, the smallest residential grouping beyond the household. Other hamlets of the same village were not safe, nor were all consanguineal kin, and it was also acknowledged, as in Abelam (Forge 1970:263–4), that members of one's hamlet might treacherously pass on personal leavings to outside sorcerers. Nevertheless, a man did not fear sorcery from his affines, nor, apparently, would an ambitious man openly threaten members of his own descent group. Our data on Lakalai are deficient because, under Christian influence, sorcery had become relatively unimportant in Lakalai at the time of our fieldwork, though still mentioned in connection with serious illnesses and death.[17]

The Legitimacy of Sorcery Attacks
When comparing a Kove sorcerer with those described from other parts of Melanesia, several points must be kept in mind. Rather than being identified because of his isolation during initiation (Lawrence, this volume), or by his

appearance and demeanour (Stephen, this volume), he identifies himself by boasting, threatening and accepting payment for his services. Of course, given that some men acknowledge that they practise sorcery, it is probable that others are falsely identified or divined as also being covert adepts. Nevertheless, the situation differs from that reported in some areas in which an outsider may doubt that sorcery, however frequently discussed, is ever practised (Forge 1970:261, Bowden, this volume). Furthermore, the techniques employed by Kove sorcerers do not include shape-shifting, invisibility, or any of those commonly classed in Pidgin as *sangguma*, but only ones which the most sceptical outsider would acknowledge that a human being could practise.[18] The efficacy of the techniques is not at issue; I am simply noting that there is no reason to doubt that sorcery is performed. Another point that must be stressed is that sorcerers are not usually thought to be randomly malicious—unlike, for example, the Tangu *ranguma* (Burridge 1965:231). The Kove sorcerer's motives—including ambition, vengeance, the desire for wealth, and even envy— are shared by everyone, and not blameworthy in themselves, however one may dislike falling victim to the activities they inspire. Speaking of New Guinea as a whole, Forge (1970:258) says: 'Sorcery in the abstract is bad, but in actual life it is morally neutral', but a Kove is more likely to regard it dispassionately in the abstract, and be neutral in his attitude towards a specific sorcerer unless that sorcerer attacks him. Indeed, a father who knows sorcery may be a source of pride. Furthermore, the closest kin of a victim may admit that he invited retaliation by his misbehaviour, though they may express mild disapproval of the sorcerer's ignoring of kin ties. The belief that sorcery may be evil in itself was expressed to me only by one man, who 'died' and saw the sorcerer responsible walking on a stony and difficult path while his own soul was on a pleasant one. He told me that upon recovery (which depended on his identification of the sorcerer) he decided to abandon sorcery himself for fear that sorcerers would suffer in the afterlife. Almost certainly Christianity had influenced his ideas.[19]

Because sorcery is not intrinsically evil, a man need not feel insulted if he is accused of being a sorcerer.[20] A man may, however, resent being held responsible for a particular death; an outsider cannot determine whether the resentment indicates innocence or fear of retaliation.

Sorcery and Group Fission
Occasionally sorcery accusations do lead to the emigration of the suspect, either voluntarily or by expulsion, but they do not seem to lead to the neat fissioning described for African societies (Douglas 1970:xxvii). When villages do break up, quarrels about other matters such as adultery tend also to play a part, and although it is reported that villages have been abandoned following many deaths, the splits are not necessarily along lineage or hamlet lines. Given the wide range of subjects about which the Kove quarrel, and the mild inhibitions on open displays of anger between lineages, within the lineage, and between most categories of affines,[21] sorcery accusations are often made between the same people who disagree openly, rather than being an alternative to violent conflict (cf. Marwick 1965: 294).

It is nevertheless true that the existence of factions where they should not exist—within the hamlet—can be detected by covert sorcery accusations. In one case, each of two men separately told me that the other was responsible for killing the child of a third, all being residents of the same hamlet, though the informants were not in the same men's house. (At the time, the father of the dead child was in Rabaul, and according to one informant would not return because of fear and rage, while the other said that he would come back when his grief had lessened, as indeed he did.) If these accusations were made publicly, one of the men would almost certainly have to leave; as it was, the range of malicious gossip in which the two indulged, which included accusations of incest, indicated that they were separated, and indeed opposed, in their own minds if not in their places of residence. It could be argued that this case would justify putting the Kove into Douglas's (1970:xxvii) category of societies in which the witch or sorcerer is an internal enemy and the 'function of accusation [is] . . . to redefine faction boundaries or realign faction hierarchy or split community'. Sorcery accusations in Kove do not, however, usually split the community; indeed, given that they occur between brother and sister (and, in the case of a transvestite said to have been killed by his shamed kin, brother and brother), they do not necessarily split a lineage.

In Kove, social acceptance of the reasonableness, if not always the justice, of the sorcerer's action allows him to remain within the group which also contains his victim. Douglas (ibid.) does not really consider the possibility that in-group sorcery might be tolerated; she assumes that such attacks 'tend to make the body of the victim into an image of the betrayed community: its internal strength is sucked out or poisoned by someone who can get into very close contact'. Almost all Kove sorcery techniques do involve close contact, and if not carried out with the aid of a helper, as when a man tries to kill his brother-in-law, require the sorcerer to approach the potential victim's person, house or belongings (such as betel-chewing equipment left temporarily in a garden hut). He can try to work by stealth at night, but most Kove villages are on offshore islands, and strangers coming ashore at night usually arouse the dogs. Sorcerers operating by daylight must have a legitimate reason for being near the victim, and so are at least on terms of apparent amity with him, if not necessarily residents of the same community.[22]

The Effects of Social Change

Lindenbaum (1981:119) sees the 'effects of colonisation' in 'a shift from what might be called exo-sorcery to endo-sorcery'. Undoubtedly there are many societies in which it is reported that 'endo-sorcery' is a recent phenomenon, including the Kilenge, with whom the Kove frequently interact and sometimes intermarry (Zelenietz 1981:110). I have heard similar statements from the Molima of the Milne Bay Province, who blame depopulation on the uncontrolled actions of female witches whom they are no longer allowed to kill and who, with the breakup of consolidated villages following pacification, no longer feel loyalty to a large group of co-residents (Chowning 1959). The Kove, however, do not report either that in-group sorcery is a recent phenomenon or (in contrast with many other Melanesian societies) that they are more threatened by sorcery than in the past, except in so far as it is a substitute for physical violence. Furthermore, although they think some foreign sorcery, as that of the Tolai, is more powerful than their own, they do not, as a group, feel particularly menaced by outsiders, whether Europeans or other Papua New Guineans. The Kove are well known for their pride and ability to coerce others; in their own eyes, they are the dominant society in West New Britain.

In-group sorcery cannot be attributed to the disappearance of some former state of 'mutual trust and support which magnetised communities from within' (Lindenbaum 1981:122), nor can it be said that 'new sorcery powers, not well institutionalised, stand outside the most respected sources of local authority' (ibid.:125). Although *mahoni* were esteemed for their genealogical connections with the first settlers and for their ability to dispense large amounts of wealth at ceremonies, their real power always derived largely from their ability to use sorcery or employ sorcerers. In contrast to so many of the societies discussed by Lindenbaum (1981:126), the Kove never seem to have been egalitarian, with 'emphasis on long-term equivalence'. A person who is able to accumulate and distribute enough wealth so that none of his creditors complain acquires the kind of prestige that makes other Kove try to surpass his achievements; what he has hoped for is long-term superiority over everyone else, even if he should not over-emphasize his individual achievements and should give due credit to the kin who helped him. I suspect that a fully traditional *mahoni* did not feel such inhibitions judging from the way I have seen older men act; it may be the fear that younger men can easily take revenge if offended that has brought about changes in tolerated public behaviour.

The failure of missionaries greatly to alter Kove attitudes towards sorcery is simply one of many indications (along with the retention of polygyny and of various traditional ceremonies) of widespread disregard of Christian teachings. It is, of course, extremely rare for missionaries to succeed in abolishing belief in sorcery, but certainly in many Melanesian societies practitioners have been persuaded to destroy their paraphernalia and not pass on their knowledge (Tonkinson 1981:86; Zelenietz 1981:103—but see Lawrence, this volume). In Kove, however, if informants' memories are to be trusted, attitudes towards sorcery seem to have undergone no radical change in recent decades. The danger of being sorcerized, and the reasons for becoming a victim, are also viewed as no greater, and neither is discussed with horror. A Kove woman calmly announces both that her brother gives her presents because he 'loves' her[23] and that he will sorcerize her if she does not repay him; she accepts that it is up to her to influence her husband so that he will keep her brother content. Fear of sorcery rarely seems to inhibit the ambitious, as it is said to do in so many parts of Melanesia (Tonkinson 1981:78). For the Kove, to be inhibited by dread of the envious is to condemn oneself to mediocrity, at best, and ridicule, at worst. Kove children are taught a repertory of insults in which they ask each other who their fathers were and what they accomplished. Lindenbaum (1981:123) notes that 'Kilenge sorcerers are men who partially remove themselves from the web of kinship obligations, conveying an image of autonomy'. Like many Melanesian bigmen, this is precisely what the Kove *mahoni* could always do, and it might be argued that nowadays all Kove desire such autonomy, as the burgeoning exchange system renders kinship obligations so onerous. For men who choose to live within the society, the easiest way to achieve a measure of autonomy and to manipulate the kinship system is to acquire a reputation for knowing some sorcery.

To an outsider, it seems that nowadays many more men are thought to have access to the means to kill by stealth, and it may be that in time intra-community relations will be so affected that sorcerers will come to be generally regarded as immoral. At present, however, the increase in the number of reputed practitioners is balanced by the perceived diminution in activity by older men. As the Kove themselves depict recent social change, the special powers and privileges of a few *mahoni* are gradually being claimed by other men who wish to obtain the reputation and title. With the aid of innovations such as manufacturing their own shell money, obtaining other goods by selling carvings to tourists, and providing alcohol to their creditors

(Chowning 1978, 1982), but also with the use of traditional sanctions ranging from public shaming to sorcery threats, men strive to outdo each other. As competition increases, it has become necessary for the ordinary man to try to surpass others just in order to maintain self-esteem. Typically, his wife shares his ambitions just as she shares his status, and in addition to helping her husband put on ceremonies, she may also threaten and shame him to keep him up to the mark. She may also try to restrain him, however. The wife of one elected village official told me that she asked her husband to stop lecturing people on proper behaviour (as he was supposed to do) lest he be sorcerized. In the past, only the *mahoni* had the right to lecture others, and this young man, though ambitious, had yet to achieve that status.

If any religious sect did succeed in eliminating the open threat of in-group sorcery, social sanctions involving pride and shame might well sustain the competitive exchanges in something like their present form, though the taboos on female knowledge of male rituals would probably disappear. It is harder to imagine the acceptance of new explanations of intractable illness and sudden death. For the Kove to attribute all such attacks to foreign sorcerers would require them to see themselves as the victims of outsiders they now despise,[24] while it would require an enormous shift in their worldview for them to blame all major misfortunes either on the Christian God[25] or on chance (Tonkinson 1981:86).

The spread of in-group sorcery may strike an outsider as indicating the breakdown of moral codes (Lindenbaum 1981:123), but among the Kove it upholds a distinctive way of life which is valued as uniquely theirs. Sorcery maintains the present society just as it maintained the older more hierarchical one from which it derived. The Kove consider sorcery powerful, whatever some ignorant Europeans may say, and despite the dangers associated with practising it openly, the individual still finds it advantageous to use that power when he can, and tolerable to live his life with the knowledge that the same power may be used against him by his fellows.

NOTES

[1] If magic is designed to cause famine, of course it can reasonably be classified with sorcery in this narrow sense. Some Kove use the terms for 'sorcerize' to designate rain magic and magic that destroys the fertility of garden land, as well as spells to kill a dog or make a man or dog get lost in the bush.

[2] It may be that in some cases the foreign substances, such as 'lime' reputed to be made of human bones, are thought to have had magic performed over them during manufacture, but I do not think that European chemicals such as battery acid are thought to have specifically magical potency, which in Kove derives from the performance of ritual. Whether they are considered supernaturally powerful for other reasons is a different question. It is interesting that the Kove (unlike the Lakalai) do not try to poison each other with locally grown derris, though it is used for suicides, but the reason may be that the symptoms of derris poisoning, and antidotes, are well known (though the antidotes are not always successful).

[3] Fieldwork in 1966, 1968 and 1969 was supported by the Australian National University, and in 1971-72, 1972-73 and 1975-76 by the University of Papua New Guinea, and in 1983 financial aid was received from the Internal Research Fund of Victoria University of Wellington. In 1978 I visited Kove under the auspices of the Papua New Guinea Office of Conservation and the Environment.

[4] It is only the acts of the wife that may be feared. In any case, cousins are not trusted blindly (see below).

[5] The Kove know of one flying witch who lives in a mixed Kove-Bakovi village but she is reputed simply to eat corpses rather than to bring about deaths. Another, described as appearing in a Kove village, seems to be a spirit rather than a human being.

[6] Kove women are not wholly consistent on this point, occasionally accusing each other and then receiving such replies as: 'Our lineage doesn't know sorcery. Anyway, women don't practise it'.

[7] Caused by dino-flagellates which periodically increase and render shellfish which ingest them poisonous.

[8] Apart from the case of the transvestite mentioned below.

[9] On my earlier trips, I never heard a man below middle age actually accused of practising sorcery, but now men in their thirties may be suspected.

[10] Certain omens, especially visits from a particular bird, are taken as evidence that someone in the hamlet has been sorcerized.

11 An identical method is practised by the Kaliai just to the west (Counts 1974:139) and apart from the central role of the cross-cousin, by the Lakalai on the other side of the Willaumez Peninsula to the east of Kove (Valentine 1965:174).

12 Some argued that, even so, sorcery had prevented her having the baby in hospital where she might have been saved.

13 A variety of reasons were given for the failure, from incorrect handling of the pole to counter-magic performed by a woman afraid of ghosts.

14 The dead woman had earlier told me that she was as responsible as her husband for the allocation of payments and that her father had protested the neglect of his nephews and contributed some of his own share to them, but commentators consistently assumed that the men had made the decisions. Several suggested that one of them should have died rather than the presumably innocent woman.

15 A person ill from one sorcery attack can be easily finished off by techniques that would not usually be so harmful, such as throwing stones on to his house roof. One man, for fear of such attacks, moved for a lengthy period to an uninhabited island until he had regained his health.

16 The Kove both describe many changes that have taken place during this century and assert that they are doing everything just as the ancestors did.

17 Lawrence and Meggitt (1965:16) incorrectly state that sorcery had 'only moderate significance' among the Lakalai. As Valentine notes, he simply omitted from his discussion of Lakalai religion 'the large body of Lakalai magic that has no direct connexion with spirit-beings' (1965:163).

18 By contrast, the powers (as of invisibility, shape-shifting, or flight) and behaviour (such as sending fireflies to locate victims) attributed by the Sengseng to foreign sorcerers and the Molima to witches, suggest that both of these types of practitioner are imaginary. Some Sengseng men have told me that they do practise less dramatic forms of sorcery.

19 A contrast with Lakalai was the cargo cult, which stressed the elimination not so much of sorcery and illness as of permanent death. When the millennium comes, the Kove will be able to return to life shortly after dying, as they believe that at least some Europeans do; eternal life obviously is even more to be desired than avoidance of an early death. The Lakalai cargo cult myth depicts sorcery as a recent (but pre-European) evil, along with polygyny and other practices deplored by missionaries.

[20] One lineage did condemn to me the behaviour of another, the senior of the village, saying that men of the latter were only sorcerers and never warriors. The complaint was an expression of interlineage rivalry, but hardly a condemnation of sorcery, which the complainants also boast of practising.

[21] Affines of different generations should observe various forms of respect behaviour, but those of the same generation may behave freely to one another.

[22] One man was accused of destroying a whole family, from another village, by practising sorcery over their house when it was temporarily abandoned during World War II. Interestingly, he was a close patrilineal kinsman of his victims; the quarrel had arisen after an affair between his daughter and their son who had been judged too closely related to marry.

[23] The English word 'love' was used in an account being given in Pidgin. (I was told that my brother did not love me when I said that he did not constantly give me gifts.)

[24] The Kove do not fear sorcery from any of their near neighbours whom they see themselves as dominating; the groups whose sorcery is particularly feared live very far away. By contrast, the Sengseng greatly fear sorcery by their nearest neighbours, the Kaulong, and dislike travelling through their territory to reach the government station. In Sengseng, most but not all sorcery attacks are attributed to unidentified foreign sorcerers who travel invisibly, but sorcery within the tiny residential unit is occasionally threatened or suspected.

[25] The Kove long ago identified their departed culture hero Moro with the Christian God, and the identification is explicit in the cargo cult myth. Moro's departure (and their behaviour to him) did bring them many evils, but he is now far away and does not intervene in their everyday life. As has been noted earlier, accidents are occasionally blamed by some Roman Catholics on God's anger, but few Kove offer or accept such explanations. For most of them accidents are caused by human beings.

REFERENCES

Berndt, R. M.
    1972   'Social Control'. In *The Encyclopaedia of Papua and New Guinea*. Carlton: Melbourne University Press:1050-65.
Burridge, K. O. L.
    1965   'Tangu, Northern Madang District'. In Lawrence and Meggitt (1965:224-49).

Chowning, A.
1959 'Witchcraft among the Molima of Fergusson Island'.
Bulletin of the Philadelphia Anthropological Society 12:1-
2.
1972 'Ceremonies, Shell Money, and Culture Change
Among the Kove'. *Expedition* 15:2-8.
1974 'Disputing in Two West New Britain Societies: Similarities and Differences'. In Epstein (1974:152-97).
1978 'First-child Ceremonies and Male Prestige in Changing
Kove Society'. In N. Gunson (ed.): *The Changing
Pacific: Essays in Honour of H. E. Maude.* Melbourne:
Oxford University Press:203-13.
1982 'Self-esteem and Drinking in Kove, West New Britain'.
In M. Marshall (ed.): *Through a Glass Darkly: Beer and
Modernization in Papua New Guinea.* Boroko: Institute
of Applied Social and Economic Research:365-78.

Chowning, A. and Goodenough W. H.
1971 'Lakalai political organization'. In R. M. Berndt and
P. Lawrence (eds): *Politics in New Guinea.* Nedlands,
Western Australia: University of Western Australia
Press:113-74.

Counts, D. and D.
1974 'The Kaliai Lupunga: Disputing in the Public Forum'.
In Epstein (1974:113-51).

Douglas, M.
1970 Introduction to M. Douglas (ed.): *Witchcraft,
Confessions and Accusations.* London: Tavistock:xiii-
xxxviii.

Epstein, A. L.
1974 Introduction to A. L. Epstein (ed.): *Contention and
Dispute: Aspects of Law and Social Control in Melanesia.*
Canberra: Australian National University Press:1-39.

Evans-Pritchard, E. E.
1937 *Witchcraft, Oracles and Magic among the Azande.* Oxford:
Clarendon Press.

Forge, A.
1970 'Prestige, Influence, and Sorcery: A New Guinea
Example'. In Douglas.(1970:257-75).

Hau'ofa, E.
1981 *Mekeo: Inequality and Ambivalence in a Village Society.*
Canberra: Australian National University Press.

Lawrence, P.
1973 'Religion and Magic'. In I. Hogbin (ed.): *Anthropology
in Papua New Guinea: Readings from the Encyclopaedia
of Papua New Guinea.* Carlton: Melbourne University
Press:201-26.

Lawrence, P. and Meggitt, M. J.
  1965 Introduction to P. Lawrence and M. J. Meggitt (eds): *Gods, Ghosts and Men in Melanesia: Some Religions of Australian New Guinea and the New Hebrides*. Melbourne: Oxford University Press:1-26.

Lindenbaum, S.
  1979 *Kuru Sorcery: Disease and Danger in the New Guinea Highlands*. California: Mayfield Publishing Company.
  1981 'Images of the Sorcerer in Papua New Guinea'. *Social Analysis* 8:119-28.

Malinowski, B.
  1926 *Crime and Custom in Savage Society*. London: Routledge and Kegan Paul.

Marwick, M. G.
  1965 *Sorcery in Its Social Setting: a Study of the Northern Rhodesian Ceŵa*. Manchester: Manchester University Press.

Monsell-Davis, M.
  1973 'Thoughts on Roro Leadership'. Unpublished paper.

Patterson, M.
  1974-5 'Sorcery and Witchcraft in Melanesia'. *Oceania* 45:132-60, 212-34.

Royal Anthropological Institute of Great Britain and Ireland
  1951 *Notes and Queries on Anthropology*. London: Routledge and Kegan Paul.

Seligman, C. G.
  1910 *The Melanesians of British New Guinea*. Cambridge: Cambridge University Press.

Tonkinson, R.
  1981 'Sorcery and Social Change in Southeast Ambrym, Vanuatu'. *Social Analysis* 8:77-88.

Valentine, C. A.
  1965 'The Lakalai of New Britain'. In Lawrence and Meggitt (1965:162-97).

Zelenietz, M.
  1981 'One Step Too Far: Sorcery and Social Change in Kilenge, West New Britain'. *Social Analysis* 8:101-18.

6

Sorcery, Illness and Social Control in Kwoma Society

ROSS BOWDEN

The purpose of this article is to offer a description and interpretation of the institution of sorcery as it is found among the Kwoma, a non-Austronesian people in the East Sepik Province of Papua New Guinea. In particular, I wish to focus on the way in which sorcery beliefs in this society are related to concepts of illness and the curing of illness, and also the way in which they contribute to the resolution of social conflict.

My interest in this topic derives from the fact that during the sixteen months' fieldwork that I carried out among the Kwoma, from October 1972 to January 1974, sorcery formed an almost daily subject of conversation among the people with whom I lived. In the course of listening to discussions about sorcery over several months, and observing the rancorous and often fiery debates on the topic that took place in village men's houses, two things soon became apparent: first, that people's interest in the subject was greatly heightened by particular events, notably serious illnesses, accidents and deaths; and second, that their responses to sorcery, or at least the illnesses that allegedly manifested it, were highly patterned. But there was another aspect of Kwoma sorcery that intrigued me, and that was that no one ever directly accused anyone else of practising it (although imputations were commonly made in private), and no one ever admitted in public or in private to knowing anything about how it was practised—at least not in any detail. Moreover, on the evidence available to me I became convinced Kwoma actually did not possess the sorcery substances or 'poisons' that they feared so greatly, and that people rarely if ever performed the techniques that sorcerers were thought to employ. So I found myself living in a community in which people were greatly concerned about sorcery and constantly alive to the possibility of being 'poisoned', but where there was no firm evidence that anyone actually *did* anything.

Before describing how sorcery beliefs relate to concepts of illness and conflict resolution, I propose to place the phenomenon in its wider social setting by giving, first, a brief account of Kwoma group structure (since this is necessary for an understanding of the contexts in which imputations of sorcery occur), and second, a summary account of the techniques that sorcerers are thought to employ to harm others. By 'sorcery' in this article I refer to the belief that a person intentionally can do another harm by 'magical' or other than ordinary physical means (striking, spearing etc.; cf. Patterson 1974–75:132). The Kwoma term for sorcery is *siiga kapa*, which derives from the names of the two most well known substances which sorcerers allegedly use when practising their art. A sorcerer is termed *siiga kapa niik tawa ma*, a man (*ma*) who 'holds' (*niik tawa*, i.e. stores and manipulates) *siiga* and *kapa*. (I describe these substances in more detail below.) The Pidgin term for sorcery is 'poison'. In the Kwoma view 'poison' and 'poisoning' represent the major means of attacking and injuring another person other than by direct physical violence. Some sorcery techniques are said to involve the recitation of spells (*yaba*); I never succeeded in recording any of these, however, and thus cannot say whether they invoke spirits (*sikilowas*) or other supernatural agencies (e.g. ghosts). Indeed it is unclear whether the institution of sorcery has any direct relationship to the people's rich mythological and ritual traditions. Kwoma themselves think of it as a straightforward 'empirical' technique (albeit a different one from direct physical assault) for harming others.

I

The Kwoma, or 'hill people' (*kwow*, hill; *ma*, people), number approximately 2000 and live in a chain of low mountains, named the Washkuk Hills, located immediately to the north of the Sepik 250 river-miles west of its mouth. The society is composed of four named politically autonomous tribes (*magwil*): the Hongwama, Koriyasi, Urambanj and Tongwinjamb; these range in size from about 350 to 700 persons (Bowden 1983:20).

Each tribe is composed of a large number of small exogamous patrilineal and patrilocal clans (*magwil*).[1] Clans, rather than tribes, are the basic social units. Each independently owns land and manages it in its own interests; builds its own ceremonial men's house and sponsors performances of rituals in it (which members of a tribe as a whole attend); and independently organizes the inter-clan prestations of wealth that focus on puberty, marriage and death (Bowden 1983:35–45). There are probably between sixty and eighty clans in the society as a whole. The Hongwama ('Honggwama') tribe, in which I conducted the bulk of my fieldwork, contains twenty-four. On average, Hongwama clans contain six married male members each; they range in size from one to twenty-nine married male members.[2]

Traditionally, warfare (i.e. fighting with spears with the intention to kill) commonly took place between all four Kwoma tribes, and between each and neighbouring non-Kwoma groups. By common agreement among the groups involved, warfare did not take place among the clans that made up a single tribe. This prohibition was not backed by formal political or legal sanctions, but was based simply on the recognition that the security of individual clans was best guaranteed by each tribe suppressing violent conflict within its boundaries, and presenting a united front *vis-à-vis* other tribes. However, clans in the same tribe were, and still are, believed to practise homicidal sorcery against each other, and men openly describe the members of all other clans, including those in the same tribe, as 'enemies'.

In common with many other Melanesian societies, Kwoma lack hereditary leaders or chiefs, and leadership is exercised by men who rise to positions of influence and prestige on the basis of their personal abilities: on the strength of their personalities, their negotiating skills in intra- and inter-tribal affairs, (traditionally) their prowess in warfare, and their greater knowledge of ritual and artistic matters. Each clan usually has one or two acknowledged leaders who people refer to as 'big men' (*hisawa ma*; *hisawa*, big, tall; *ma*, man).

Prior to about 1940 each tribe formed a large, but discrete, settlement group located, for defensive purposes, on the back of a high ridge, or contiguous series of ridges, at the northern end of the Washkuk range. Following the suppression of warfare by the Australian administration in the late 1940s Kwoma moved their tribal settlements to sites lower down the hills next to or near waterways. In the course of these moves the Koriyasi tribe divided into two sections, each of which now forms a separate village on the western side of the range, namely Meno and Beglam, and the Hongwama tribe divided into three—represented by the contemporary villages of Washkuk, Melawei and Bangwis. (I will say more about the fragmentation of the Hongwama tribe at the end of this paper.) The two other tribes retained their residential solidarity in the course of these moves and presently form discrete villages at the northern end of the range.

II

Kwoma believe that sorcery is practised in three different ways. These correspond broadly to types that are found very commonly elsewhere in Melanesia (Glick 1973; Patterson 1974–75:141ff).

The first involves the introduction of a supposedly highly toxic substance, called *kapa*, into the victim's food. None of my informants was able to say what *kapa* consisted of, or how it is obtained, but several expressed the view that it was made from the ashes of burnt human skulls. The substance is thought to be so deadly that even the minutest portion of it added to the victim's food, or rubbed on his cigarette tobacco, ensures a swift and sudden death. People take the possibility of being poisoned with *kapa* very seriously, and to ensure that they are not, are generally very circumspect about whom they accept food from.

On a number of occasions during fieldwork I had the opportunity to observe the length to which men will go to avoid accepting food from people they suspect might be sorcerers. For instance, I once visited the Mayo-speaking village of Neweri with the Bangwis village councillor. The journey was a long and hot one and as we approached Neweri, not having eaten all day, we began to plan our evening meal. But shortly after we arrived, and before we had an opportunity to cook any of our own food, the Neweri councillor presented my companion, his Bangwis counterpart, with a large and very generous supply of cooked sago and other foods. Fearing (as I later learned) that the food might be poisoned my Bangwis friend immediately told our hosts, quite mendaciously, that he had eaten a huge meal on the way, and was no longer hungry. But pointing to me he said coolly, 'Give it to him; he'll eat it'. To give another example, whenever I visited Melawei I took with me from Bangwis (my field base) a young man whose mother lived at the village, and whom he was always pleased to visit. At Melawei this young man invariably insisted that I sleep between him and the door of the house in which we stayed. When I asked him about this, he explained that he knew that he slept with his mouth open and that he was afraid that if he slept near the door a sorcerer would drop some *kapa* in his mouth during the night and poison him.

The second technique that sorcerers are thought to employ to 'poison' people is called *süga* and involves the obtaining of something that has been in association with the intended victim, such as a scrap of food, cigarette butt, or particle of body waste (saliva, sweat etc.), and heating (*hiyutow*) or 'cooking' it, to the accompaniment of appropriate spells, over a fire deep in the forest (cf. Forge 1970:260–1). Kwoma believe that if a sorcerer simply heats the leavings (*süga*), the victim will become seriously ill, and stay ill so long as he continues periodically to do so. But if he throws the leavings into the fire and completely incinerates them, the victim will die.

One consequence of the belief that sorcerers can use people's leavings to make them seriously ill, or even kill them, is that villages are spotlessly clean. Indeed, people routinely go to great lengths to ensure that their personal leavings do not fall into the hands of potential sorcerers. Following a meal, for instance, they either carefully burn the leftovers in the fire, or wrap them up and later dispose of them in the forest or in a river where they will not be found. I recall vividly once watching some men sitting around a fire eating fish. A number of half-starved village dogs, as they are accustomed to do, were standing around watching the men eat, hoping that they would be thrown a few scraps. But after picking the bones clean, the men carefully placed them in the fire, and burnt them. Suspecting that they were doing this out of fear of sorcery I asked them why they didn't throw the bones to the dogs. One of them gravely explained that Kwoma never did that, since dogs are in the habit of dropping small particles of food when they eat, and if these were found by sorcerers they could be used against the people whose leavings they were. In fact to practise the *süga* technique, the same man said, a sorcerer needed only the tiniest fragment of food. Thus, if a sorcerer were walking past a house and saw an ant carrying a crumb left over from a meal, he would immediately take the crumb away from the ant, wrap it up and keep it for future use.

The third type of sorcery Kwoma call *güra*; this corresponds to the type Glick (1973:183) describes as 'assault' sorcery. A sorcerer is said to lie in wait for someone beside a track in the forest and when he (or she) passes magically stuns the victim. The sorcerer then comes out of hiding, performs various operations on the victim, such as thrusting long slivers of bamboo into his body, or entirely removing certain organs, and then revives the victim and sends him on his way. The victim is conscious only of having stumbled on the track; but within twenty-four hours he becomes seriously ill, and within forty-eight hours is dead. Although both men and women are thought to be equally vulnerable to *güra* attack, people believe that it is practised predominantly against women. Consequently when a woman stumbles on a forest track, especially if she has been walking alone, her immediate concern is whether she has been the victim of *giira*.

Kwoma believe that all adult men have roughly equal access to sorcery powers. The techniques and spells associated with them are thought to be relatively simple, and if a man does not have a father who can teach them to him, he can generally 'buy' knowledge of them, with shell valuables, from someone else. If a man does not himself possess knowledge of sorcery techniques, and is not interested in learning them, he still has access to sorcery since he can always 'pay' a member of his own or another clan to perform the techniques on his behalf. Women are also thought to have access to sorcery, for although they themselves do not practise it—because of their sex they are believed to be unsuited to it (see below)—they can similarly 'buy' the services of a sorcerer, generally a brother or some other agnate. In Kwoma society there is no class of publicly identified 'professional' sorcerers comparable to those found in some other Papua New Guinea societies (cf. Stephen this volume; Malinowski 1967:85–6 et passim); but some men, generally those who are experts in other areas of ritual and magic as well, are thought to be more skilled at sorcery than others, and are believed to practise it period- ically on behalf of fee-paying clients. Such men, although never publicly identified as sorcerers, are said to be rec- ognizable by their unusually large testicles (traditionally Kwoma went completely naked), and by their 'black' (*kehapa*) hands. The latter characteristic is said to result from spending a lifetime handling 'hot' (i.e. powerful) magically- charged substances (Forge 1970:260).

To practise successfully the techniques described above Kwoma say that a sorcerer must be in a ritually 'hot' con- dition (Bowden 1983:188–96). A man achieves this by refraining for several days from sexual contact with women, by eschewing 'cold' (*niikiiriyaw*) foods such as day-old boiled sago or food cooked and handed to him by a woman, and by the consumption of specially prepared 'hot' soups (cf. Whiting 1941:109; Bowden 1983:195–6). A man similarly must be in a ritually 'hot' condition to perform successfully other forms of magic (e.g. yam-planting and love magic) as well as all specifically masculine tasks such as painting, carving, pottery-making, learning and teaching esoteric knowledge, and (traditionally) warfare. To fail to be in a 'hot' condition entails that he will perform these tasks badly; thus a potter's bowls will break when they are fired, a painter will make mistakes in his design, and a student of ritual knowledge will forget the songs and other esoterica being taught him. In contrast to men, women, because of their sex, are thought to be intrinsically 'cold' (*niikiiriyaw*) and thus incapable of performing magic or other traditionally masculine tasks. No woman, therefore, could aspire to be a sorcerer or an expert in any other branch of ritual knowledge.

III

In this paper I am not concerned with the question of the efficacy or otherwise of Kwoma sorcery techniques. Suffice it to say that there is no firm evidence that Kwoma actually possess and use poisons, or that the different forms of sorcery have the effects they are believed to have. Here my concern is with sorcery as a belief system, and with the role these beliefs play in social life. In this section I comment on and illustrate Kwoma sorcery beliefs under three separate but related headings: as an explanation for misfortune; as a social sanction; and as a means of resolving conflict.

First, much as Evans-Pritchard and others have argued for societies in Africa, and elsewhere in Melanesia, the belief in sorcery provides Kwoma with a personalized and psychologically satisfying explanation for misfortunes—notably serious illnesses, accidents and death. Such explanations, furthermore, are phrased in terms of what Marwick has called disturbances in the 'moral relationships between persons' (Marwick 1965:281; Evans-Pritchard 1937:26, 63–70, 170 et passim; Douglas 1970:xix; cf. Patterson 1974–75:137). The only serious misfortunes that Kwoma do not attribute to sorcery are deaths that occur in battle (Forge 1970:259), and, occasionally, deaths of women which they attribute to incompetently performed love magic. In the hands of an unskilled practitioner love magic, it is thought, can be made much more potent than it need be, such that it accidentally kills, rather than attracts, the woman at whom it is directed.

In his study of witchcraft beliefs among the Azande— and in this respect Azande witchcraft functions in the same way as sorcery in Melanesia—Evans-Pritchard (1937) states that Azande reject, or at least regard as inadequate, explanations of misfortunes (e.g. illness and accidents) by reference to chance. Thus, if a person knocks his foot against a stump of wood on a track and the wound unexpectedly becomes badly infected, a Zande will want to know why on that occasion and not on many others when he has walked along that track, including times when he has knocked his foot on stumps, the wound became infected. This he will explain by reference to witchcraft: to the fact that someone with witchcraft powers bears a grudge against him and caused him to have the accident. Evans-Pritchard emphasizes that Azande do not attribute all events, or general patterns in events, to witchcraft, but only those that are unusual or atypical.[3]

Inasmuch as Kwoma attribute serious misfortunes to sorcery they think in exactly the same way as the Azande. If a person becomes ill and does not recover within a few days, or suffers repeatedly from a debilitating ailment, they explain this by reference to the malevolent actions of a sorcerer, i.e. someone who harbours a grudge against the victim (or is acting on behalf of such a person) and wishes him ill. For Kwoma, in other words, no serious illness or death is the result of 'natural' causes.

Significantly, Kwoma do not regard Western medical explanations for illness, in terms of germ theory, as in any way contradicting their belief in sorcery. Kwoma, in fact, are willing to accept that there are such entities as germs, and that if these entities get into your body they can make you ill. They are also quite willing, and indeed are avid, to be treated with Western medicines, since they acknowledge that these do alleviate or cure some illnesses. But Kwoma reject the assertion that a person's illness is adequately explained by the fact that he has germs in his body. They take the view that the only reason a person becomes ill, including why he has germs in his body, is because of sorcery: because someone bears a grudge against him, and has made him ill—'by putting the germs in his body', as they often say nowadays.

Let me give one concrete illustration of the way in which Kwoma rationalize misfortunes. This case illustrates the rather tortuous reasoning that Kwoma often employ to explain an event, and also the fact that sorcery is believed capable of going astray and 'striking' the wrong person. None of my informants, however, was able to explain precisely how this happened.

In October 1973 a married woman named Bwiyakay of Melawei village fell out of a breadfruit tree and killed herself. (Falling out of trees is not an uncommon cause of death in this society.) Knowing that the accident would be attributed to sorcery I asked my nearest neighbour in Bangwis, Tudimi, who he thought had caused her death. Tudimi explained that it was much too early to formulate a clear view of what had happened, but that over the next few months, after the husband's 'anger' at his wife's death had subsided,[4] 'gentle breezes would begin to blow' (i.e. rumours would begin to circulate) and he would have a better idea. When I approached him again, some months later, he said that the full story had still not emerged, but that he had heard that the woman had died from *siiga* sorcery intended for her husband. Apparently, two years earlier, the elder brother of the husband of this woman had died. His widow had come to live with Bwiyakay and her husband, Amasay, until the second burial had taken place (which formally ends the period of mourning) and until another husband could be found for her. While she was living with them another Melawei man, Merek, conceived a violent passion for her, and tried repeatedly, but unsuccessfully, to persuade her to marry him. Merek even made a special journey to Ambunti to ask the senior government officer there to order the woman to marry him. However, following the second burial (when the surviving spouse becomes free to remarry) the widow decided to marry another man altogether, from Washkuk village. According to my neighbour's information, Merek believed that Amasay, who he did not get on well with, had actively encouraged the woman to marry someone else, to slight him; and in retaliation had performed sorcery against Amasay. But for some unknown reason the sorcery missed and struck his wife instead, causing her to fall out of the tree and kill herself. On the morning of her death Amasay is said to have had a premonition that his wife would meet with a serious accident if she went out that day, and advised her to stay at home. But with uncharacteristic stubbornness Bwiyakay refused to heed her husband's advice, and subsequently fell to her death. This uncharacteristic stubbornness on Bwiyakay's part in refusing to listen to her husband, my neighbour said, was a sign that *siiga* was being practised.

The second aspect of sorcery that I wish to comment on here concerns the way in which it acts as a social sanction and force for social control. It does this by discouraging, through fear of reprisal, behaviour which is socially unacceptable (Patterson 1974–75:133; Malinowski 1967:93).

Kwoma acknowledge openly that the threat of sorcery is one of the main reasons why people in this society respect the rights of others and honour their obligations to them. They point out, however, that sorcery, or at least the threat of it, only operates as a sanction in two specific contexts: in relations generally between members of the same tribe, and in relations between members of different tribes who are connected by close affinal or uterine ties. The significant analytical point here is that disputes between individuals or groups in either of these two contexts normatively should be resolved by conciliation rather than by the threat, or use, of physical violence (cf. Patterson 1974–75:148). With regard to the distinction between inter- and intra-tribal relations, for instance, men stated bluntly that in the past when warfare was still a feature of their society, the primary sanction that maintained orderliness in *inter*-tribal relationships was the threat of physical attack, a threat that was commonly carried out. But physical violence, as I have already indicated, was not an acceptable response to conflict in *intra*-tribal contexts, since by common agreement among the clans involved warfare at this level was prohibited. According to my informants, therefore, at the intra-tribal level the sanction that in the end compelled people to respect the rights of others, and honour their obligations to them, was the threat of attack by magical means, that is, by sorcery. Since Kwoma believe that every adult, directly or indirectly, has access to sorcery powers, this means that a person believes that he (or she) is at least potentially at risk of being sorcerized by every other member of the community in which he lives. And, as any Kwoma knows, these are the persons with whom an individual will interact (and potentially come into conflict) most frequently.

This association that Kwoma make explicitly between warfare as a sanction in inter-tribal relationships, and sorcery as a sanction in intra-tribal contexts (or, more accurately, in contexts where warfare was not a socially acceptable reaction to conflict), is supported by my case material on actual disputes. Of several dozen disputes involving imputations of sorcery that I was able to document not one involved a dispute between individuals or groups which, traditionally, could have resolved their differences by resorting to warfare. All involved disputes either between members of the same tribe or closely related members of different tribes; many involved disputes between members of the same clan—political allies *par excellence*.

Sorcery, then, both in popular opinion and in fact, is a sanction that operates only in contexts where disputes cannot be resolved by resorting to, or threatening, physical violence. This correlates neatly with what we know of sorcery and witchcraft in Africa. Marwick notes that in Africa believed sorcery (or witchcraft) attacks *only* occur between persons linked by close social bonds (1970:280; see also Evans-Pritchard 1937:26,102–7,170) and typically between persons who, because of their close relationships, do not have access to other, institutionalized means of settling disputes. For instance, in Ceŵa society, the southern African group that Marwick studied, believed sorcery attacks typically attend disputes between close matrilineal kin: people who, because of their membership in the same kin group, cannot take their disputes for settlement to the chief's court, as *non*-kinsmen can (Marwick 1965:3,210ff).

The fact that in Kwoma society sorcery is believed only to be practised between members of the same tribe (i.e. the autonomous political unit), or between closely related members of different tribes, contrasts markedly with the situation that some anthropologists contend obtains generally in Melanesia. In this region sorcery is thought to be practised typically, or even exclusively, between members of *different* groups. Indeed, Marwick himself believes that this feature distinguishes sorcery beliefs in Oceania from those in Africa (1970:280–1). More specifically, Patterson has argued that in Melanesia a distinction needs to be made between sorcery accusations that follow illness and those that follow death. The former, she says, tend to conform to the 'African paradigm' in that they are usually directed at other members of the same 'local group'; moreover, such accusations highlight conflicts that normatively should be resolved non-violently, i.e. 'by the payment of compensation on the part of the sorcerer or by a reciprocal exchange between alleged sorcerer and victim' (1974–75:148). Sorcery accusations that follow deaths, on the other hand, are 'almost exclusively' levelled at members of other or 'out-groups' (1974–75:149); as Patterson explains it, 'The characteristic of these situations is that, while it is possible to conceive that an individual may bring about the misfortune [through serious illness] of a fellow group member, it is *not conceivable* that he should wish to cause his death' (1974–75:149; my emphasis). In addition to the fact that accusations of homicidal sorcery occur between groups, Patterson argues, they frequently occur as an expression of 'pre-existing hostile relations', and are the concomitants of 'feud and warfare' (1974–75:149).

The anomaly here is highlighted by the fact that Kwoma group structure corresponds broadly to that of Patterson's 'Type B' societies (1974–75:154–5), which, she says, exemplify the generalizations I have summarized above. However, the difference here might be more apparent than real; for I suspect that as more ethnographic data become available it will be found that sorcery in Melanesia is practised between members of the same local group much more commonly than is presently thought.[5] Indeed Patterson cites, but glosses over, one paper relating to another Sepik society that supports this point. In his study of the Abelam, Forge indicates clearly that although sorcerers are thought to practise their art only against members of 'enemy' villages, they always perform it *on behalf of* someone 'in close relationship with the victim, if not actually in his village' (1970:263). My own fieldwork in different parts of the Sepik suggests that a similar situation obtains in at least a number of other societies in the same region.

The role that Kwoma sorcery plays as a social sanction, principally in intra-tribal contexts, is manifested in three ways. First, people expect that sorcery attack resulting in illness or death will be the inevitable outcome of all long-standing and unresolved disputes arising out of breaches of basic social norms. These include adultery with a married woman where no compensation has been paid to the husband; repeated theft of garden produce; incest; violations of marriage rules; the refusal to make a marriage payment or other obligatory payment to affines; and failure to make a pig sacrifice in the men's house after a ritual offence has been committed.

Second, Kwoma attribute the great majority of past deaths to unresolved disputes between close kin. For example, Manal Kapay of Bangwis village attributed the deaths of his two older brothers to vengeance sorcery practised by (or on behalf of) another member of his own clan following a dispute with his father over land. Some years ago Kapay's father ceded rights of use in an area of sago forest that he did not require for his own purposes to an agnate named Kupudu. The understanding was that Kupudu could use this land for the duration of his life. Kupudu cleared the land of unwanted trees and exploited the sago productively for many years. However, shortly before he died Kapay's father demanded the land back, to give to his sons. In doing so he effectively dispossessed Kupudu, since the latter owned no other sago stands in the vicinity. This forced Kupudu to move elsewhere and attach himself to an unrelated clan to gain access to sago. Not long after, Kapay's two brothers (the recipients of the land) suddenly died—the result, Kapay said, of homicidal sorcery practised by Kupudu in retaliation for losing the land he had cleared and tended so carefully.

Third, people explicitly acknowledge that the threat of sorcery constitutes a powerful incentive for doing what others can reasonably expect of you.

One of the basic principles governing relations between male members of the same clan is that all should have roughly equal access to wealth in the form of shell valuables. In this society the major source of wealth open to a man consists in the clan sisters he gives away in marriage. In exchange for giving up a sister in marriage a man receives a bridewealth payment; small quantities of shell valuables in return for gifts of food from her husband throughout his sister's married life; and when she dies, a large and valuable death payment. Kwoma recognize that a man with no (or few) sisters is in a seriously disadvantaged position, in terms of wealth, *vis-à-vis* men with several, and to overcome the inequalities entailed, men with several sisters (or daughters) cede exchange rights in one or more of them to less privileged agnates. For instance, Tudimi of Nowil Tek clan has three daughters and only one son. His next closest kinsman, Mekapoyena, has only one sister, and is thus in a relatively disadvantaged position *vis-à-vis* Tudimi's own son, Apen. To rectify this imbalance Tudimi, on his young son's behalf, ceded exchange rights in his eldest daughter to Mekapoyena. This resulted in Mekapoyena and Apen having two sisters each. When I asked Tudimi why he had done this he made a simple, but telling, one-word reply: 'Poison'.

In arguing that sorcery constitutes a social sanction, I am not suggesting that the belief in it is sufficient to keep everyone, all of the time, on the straight and narrow path of morality. People do offend and injure others, and some people acquire reputations as trouble-makers, constantly violating or bending social norms, or endeavouring to manipulate them to their own advantage. But such persons are generally well aware of what they are doing, including what others think of them, and to prevent themselves from being 'poisoned' in retaliation, take great pains to ensure that their leavings do not fall into the hands of persons they have offended. Politically ambitious men, who endeavour to maximize their wealth at the expense of others, often acquire reputations for being obsessive in this regard.

But there is one institution in Kwoma society that undermines the attempts of even the most careful man to protect himself from sorcery; I refer to the fact of clan exogamy. Since men must obtain their wives from other clans, a man's wife, as Kwoma say, is the sister of an enemy. Thus, if a man persistently reneges on, say, his clearly defined obligations to his wife's kin, Kwoma believe that his wife will not hesitate to pass some of his leavings to her brother so that he can sorcerize him, or to place poison that her brother has provided in his food. In the Kwoma view, therefore, a man's wife is both his best friend and potentially his worst enemy, since she is the one person in this society who has unlimited access to his food and personal leavings. It is understandable, therefore, that when a man becomes seriously ill, one of the first persons he suspects of sorcery is his wife. The fact that women have unlimited access to their husbands' food, incidentally, also serves to protect the rights of wives generally; for men believe that if they persistently deprive their wives of anything to which they are entitled (including company and sexual attention) they will not hesitate to poison their food, or pass some of their leavings to a sorcerer.

The third aspect of sorcery that I wish to comment on here concerns the way in which it contributes to the resolution of social conflict. To understand how sorcery operates in this respect it is necessary to be clear about precisely what happens in contexts where sorcery is thought to have been practised. In contrast to what Kwoma themselves believe, one does not have a situation where a sorcerer first performs a certain act, and then people wait expectantly to see if the intended victim becomes ill or dies. What one finds in fact is precisely the opposite. First, a person becomes ill. If he (or she) does not recover within a few days he and his kinsmen then begin to speculate about who might have a grudge against him such that they would want to injure him through sorcery.[6] Significantly, when a person has isolated someone he suspects might be sorcerizing him, he does not directly accuse that person of having made him ill. The reason for this, Kwoma explain, is that if that person in turn were to become seriously ill, he and his kinsmen would immediately suspect the accuser of having caused his illness (through sorcery) and would retaliate with further sorcery. Since no one is ever directly accused of sorcery, it is not surprising, therefore, that no one ever publicly admits to having practised sorcery. Rather, when a sick person has identified a likely sorcerer, he (or close kinsmen on his behalf) sets about trying to *remedy the conflict situation* that has given rise to the sorcery being practised. For Kwoma reason that until the conflict *is* resolved, the sorcerer will have no reason for relenting, and consequently the sick person will not recover (cf. Malinowski 1967:86).

If a person who is ill is successful in resolving some dispute in which he has been involved (e.g. by the payment of an outstanding debt, or compensation for an injury) and recovers soon after, he will conclude that the person with whom he was in dispute was indeed the sorcerer responsible for his illness, but has now withdrawn his magic. But if the sick person does not recover, he will not conclude that something other than sorcery was responsible for his illness, but will take the view that he has not yet identified the sorcerer responsible. He will thus set about trying to identify another conflict situation which could have given rise to sorcery being practised, and attempt to resolve that situation in turn. If he does not recover then, he will look for yet another possible source of conflict, repeating the process until he finally regains his health.

What happens if the alleged sorcery victim dies? In this situation his kinsmen, although greatly 'angered' by his death, can only conclude that he was unsuccessful in identifying the conflict situation responsible for his illness. Alternatively, they might conclude that he had in fact successfully identified the relevant conflict, and hence the sorcerer in question, but that the conflict was such that it did not lend itself to easy resolution. To give a brief example of the latter alternative, one old Bangwis man who had formerly been the village *luluai* or government appointed village leader, attributed the tuberculosis from which he was suffering, and from which he died soon after I left the field, to sorcery practised by a younger politically ambitious member of his own clan who aspired to take over his position of village leader, which he in fact did when he became ill. The old man explained his continuing ill health by the fact that his rival, to prevent him from returning to active political life, was still periodically 'cooking' (i.e. heating) the leavings that he had in his possession.

Viewed, therefore, as a theory or explanation of disease, sorcery may be regarded as a means of resolving conflict (although not invariably a successful one) for the reason that illness, which is its symptom, forces people to take conflict seriously. Since people in this lowland tropical society are constantly falling ill from such diseases as malaria, dysentery and tuberculosis, they are constantly being forced *for the sake of their health* to recognize and actively work at repairing damaged social relationships. These relationships, moreover, typically involve people who are connected by close, multiple and overlapping social and economic ties (cf. Marwick 1965:290).

In addition to responding to their own illnesses in this way, Kwoma commonly respond to the illnesses of close kin, such as parents or children, along similar lines; for just as sorcery occasionally misses its mark and strikes the wrong person by mistake, it is thought that a sorcerer sometimes intentionally makes someone other than his real target ill to scare the person who is its real object into recognizing that all is not well with his social relationships, and into doing something about it. Let me give two examples which illustrate both this last point and the argument generally in this section.

The first concerns a dispute arising out of the failure of a group of three brothers to 'pay' (*tokitow*) their mother's brother with shell valuables for a quantity of pork he had given them some months earlier. In this society one of the closest of all social relationships it that between a mother's brother (MB) and a sister's son (ZS) (Bowden 1983:64–5). Although they are members of different clans, a MB is obligated to 'look after' (*aboboy hawa*; lit. 'feed', 'nourish') his ZS by giving him regular gifts of food, by helping him with such activities as gardening and housebuilding, and, traditionally (if they were members of different tribes) by acting as an ally in war. Thus, a MB was obligated to inform his ZS of impending attacks on his settlement by his own or other tribes, to refrain from participating in such raids, and to provide him and his family with refuge (if need be) at isolated bush houses following or in the face of hostilities. A sister's son reciprocates these services. In the case in point a man had given three sororal nephews a valuable gift of pork. There is no fixed time by which such gifts must be 'paid for', as Kwoma say, but ideally the payment should be made promptly. In this case several months had passed with no sign that the payment would soon be forthcoming. Suddenly the aged father of the three nephews became seriously ill. When he showed no signs of improvement after about a week, he, his sons and other close agnates began to speculate about possible reasons for his illness. The father himself suggested that it might be the result of sorcery practised by the above MB, but directed at him, rather than his sons, to scare them into making the payment they owed him. At first the sons were sceptical, but when their father had not recovered after about another two weeks, and fearing that there might just be something in it, they quietly got together the necessary wealth and made the payment—to their MB's complete satisfaction. The father, as it happened, did not recover and despite numerous attempts to isolate and conciliate several other potential sorcerers over the ensuing months, subsequently died for reasons which his sons were never able to discover.

The second case involves a dispute over an incorrect marriage. A young married Bangwis man had an affair with an unmarried girl,[7] and then announced that he intended to marry her. The fact that the man in question was already married was no formal obstacle to the union since Kwoma still practise polygyny. The problem lay in the fact that he had not yet made the bridewealth payment for his first wife, and convention dictates that a man shall not take a second wife until he has 'paid' for the first. In addition, the first wife, as she was formally entitled to do, stated emphatically that she would not agree to the marriage until her husband had 'paid' for her. In this she was supported by the rest of the village. Notwithstanding the opposition to the union the couple went ahead with their plans to marry and the girl moved to her husband's house.[8] One morning shortly after this the first wife, indignant and angry at what had happened, picked up a digging stick and struck the second wife over the head, seriously injuring her. Several weeks later, after the second wife had recovered from her injury, one of the first wife's young children became seriously ill. People immediately suspected that the second wife had passed some of its leavings to her father, reputedly a powerful sorcerer, and 'poisoned' it in retaliation for the first wife's attack. The child's illness brought the dispute out into the open and made it a major subject of debate in the men's house. One vocal participant in debate was the father of the first wife, who not only endeavoured repeatedly to persuade his daughter's husband to give up his second wife, but implied on several occasions that if his grandchild died, her death would be avenged. The husband's response was to wait and see if his child recovered. When it did not—indeed its condition temporarily worsened and it had to be hospitalized—and fearing (as he told me) that his father-in-law's threats of retaliatory sorcery would seriously escalate the dispute, he announced in the men's house one morning that he intended immediately to begin accumulating the wealth required for the bridewealth payment for his first wife. This decision, everyone agreed, effectively removed the root cause of the conflict, and when the payment was eventually made, the two wives became reconciled. The sick child, by this time, had long since recovered.

IV

In arguing in the previous section that sorcery beliefs in Kwoma society constitute a means of resolving social conflict, I did not wish to imply that imputations and suspicions of sorcery in all contexts necessarily operate as a force for social cohesion (Malinowski 1967:93; Marwick 1965:247). Clearly they will only do so if the individuals that make up the groups within which sorcery is thought to occur have an overriding commitment, or are compelled for various social, economic or political reasons to remaining a cohesive unit. But in changing internal or external conditions, suspicions or imputations of sorcery can have the effect not of reconciling groups and preserving the status quo, but of tearing them apart and permanently altering social and political alignments. In an African context Marwick has drawn attention to this double aspect of sorcery. On the one hand, he argues, sorcery accusations provide a means by which 'tense [social] relationships may be formulated, and sometimes redressed, as a result of their clearer, more incisive, or even more explosive, expression' (1965:283); but on the other hand they can permanently rupture and terminate relationships that have become, in his words, intolerable or redundant (1970:293; see also 1965:147. Cf. Thomas 1970; Macfarlane 1970).

To illustrate the potentially fissive consequences of sorcery beliefs in Kwoma society I take an example from the post-contact history of the Hongwama.

In 1928 men belonging to clans now located at Washkuk killed two native policemen in retaliation for the alleged rape by them of one of the men's wives. The government responded to this event by sending several armed patrols into the Washkuk hills to apprehend the murderers; while searching for them the patrols burned down numerous houses (including a number belonging to clans not involved in the killings) and indiscriminately shot and killed about twenty people.[9] In the face of this violence the Hongwama abandoned their settlement and fled to the bush where they remained for two years. During this period two bitterly opposed factions emerged, which came to be known as 'Washkuk' and 'Bangwis'. The former consisted of those clans that were directly involved in the killings, and the latter of those that were not. In 1930, after the policemen's killers had finally been arrested and the dispute with the government resolved (McCarthy 1963:56–62), the tribe as a whole emerged from hiding. But instead of rebuilding their settlement, the people moved to a new site several miles to the south. There the clans reoriented their hamlets along the new factional lines. According to Bangwis informants, this second settlement was never a happy one and relations between the two factions, characterized by open animosity and suspicions and imputations of homicidal sorcery, rapidly deteriorated. Late in the 1930s two events took place that brought these divisions into the open and split the community into two distinct parts. Both involved sorcery. First, following the death of a woman in the Washkuk faction, allegedly as the result of 'Bangwis' sorcery, a leading Bangwis bigman (of Nowil Tek clan) came to the dead woman's house—in the traditional manner—to pay his respects to the deceased. When he approached the house, a 'Washkuk' man leaped to his feet and threatened him with a spear. The Bangwis man, fearing for his life, promptly turned on his heels and fled back to his own hamlet. Later that afternoon a number of Washkuk men, after performing a type of sorcery divination known as *haba*,[10] went to a yam storage hut owned by another member of the Bangwis man's clan, and there defecated on his yams. This provocative and highly insulting action[11] was an open challenge to fight, and if it had occurred in an inter-tribal context would certainly have led to war. Although younger members of the clan in question were willing to take up the challenge, older and wiser heads, fearing that open warfare between the two factions would irremediably weaken the Hongwama as a political unit *vis-à-vis* other tribes with which they were still periodically fighting, counselled that the clan that had suffered this insult should .immediately abandon the tribal settlement and build a new village for itself several miles away. This it did without delay.

The other 'Bangwis' clans stayed put, but not for long. Following the deaths of several children in the Washkuk faction, a group of Washkuk men raided a Bangwis hamlet and killed a man who they believed was acting as the conduit through which leavings belonging to their group were passing to Bangwis sorcerers. Although no further overt violence took place, this killing brought the old political unity of the tribe to an abrupt end. Fearing that they would now become the object of all-out homicidal sorcery, if not warfare proper, by the Washkuk faction, the remaining Bangwis clans moved to the new village founded by Nowil Tek (and which had been named Bangwis) where they are still located. During the late 1940s and early 1950s, when the administration had finally suppressed inter-tribal warfare, the 'Washkuk' clans similarly abandoned the Hongwama settlement and moved to their present sites at Washkuk and Melawei villages. (The clans at Melawei established a separate settlement from those that founded Washkuk to be within easy reach of extensive sago stands they owned in the vicinity.) During the last fifty years, therefore, the Hongwama tribe has undergone major changes in settlement patterns and internal political alignments. Although sorcery was not the cause of any of these changes, it unquestionably provided a means, in Marwick's terms, of dramatizing strains in inter-clan relations and facilitating adjustments to them.

V

The final topic I wish to comment on here concerns changes that are currently taking place in the range of persons who are thought to practise sorcery against each other. I noted earlier that Kwoma conceive of warfare and sorcery as two different ways in which an individual or group can attack and inflict injury on another (cf. the distinction the neighbouring Abelam make [Forge 1970:259] between the 'spear by day', i.e. warfare, and the 'spear by night', i.e. sorcery). Warfare, in the Kwoma view, is the appropriate form of attack, and ultimately the only means of avenging injuries, in inter-tribal contexts; whereas sorcery, which does not involve overt physical violence, is the means by which people endeavour to avenge wrongs in contexts where warfare is prohibited. Traditionally, according to my informants, there was no reason why sorcery could not have been practised against a group with which one also fought; it was simply that it was *unnecessary*. After all, people would say, why sorcerize an enemy when you could spear him?

Since the establishment of the Pax Australiana in the late 1940s, warfare is no longer a possible response to intertribal conflict. Although none of the sorcery disputes which I documented involved persons who, traditionally, could have resolved a dispute (in a socially approved manner) by threatening or resorting to physical violence, one consequence of the suppression of inter-tribal warfare has been that people now believe that they are at risk of sorcery from a much wider range of persons than they were previously: notably from former military opponents as well as allies and kinsmen (cf. Lawrence and Meggitt 1965:17–18; Lewis 1976:82). Formerly, people would say, relations between tribes, although often tense, were at least not complicated by fears of sorcery. But now a person must be on his guard against all Kwoma; for if a man (or woman) with a legitimate grievance against a member of his own *or another* tribe cannot obtain satisfaction by such means as compensation or negotiation, or, nowadays, through the courts, the only means left open to him is 'poisoning'.

NOTES

[1] The orthography used for Kwoma words in this paper follows that proposed by Kooyers et. al. (1971). Note that 'b', 'd', 'g' and 'j' are all prenasalized and are equivalent to 'mb', 'nd', 'ngg' and 'nj' respectively. Thus *magwil*, the Kwoma term for tribe and clan, is pronounced 'manggwil' (alt. 'menggwil').

[2] Kwoma share their language and most elements of their culture with five Nukuma ('headwater people') villages immediately to the north and north-west (see Bowden 1983:9), but following local usage I restrict the term Kwoma in this paper to the inhabitants of the Washkuk Hills, the 'hill people' proper.

[3] Contrary to what is often implied about tribal peoples, Kwoma have a well developed notion of chance which they express in Pidgin by the word 'pasin' ('fashion'). Thus, if a man chops a tree down and it unexpectedly falls one way rather than another, this is put down to chance: it is simply the 'pasin' of a tree to do such things. But for Kwoma chance operates only in contexts that are socially inconsequential. In others, sorcery is invoked to explain unpredictable events. Hence if a tree falls on someone and injures or kills him, this is not the result of chance, but sorcery.

[4] Kwoma deliberately refrain from speculating publicly about the possible identity of a sorcerer immediately after a death lest close relatives of the deceased, in the heat of the moment, spear the suspected poisoner. Such an action, they point out, would not only automatically be avenged by another spearing but would split a community asunder.

[5] Mr Nigel Oram informs me that at Hula, a Motu-speaking community east of Port Moresby, sorcery is typically thought to be practised *within* the village. The same is apparently the case in a number of other coastal Papuan societies (see, for example, Hau'ofa 1981:82,96,123 et passim).

[6] To my knowledge Kwoma do not (and did not) perform any kind of divination to determine the individual identity of suspected sorcerers. However, they did perform at least one type of divination (known as *haba*; see note 10), following a death, to determine the clan of the sorcerer.

[7] Kwoma disapprove strongly of sexual contact between unmarried people.

[8] In Kwoma society a marriage is not celebrated ritually, but is marked by the removal of a girl from her parents' house to that of her husband, and by the couple establishing a sexual and domestic relationship.

[9] My information on this period derives from reports by patrol officers, both published and unpublished (e.g. McCarthy 1963:56-62), the reports of the anthropologists Whiting and Reed (Whiting and Reed 1938-39; Whiting 1941) who worked among the Hongwama in 1936-37; and from Kwoma and other informants in the Ambunti area who were alive at the time.

[10] *Haba* is one type of divination Kwoma perform to determine the clans of sorcerers. The technique involves holding aloft a length of bamboo of the *haba* species, which, following the reci-

tation of certain spells, is said to fly through the air and land on a house belonging to a member of the sorcerer's clan. On this occasion it was performed to test the suspicions of the man who threatened the Nowil Tek visitor.

11 As elsewhere in the Sepik (e.g. Tuzin 1972; Forge 1966) men tacitly equate themselves with the yams they have cultivated (Bowden 1983:186-96). To defecate on a man's tubers, therefore, is tantamount to defecating on the man himself.

REFERENCES

Bowden, R.
  1983 *Yena: Art and Ceremony in a Sepik Society.* Oxford: Pitt Rivers Museum.
Douglas, M.
  1970 (ed.)*Witchcraft Confessions and Accusations.* London: Tavistock Publications.
Evans-Pritchard, E. E.
  1937 *Witchcraft, Oracles and Magic Among the Azande.* Oxford: Clarendon Press.
Forge, A.
  1966 'Art and Environment in the Sepik.' *Proceedings of the Royal Anthropological Institute for 1965*:23-31.
  1970 "Prestige, Influence and Sorcery: a New Guinea Example.' In Douglas (1970:257-75).
Glick, L. B.
  1973 'Sorcery and Witchcraft'. In I. Hogbin (1973:182-6).
Hau'ofa, E.
  1981 *Mekeo: Inequality and Ambivalence in a Village Society.* Canberra: Australian National University Press.
Hogbin I.
  1973 (ed.)*Anthropology in Papua New Guinea: Readings from the Encyclopaedia of Papua New Guinea.* Carlton: Melbourne University Press.
Kooyers, O. and M. and Bee, D.
  1971 'Phonemes of Washkuk'. *Teo Reo* 14:37-41.
Lawrence, P. and Meggitt, M.
  1965 (eds)*Gods, Ghosts and Men in Melanesia: Some Religions of Australian New Guinea and the New Hebrides.* Melbourne: Oxford University Press.
Lewis, I. M.
  1976 *Social Anthropology in Perspective: the Relevance of Social Anthropology.* Harmondsworth: Penguin Books Ltd.

McCarthy, J. K.
1963 *Patrol into Yesterday: My New Guinea Years.* Melbourne: F. W. Cheshire.

Macfarlane, A.
1970 'Witchcraft in Tudor and Stuart Essex'. In Douglas (1970:81-99).

Malinowski, B.
1967 *Crime and Custom in Savage Society.* Totowa: Littlefield, Adams and Co. (First published 1926.)

Marwick, M. G.
1965 *Sorcery in Its Social Setting: a Study of the Northern Rhodesian Ceŵa.* Manchester: Manchester University Press.
1970 'Witchcraft as a Social Strain Gauge.' In M. Marwick (ed.): *Witchcraft and Sorcery: Selected Readings.* Harmondsworth: Penguin Books Ltd.:280-95.

Patterson, M.
1974-75 'Sorcery and Witchcraft in Melanesia'. *Oceania* 45:132-60, 212-34.

Thomas, K.
1970 'The Relevance of Social Anthropology to the Historical Study of English Witchcraft'. In Douglas (1970:47-79).

Tuzin, D. F.
1972 'Yam Symbolism in the Sepik: an Interpretative Account'. *Southwestern Journal of Anthropology* 28:230-54.

Whiting, J. W. M.
1941 *Becoming a Kwoma: Teaching and Learning in a New Guinea Tribe.* New Haven: Yale University Press.

Whiting, J. W. M. and Reed, S. W.
1938–39 'Kwoma Culture: Report on Fieldwork in the Mandated Territory of New Guinea'. *Oceania* 9:170-216.

PART FOUR:

Witchcraft in a Changing World

7

Kalam Witchcraft: a Historical Perspective

INGE RIEBE

The Kalam live in the valleys of the Simbai and Kaironk rivers and their tributaries, their territory extending to the Ramu foothills of the Schrader ranges and to the western fringes of the Bismark mountains. They live in scattered homesteads, the composition and distribution of which alter in accordance with changing affiliations and the demands of a shifting agricultural system. A homestead is supported by a number of gardens of varying kinds and at varying stages of use, including fallowing under casuarina. Some gardens are close to, others at a considerable distance from, the current dwelling. Kalam keep pigs and, in smaller numbers, poultry and cattle. They also hunt, and they husband highland pandanus. I worked mainly among Upper Kaironk Valley residents whose interests, including land interests, extended to the northern and southern valleys and into the Upper Simbai Valley.[1] These residents were estimated at 1500 in 1965 and had increased to just under 2500 by 1977. Residential and operational groupings among Kalam are not stable in composition, name or territorial affiliation. Individuals describe their ties and loyalties in terms of interlinked networks of kin, the kin of kin, and associates given putative kin names; and their land claims are based on sequences of earlier residences, both their own and those of their ancestors.

The Kalam year is organized around the *smy* festival. The *smy* is a time for the transacting of all forms of outstanding exchanges, as well as for initiation ceremonies and intergroup hosting of festival dancers. The initiation ceremonies and pig kill can be understood as adjusting reciprocities with ancestral beings; the hosting of groups of dancers as symbolizing and readjusting current intergroup alliances. The exchanges, whether the calling in of a debt or the paying of creditors, can relate to marriage obligations, trade exchanges, the equalizing of generalized support over the past years, or payment for killing ventures. Witch beliefs have come to play a central part in the exchange system. In this paper I will discuss the introduction and development of the concept of witchcraft and describe its pivotal role in current Kalam ideology.

The Introduction of Witchcraft Beliefs in the Nineteenth Century

From a large body of self-consistent oral evidence (Riebe 1974:539–54) it seems that deaths in the Upper Kaironk Valley began to be attributed to witchcraft (*koyb*) at the end of the nineteenth century. Kalam informants think it possible that people may have died of *koyb* as early as the 1860s, though the people of that time were not aware of its presence among them. During the 1890s Upper Kaironk Valley Kalam travelling in the valleys to the north were told that some people living in their own area had already acquired the *koyb* techniques and that some among them were dying from it. Before this they had been aware of witchcraft practices among the Kopon to the west (which were known as *yawt yawt nwlk*); and among the Maleng to the east (known as *kwm*), but neither of these techniques were thought to be practised by Kalam.

Previously Kalam had attributed deaths to physical violence, to *kwj* practised by other Kalam, or to non-human agencies (the last of these I am not concerned with here). *Kwj* could be both beneficial and malevolent. Different forms were important for success of gardens, festivals, economic transactions, love, marriage, etc. It was used to prevent and cure illness, to strengthen warriors for battle and to help weaken the enemy. Certain kinds could be used to kill the enemy outside of battle. The power of *kwj* was contagious. It could be transmitted by wind or water or through direct tactile contact. Selected individuals might be killed by *kwj* if they could be induced to ingest affected material.[2] More usually, however, it was transmitted against a distant enemy by wind and was not selective of individuals. Pigs as well as people were vulnerable to it. An extended household or a number of such households forming a fighting unit had special houses in which war *kwj* items were stored. A resident or non-resident kinsman could be the main war *kwj* practitioner for a campaign. He was known to the allies and often his identity also became known to the enemy. Healing *kwj* was often practised by bigmen as part of their service to followers. There were also male and female healers whose reputation was for healing alone. They might be sought from far afield, as well as by their own kith and kin. Any practitioner of *kwj* needed to observe a variety of taboos, especially food taboos, and exercise great care in handling *kwj* substances to avoid damaging himself or his close associates.

The concept *kwj* covers both magic and sorcery, whether beneficial or malevolent. However, 'malevolent' should not be taken to imply a negative moral judgement. War sorcery aimed to kill, but a war sorcerer was an entirely respected person. The sorcerer who helped the enemy in battle was a prime target for revenge killing not because of any moral judgement against him, but because he was a great asset to the enemy. It was possible to misuse *kwj* but the ethical precepts judging misuse were complex ecological ones: attempts to increase crop yields if taken too far might cause a polluted crop causing illness; love magic used too continuously to attract a particular woman might cause her urinary infections or other abdominal troubles; carelessly made *kwj* directed at an enemy might kill at home.

The newly introduced concept of *koyb* came from the north and shared characteristics with the *sangguma* syndrome found on the coast and hinterland. According to Kalam folktale the source of the witchcraft introduced to them was on the Ramu flats. From the beginning *koyb* was manifest as a small snake-like creature held in the abdomen of the human host, enabling the host to kill with super-natural power. Other details were added through later contact with peoples with *sangguma* type beliefs. These included the abilities to: change into animals, or other humans, become invisible, move at incredible speeds, or be in two places at once, kill without direct or indirect physical contact with the victim, and the ability to sew together and temporarily resuscitate people killed with conventional weapons. Witches were also said to have a greed for human flesh.

Koyb was used, initially at least, to explain sudden and unexpected deaths. The character of a human host was described as sullen, stingy, unfriendly and greedy. Witches worked secretly and no material evidence of their activity was expected; nor did anyone admit to being a witch. To kill with witchcraft was considered evil and anti-social. Once the concept was current among Kalam, however, there were ways in which it changed.

The small snake-like creature in the abdomen of the human host came to be regarded as controllable by its rightful owner. The idea that someone might be possessed by the witchcraft creature was retained, but this was thought to occur only when it entered the wrong person; then that person would kill without reason, driven only by hunger for human flesh. No instance of this occurring was ever given. The correct host could control the power and killed only at will, that is, deliberate human will. Moreover, witches were thought only to kill when paid to do so by normal humans. A witch was said to kill at its own behest, only if payment was promised and not forthcoming. The Kalam thus developed a concept of witchcraft subsumed under the social order—a somewhat paradoxical picture of rational biddable witches.

The introduction of witchcraft into Kalam culture did not differ from the introduction of a new form of *kwj*. The claim that the first Kaironk Valley practitioners were taught witchcraft by contacts in the northern valleys competed with the belief that witchcraft could only be transmitted from parent to child. Kalam sometimes declared that there could only be a very few witches, all of whom must be descended from witches. At other times, they claimed witches were prolific and accused people whose parents were not only not witches, but to whom they themselves were related. These contradictions presented no difficulties to Kalam informants because people happily professed ignorance as to what was in fact the case, thereby asserting their lack of involvement in matters of witchcraft.

Belief in witches added a new dimension to the Kalam repertoire of explanations for death because an accusation of killing with witchcraft could not be disproved. Identity as a witch could not be proven or disproven, admission was not expected and, unlike those of sorcerers, the activities and status of witches was not known to intimates. Anyone could be a witch without people knowing it. Thus any accusation of witchcraft was at least tenable. Anyone might be a witch, any exchange of wealth might, under cover of some other stated purpose, be in truth a payment to a witch. Such an accusation, to hold a measure of conviction, required only that a person with a motive to kill the deceased engaged in some economic transaction. The latter could even be dispensed with as witches and their clients were thought to become increasingly devious and agreed to delay payment until well after a death, in order to allay suspicion.

Enemy and competitor alike could, with the new concept of *koyb*, be accused of causing a death and be killed in return. Kalam informants have told me: 'We wanted to kill him, so we called him a witch'. The witchcraft explanation for death allowed conflicts between people to be aggravated into a matter for killing without an earlier history of violence between them. Because the accusation could be either of being a witch, or of paying a witch to kill, people of high social standing who had no witch-like personality traits could also be accused.

The introduction of the witchcraft concept made explanations for otherwise inexplicable deaths possible, and it attributed these deaths to human agency. Were there in fact fatalities requiring new explanations in the late nineteenth century?

Older informants said that in their grandfathers' times there had not been the speedy, inexplicable deaths that favoured a witchcraft explanation. Some gave examples of deaths in the period 1890–1910 which their fathers had remarked were the first deaths of that kind known to them. Kalam also maintained that deaths of adults in their prime generally increased at this time. It is certainly possible that during this period diseases introduced by Europeans in the north coast and Ramu flats had spread to the mountains.[3] There is some evidence of dysentery epidemics in various parts of Papua and New Guinea during this period. (Sack and Clark 1979:66, 281, 360). Increased contact with lowland people, and through them indirect contact with European gold miners and explorers (Sack and Clark 1979: 124,135–6,146,167), could account for the introduction of both new diseases and *sangguma* beliefs, the former setting the stage for the acceptance of the latter.

In detailed migration and settlement histories I collected there were a number of instances, around the turn of the century, of people moving from settlements in the northern valleys to join kin in the Upper Kaironk Valley after many of their co-resident kin in the north had died. In each instance, some of the Upper Kaironk Valley kin they had joined subsequently died, while the newcomers remained healthy. This led to the newcomers being suspected of witchcraft, having, it was thought, probably killed their relatives at home as well as their new co-residents. Recently arrived settlers from the northern valleys, or people who maintained close contacts there, continued to be regarded as more likely to have witchcraft powers. This pattern is of course suggestive of newly introduced infectious disease.

Apart from the increase in deaths of adults in their prime, there were other changes around the turn of the century that may well be associated with the acceptance of the witchcraft explanation for death. There was a gradual increase of population in the Upper Kaironk Valley during the nineteenth century. This was due partly to natural increase and partly to in-migration. In this same period domesticated pigs were introduced. In the mid Upper Kaironk Valley, the first *smy* at which pigs were slaughtered was in 1845.[4] There were still not enough pigs or shell wealth to pay for the first revenge killing in 1875; payment was made with land and hunting rights. Early pig fences around gardens were built in the 1890s by a man who was renamed *Kajwaty* (pig fence). The revenge killing paid for in 1875 marked the beginning of reciprocal killings in the valley (Riebe 1974:543).

The end of the nineteenth century thus marked the beginning of a change in this valley from a people-hungry to a resource-hungry community. The resource conflicts developing during this period may have found expression in witchcraft accusations.

It is significant that in the first half of the twentieth century such accusations were more frequently made against the accuser's mother's brother's sons than against other kin. These were kin who, although often not part of the immediate working circle and with whom the accuser most probably did not grow up, had strong claims on a share of resources because their father had given his father a wife. Not all cross-cousins were in conflict, many were closest friends; but when the bridewealth transactions between the fathers were incomplete, or when the mother's land rights were in dispute, intolerable conflicts over resources could arise. An accusation of witchcraft, and acting upon it with an ambush killing, made possible the rather one-sided solution of such conflicts.

Because witchcraft accusations were part of a conflict situation, there were winners—people who benefited from the effect of the accusation on the accused, whether this was loss of status, loss of wealth or loss of life. But hope of such gains, while important, was not sufficient to explain the increase in witchcraft accusations. The process and results of accusations were not so predictable, nor were those to gain in this way always the most determined accusers. But there were different gains to be had by manipulating the outcome of witchcraft accusations.

Once the identity of a killer and his supporters were known, avoidance restrictions came into operation, and these served to limit interactions between people. This was the case whether the killing was by violence or witchcraft. The concept of witchcraft served to weave all deaths into a pattern of reciprocal killings by justifying revenge killings subsequent to a non-violent death. The contractual form of the groups that co-operated in killings, the flexibility of the rules indicating who was to be avoided subsequent to a killing, and the availability of compensation payments to terminate avoidance between individuals, all served to give even individuals who could not fully control the choice of victim or accused a strategy for contracting and/or re-aligning their own and others' associations.

Among Kalam associations could lead to an assumption of kinship within one generation; also any help or gift initiated a sequence of reciprocities; and any use of land established some claim. Thus there was ample opportunity for people to maximize their access to goods, land, services and followers. The increase in scale of Kaironk Valley Kalam society in the late nineteenth century meant that Kalam welcomed the opportunity afforded by the witchcraft ideology to limit claims made upon them by the maximizing strategies of their kin. This limiting could be achieved either by direct accusation and killings, or by the manipulation of avoidance relations created by other people's killings. Thus not only leaders were able to control killing ventures, but any politically active Kalam could benefit in this way.

Witchcraft Accusations and Changes in the Economy until Pacification (1956)

The growth in scale continued through the early twentieth century with increases in shell wealth and other wealth items, as well as an increase in population. From the 1930s all these factors led to a period of elaborated exchanges, with witchcraft acusations becoming a part of lengthy sequences of revenge killings. Such sequences served the interests of politically ambitious men in two ways: (a) by influencing the choice of victim they were able to control the restructuring of social networks; (b) an up-and-coming leader who acted as an organizer between mourners and killers thereby became the key distributor in a major wealth exchange which enhanced his status and gave him control over wealth. The intertwining of witchcraft accusations and economic interest became a dominant theme from the 1930s onwards.

The Economic System and Witchcraft
The Kalam economic system was based on the distribution of agricultural produce, tools, wealth items and women

through the giving of gifts. I am using the term 'gift' rather than 'exchange' or 'transaction' because subjectively it was a voluntary gift made in contexts of hospitality and varying degrees of ceremony. People gave what they wanted to give, based on their own expectations and juggling of their resources.

The compelling aspect of the gift in a system where reciprocity is a basic social principle has been well developed in the literature since Mauss (1966). This emphasis was necessary precisely because our own subjective view of gifts is that they are voluntary. We have been made aware of the power of the gift to force its own return. It is also important not to lose sight of the fact that gifts in Melanesian society are also voluntary. The very existence of strong mores about reciprocity and sharing evince the lack of control people have over others in respect to their gifts, whether initiatory or reciprocal. The existence among Kalam of magic procedures to entice the return gift to the initial giver's house is evidence of the uncertainty of such return. Moral and personal obligations are very different from contractual rights and coercive sanctions.

By way of gifts: subsistence produce was distributed; women moved from natal to husband's household; and means of production, including land and tools, changed hands. Some of the essentials of a household's livelihood were brought to it by way of voluntarily given gifts. There was a contradiction between the essential nature of the things being given and the lack of control over their passage. There were fairly clear expectations as to what constituted a minimum or generous return, what amounted to a quick or belated return, or what was tantamount to neglect. Latitude was considerable, however, and it was difficult to predict what type of return would occur in any particular instance.

A Kalam individual made plans on the basis of expected return, but that expectation being met depended upon some other individual sharing his view of the relevant social relations. In fact people could decide that some other avenue or connection was more important to them and expand one tie at the expense of another. The 'other' might find this a source of considerable frustration and possibly hardship.

The individual was caught in the contradiction between the essential nature of the need and the voluntary nature of the gift. Gifts were judged not in terms of rights but in terms of loyalty, hospitality, gratitude and generosity. To be demanding of a return gift was socially just as likely to be dangerous as to be tardy in returning it. This created both a conflict between people and a conflict within people.

The conflict between people occurred when related people made incompatible decisions as to which social ties they wished to maintain. An example of such a conflict occurred during the year 1939–40. Maklek on several occasions asked his cross-cousins for stone axe blades. After the death of their father, in late 1940, the cousins began to wonder why Maklek had kept asking them for stone axe blades. Out of this seemingly simple question grew an accusation of witchcraft which ended in Maklek's being killed in 1942 to avenge their father.

The simple answer to the question as to why Maklek asked them for axe blades was that his family had previously lived near his cousins and had always received their axes from them because they had a good trade source. Maklek's branch of the family had moved further west but still wished to maintain that source of axe blades and, because they had moved to a heavily forested area, had a great need for axes to fell trees. The cousins did not want to maintain this relationship, and Maklek was forced to ask them for axes. The cousins, wanting to end their investment in that relationship, denied any obligation to supply the axe blades, and accordingly could not acknowledge any good reason for his asking. Yet his asking, by Kalam logic, necessarily implied some basis in past transactions. Denying one reason, they postulated a secret reason: he was claiming (by implication) to have killed someone for them with witchcraft and was demanding pay for this. Indeed the 'Why is he asking us for . . .?' was to Kalam ears already a statement of this suspicion. From this it was a short step to: 'He asked us for pay, we refused and so because we did not pay him for the earlier killing on our behalf he has killed our father'. This whole sequence of logic was so formalized that on searching for the cause of a death one of the first questions asked was 'Who has lately asked us for things that we refused?'

No one could make material gains in the circulation of gifts without reneging on some obligation. The person reneged on could do without or make demands. The former was difficult where subsistence needs were involved and also demeaning; the latter left one open to accusations of witchcraft.

The conflict within people was between desire and virtue. When a Kalam was asked for something that he did not want to give the common response was fear. This was so even in situations where there was no overt threat or unfriendliness. Where did this fear come from? The explicit ethic of Kalam society was to accept social intimacy from kin and to share all that one had. This created a conflict within the individual between using his resources to greatest advantage and behaving well. Any Kalam rejecting a kinsman's request in order to hold on to possessions, for whatever purpose, was likely to feel guilty. The anxiety caused by the transgression of internalized mores was projected on to the person one had offended. The person asking for things became the witch out of the guilt of one's own refusal.

The principle of the economic system was to pool resources in order to distribute them. This was the human world of generous giving. Social status was accrued by public distribution in the name of positive relations between kin. The underside of this world was the world of the witch— the world of greed, destructiveness and extortions under threat of witchcraft. Greed was repressed in keeping with accepted ideals. This greed denied in oneself was then projected on to the character of the witch.

Gift giving and receiving caused people incompatible emotions. They wanted to appear generous, while also feeling greed; and gifts were felt to be both a source of pleasure and a mechanism for subjugating people by creating obligations. Kalam denounced socially unacceptable transactions by saying that they were the behaviour of a witch; or were likely to lead, however falsely, to accusations of being a witch; or were likely to attract witchcraft against one. Thereby the outer boundaries of acceptable human giving and taking were marked. All transactions could be described either in terms of the good human side or the bad witch side. The boundary between what was acceptable and what was not changed according to the outcome of conflicts. A political career was a series of such conflicts, a successful career manipulating these boundaries to serve personal ambition.

Any up-and-coming leader was vulnerable to accusations of witchcraft. A man building a reputation needed to stretch his resources to the limit and, due to his volume of economic activity and his need to maximize his own resources, he could move all too easily from the easy world of generous kin to the competitive world haunted by witchcraft.

In 1953 Aybap, a man of about forty, was killed in an ambush killing (Riebe 1974:169–258). As with any Kalam killing, there was a lengthy history of earlier killings and other hostile acts that various people wanted to avenge and to which they were able to connect the victim in various ways. However, conflicts at the time of the killing between Aybap and some of his associates also played a part. These conflcits were used to make him seem a witch to his contemporaries. Aybap had demanded a pig he regarded as owed to him and was given it. Gossip denied the validity of this claim and said the debt was owed for a witchcraft killing. Aybap later took some shells from the household of the same man that gave him the pig. A co-householder claimed he stole those shells and that he was a witch. Aybap cooked some food ceremonially and gave some to friends from another valley. One rumour accused him of having done so to make payments to witches. Another rumour claimed that he had cooked an eel, a thing only a witch would do.

After some antagonism against him had already been mobilized, Aybap married a widow whom, together with her children, he and his brother had been taking care of. He had the right to marry this woman but his brother had also been interested in her and he and others felt Aybap had once again taken everything for himself. The opposition to the marriage fuelled the rumour that he had killed the woman's husband with witchcraft in order to be able to marry her. Shortly after this Aybap boasted to a close dependant that he had helped arrange a certain killing and had a claim to the payment for it. The dependant spread the story and used Aybap's own words to make it sound as if he had been the witch who did the killing.

Aybap was killed in the time before pacification when public moots, at which he might have given a defence, had not yet been developed. Moreover, avoidance by the accusers of the accused before the killing, and taboos of association after the killing, meant that even in private settings there was no opportunity to argue out accusation against defence. Thus we have no record of Aybap's explanations of the incidents used against him. It is clear, however, that he was a strong man headed for leadership in intense competition with two others, one of whom was his brother. His aggressiveness in collecting debts, his eagerness to further distant associations and his lack of conciliatory care with his marriage plans, all contributed to his downfall—his boast of the involvement with a plot to kill sealing his fate.

Witchcraft accusations that led to a killing had direct economic repercussions other than removing a competitor. One way a young man could acquire wealth was to kill for payment. Organizing such a killing, and being the principal distributor of the pool of wealth amassed for it, was the mark of having arrived among the bigmen. But, even more importantly, revenge killings, whether avenging a violent death or a witchcraft killing, were one of the bases of inheritance of wealth among Kalam. The arranging of the revenge for a deceased gave rights over the disposal of any wealth held by that person. It also gave rights over daughters of the deceased. If the sons of the deceased themselves arranged the avenging, then they retained control over marriages of their sisters and rights to the bridewealths. If, however, some other kinsman helped arrange the revenge killing, or contributed towards it, the rights over daughters were in proportion transferred to that kinsman. Thus killing ventures, as well as regulating the flow of wealth, affected the flow of women. They also affected the allocation of land.

Kalam land tenure rules developed in a situation where people not land were a scarce resource. Any person had claims to many blocks of land, either through earlier use or through ties to ancestors who cleared that land. Further, for any block of land there were many people who had competing rights over it. Who actually used land depended not only on the person's rights to the land but on their relations with neighbouring gardeners. Established killing sequences, whether with violence or witchcraft, could change amicable relations to relations of avoidance, regardless of the feelings of the individuals involved, thereby making it impossible for those people to live or garden near each other. Even in later times of growing land shortage, issues of taking up garden claims were discussed in terms of the dangers of closeness between people in an official state of enmity. Thus those able to influence the accusations of witchcraft after a death were able to influence the passage of wealth and women and the allocation of land.

Kalam themselves tended to describe the accusations of witchcraft of this period (1930–60) very pragmatically, analysing them in terms of political motivations or intergroup dynamics (Riebe 1974:486–521). At this time the behaviour of witches was well controlled by the social order; it mirrored the behaviour of men. Despite their hunger for human flesh, they were as concerned to be paid for their killings as men were, and were said to make calculations as to whether to kill alone or with help, based on the amount of wealth available. They were not described as any more promiscuous about whom they killed than men. Indeed some informants maintained that witches were open to appeals on grounds of kinship, or on grounds of non-complicity in the offence being avenged.

Throughout this period ambush kilings and open warfare occurred and concern with witchcraft waxed and waned. Only while an accusation of witchcraft was being formulated, and support for a revenge killing was being enlisted, did it constitute an item of major interest.

Witchcraft, Grief and the Revenge System
An accusation of witchcraft most commonly followed upon a death. The early expressions of grief and anger at the death of a loved one soon turned to searchings for a culprit. Freud (1957:244) states that the task of mourning is to withdraw all libido from its attachment to the loved object. This process, he states, is very painful and the task is carried through 'bit by bit, at great expense of time and cathectic energy' (ibid.:245). In the long run the work of mourning is completed and, with the libido returned to it, 'the ego

becomes free and uninhibited again' (245). Among Kalam, the private resolution from grief to recovery was paralleled publicly by the wake which merged into a sifting of information and a mobilizing of support, and thence to a killing. Compulsive concern with the death was channelled into the process of selecting the revenge victim, and a successful revenge killing was referred to as 'the avenged dead returning to the homestead'. This marked the return to wholeness and an end to grief, when the white mud donned for mourning was replaced by the soot of victory.

This progression is well illustrated in the following statements recorded over a number of days from the father of a young man who died in 1975. The father was in his seventies and this example, although from a wake after pacification, is typical of the passage of grief in earlier times. I have chosen this example because it is the first that I fully recorded and am able to produce verbatim.

> My boy sleeps in the forest among the snakes and worms and maggots. They did not kill me. How can I live when he is outside?[5]

> Nothing says clearly: 'You did this and he died'. So I grieve and wonder, where has he gone?

This refers to any killing the father was involved in that might have resulted in the son being killed in revenge and marks the beginning of the search for a culprit. A little later, taken to task for making accusations without good foundation, he said:

> True, I should not do that, but that boy died and I grieve and so I accuse all sorts of people for no reason.

Then the endless searching begins to bear fruit and the questions become more specific:

> I have considered the talk from all parts. It is the beginnings of the events that led to the killing of Wn'gy that I am not clear about. Show me the start of those events.

A little later the grieving father begins to think of the relief from mourning ahead:

> Now at this time [of mourning] I am like a woman. When my son returns to the house [is avenged] then I will be a man.

> When I catch this thing that has eaten my son I will take bird
> of paradise feathers and decorate his mother and celebrate.

Not only the immediate kin but more distant relations saw
the avenging as the resolution of their grief. A classificatory
father's brother of the dead boy said:

> I decided I would kill two people to avenge the boy and
> thereby make my belly cold.

As with all social processes, that which has its origins
in the needs of individuals develops momentum of its own.
Reluctance to avenge a death was seen as a lack of loyalty
to the dead and this exerted pressure on people. As more
distant mourners became involved in the decisions about
the avenging, concern with reputations and with the wealth
available to pay for the revenge killing became pre-
dominant. A close kinsman still dealing with the immediate
grief might find premature the move to the political. But,
however reluctantly, the struggle to retain control over the
search for the culprit and the planning of the revenge soon
totally occupied the near kin.

Part of the intensity of feeling against a witch came
from the channelling of the anger and guilt felt at the loss
of a loved one. The revenge killing system was a powerful
way to deal with grief. It was also the key to Kalam relations
with their ancestors and, as such, essential to the well being
of the society. This was very clearly stated by one young
leader in a public meeting in 1975:

> In the past we had fire [revenge homicide] in this place,
> but one thing [the kiap] has gone around pouring water
> over everything . . . In the past we killed pigs and made
> gardens and planted cordylines and asked our fathers' spirits
> to help us and we were strong in fighting. Now we bury our
> dead and we do not see their faces properly, we do not watch
> the bones appear, and we do not avenge them as we did. So
> now the spirits no longer help us and our crops are failing.
> I tell you, from now on adults who want to grow crops should
> not bury people in holes.

All deaths caused by human agency had to be avenged.
Once the witchcraft explanation of deaths became current,
only the deaths of the very young or the very old were
thought to be due to any other types of agency. Very rarely

a death might be attributed to incompatibility of forces within one person.[6] The revenge killing system satisfied both the emotional needs of the mourners, and the economic needs of the ambitious; and the witchcraft explanation of death made it possible to extend this system to non-violent deaths.

Deeper Psychological Underpinnings of Witchcraft Beliefs

Revenge against a witch was a way of dealing with grief, but this can apply to any revenge system. Apart from dealing with grief at a death there were other emotional needs that made the character of the vicious, greedy, sexually deviant, anti-social witch an attractive butt for the projection of rejected desires. The fear, disgust and anger the witch aroused in people, and allowed them to express, was cathartic. The discomfort with oneself many situations created was relieved when one's own misdeeds were explained by, or lost in, accusations against a witch. Jealousy, inhospitality, lack of generosity can all be hidden under such an accusation. From having to explain one's own anti-social and uncharitable behaviour, one could luxuriate in self-righteous accusations against the witch. Accumulated stress or incompetence in a social situation could be alleviated by the community concern for someone claiming to be molested by witches.

However, I do think that the character of the witch, not just among Kalam but in general, has an even deeper psychological appeal. Needham (1978:33) says of the character of the witch, 'this complex construction of the imagination displays a very remarkable constancy'. The characteristics he then describes are: conceptual opposition to the social ideal; physical inversion; being active at night; some form of colour symbolism; animal familiars; the power of flight and moving nocturnal lights.

Although in particular instances where witchcraft is discussed in context these elements may not all be present, they do fit the ideal of the Kalam witch fairly well. Kalam link witches with cannibalism and incest—the extremes of anti-social behaviour; with secretive night activity; they also associate black with witches at the time of death, when the appropriate colour is white, and link witches with black or black-and-white animals. Kalam also think witches can fly and associate them with moving lights. I agree with Needham that the character of the witch has at least an interesting consistency; however, there were two further characteristics common to it that particularly struck me: (a) the wide open mouth of the devouring witch which opens vertically as a vagina does rather than horizontally as a mouth does; for an illustration of this see Goya's Caprichos no. 45 entitled 'There is plenty to suck on' (I have recorded descriptions similar to this from Kalam and Milne Bay informants); (b) the frequent association with the anus: such as the licking of the anus of the black cat that the Templars were accused of, to give just one European example; while among Kalam a blue light from the anus is associated with witchcraft, the entry of the witchcraft essence is by way of the anus, as is the entry of a snake familiar that can devour the victim from within. Both these characteristics suggest a link between witchcraft beliefs and repressed anal eroticism and negative attitudes to female sexuality. This underlying energy behind the beliefs is crystallized in the Kalam description of witchcraft dealings sometimes used in rhetoric: that to hold witchcraft secrets is to a man as being pregnant is to a woman, and to act upon them or to reveal them is like his giving birth (cf. Reay, this volume).

The relevance of these speculations in this paper is that whereas the economic role of witchcraft transactions undoubtedly serves to perpetuate them, the power of the symbol, which resists attempts to eradicate the practice, or the belief in it, is in its psychological attraction. The ideological power of the concept of the witch lay in the fit between its key economic role and its psychological function.

Witchcraft Accusations following Pacification (1956–75)

With pacification enforced in the area from 1956 to 1960 by the Australian Administration, the stage was set for yet further changes in the role of witchcraft. In the early 1960s concern with a cult, involving the building of houses without any light penetration in preparation for floods and a return of ancestors, for a time took precedence over interest in witchcraft.[7]

Once violent killings were successfully suppressed, the system of elaborated exchanges that had been attached to payments for killings became attached to sequences of witchcraft killings alone. Where previously witchcraft had been a weapon for dehumanizing someone who was about to be killed, after pacification the only possible way to avenge a death was to kill with witchcraft. Instead of witchcraft being an explanation for a death utilized to organize a killing, witchcraft became the only refuge of those desiring to avenge their deceased kin. What began as a heinous anti-social crime committed only by the weak and never admitted to, became the fulcrum of the morally imperative system of revenge, and the fulcrum of the exchange system that had previously been centred around arranged ambush killings. People were now driven to enter into witchcraft trans-actions by the compelling need to avenge their dead and by the desire to make their reputations through the control of shell wealth. It was at this point that the distinction between the honourable and self-admitted war sorcerer and the dishonourable and secretive witch seemed on occasion to blur. This was because it was necessary for a leader to provide the avenues for revenge killing and from this time he was only able to do so via access to witches.

The belief that all witchcraft was evil began to be com-plemented by the more pragmatic view that the witch who kills your kin on behalf of your enemy is evil, while the witch who kills your enemy at your behest is not.

By 1968 a bigman said of the times that:

> There are very few men who are not involved. There may be only one witch that does the actual killing but there are many people who walk around with witches and help them get their pay for killings. Most people are involved in witchcraft. There are maybe a hundred people who are without it but those who are into witchcraft are numbered in thousands . . .

> A man who is poor, without shells or money, wonders what he should do to become rich. He will go and ask a man who knows how to kill with witchcraft, learn that and then kill people for no good reason and get lots of money and shells

and axes for it. Such a bigman with many things, when his child dies he can cry out for witches to avenge him and they will come and kill for him quickly because he is rich. He makes a *smy*, kills pigs and gives shells and money and axes to the witches and sometimes a wife to their relatives.

He was describing the full cycle, from pooling of wealth to its redistribution in the exchange feasts, entirely in terms of the career of a witch. Just as before pacification most politically active men, were in some way involved in the system of revenge killing, after pacification most were in some way involved in witchcraft transactions.

The central arena for the politics of witchcraft became the witchcraft moot. In the months after a wake, a death led to public discussions between ever wider ranges of kin, until public accusations brought potentially hostile groups into confrontation at a moot. The early discussions between close kin and neighbours identified more distant people to be accused. Accusations of being involved in transactions connected with witchcraft could be made against close kith or kin; but the general aim of such accusations was to prepare for a united front in later confrontations with more distant associates. Accusations of witchcraft, and the damage people tried to inflict on the careers of the accused, became more serious as the social distance increased between the hostile groups brought into confrontation. Accusations between groups aimed to expose individuals in the opposing group. When a person was irretrievably exposed, the more distant of his support group might take him to task also, and others closer to him might fail to defend him, but they might also close ranks and withdraw. The support group's reaction depended upon the person's popularity and his discretion. Thus, as was the case with ambush killings that took place before pacification, there might have been a close associate of the accused witch helping the enemy, but the core of the attack always came from further afield. The limit of the distance between accusers was reached if an accusation made publicly did not lead, in time, to a moot. Mediators were very active in mobilizing sufficient interest and concern for major moots to attract all those involved; but if social distance was sufficient to create indifference they sometimes failed.

At such moots reputations were made and broken. The ability to hold his own in rhetoric and in the handling of information was the mark of a man of status. Much of what was said at a moot was understood only by those who had a wealth of knowledge about past transactions and kept themselves well informed as to current exchanges and rumours about such exchanges. The cryptic Kalam style of speech meant that many present could hear every word without learning any more about what was going on than they knew previously. The man who handled a defence successfully or managed to sink accusation home attracted followers as protector or champion.[8] As was the case with accusations of witchcraft that led to killing, accusations of witchcraft—even without the killing of the victim—were one of the techniques for halting, if not ending, the climb to success of an economic competitor. Any man taking an active part in the pooling and distributing of wealth was vulnerable to such accusation. Where an accusation met its mark, the accused suffered both financial loss and loss of status.

Wealth passed from hand to hand: from avenging kinsman to go-between . . . to go-between . . . to go-between . . . to the witch.[9] When a death, together with some leak of information, led to a particular set of shells becoming the centre of public interest, anyone holding any of those shells was vulnerable to accusations of witchcraft.[10] Often, as the pressure built up towards a moot, people at risk returned the shells they were holding. Others were forced to agree to do so during a moot. The task of a skilled operator in a moot was to force his opponent to reveal his own dealings but to retain control of just how much was made public. The danger was that his own transactions might also be exposed or that he might force someone into a revelation that later was thought to lead to that person's death. In such a case the person forcing the exposure was open to demands for compensation or to being killed in revenge. An aspiring young bigman who was the main suspect accused in a moot held in 1973 exploited these fears in his defence and also described the mood of the moot very well:

> All of you all the time are entering into killer contracts with witches. Then when people find out some small part of them

and try to discover what is going on all of you are sweating and worrying because you are all in some way involved. Then when someone confesses to some transaction you are so relieved your bellies go cold again. But now you are accusing me I will tell all the things you people have done— all! You are all witches not men!

In handling their wealth exchanges people took care not to attract witchcraft accusations on the one hand, and to avoid having witchcraft practised against them on the other. Having large amounts of wealth was said to attract both.

Many deaths were attributed to witches killing people who received more payment than the witches themselves did for some joint killing venture. Refusal to make payments was seen to be dangerous. Hoarding wealth caused criticism and deaths were attributed to it. A classificatory brother of the old man whose son's death I mentioned earlier said after that death:

> Many people gave him shell money. They have given him so much money that the bottom of the pile is already rotting. He must have arranged something and when the witches asked for pay he did not give them enough, and so they killed his son. He should have used up all his wealth. If he had done that then his child would not have died.

Indeed the father's protestations at the wake consisted in large part of a recounting of all the compensation payments he had made and all the payments he had made to people who had killed on his behalf. He claimed to have been generous.

At another moot a man explained to the younger men:

> If a witch decides to kill someone to avenge your kinsman do you think you could pay him only once? If he did not consult you at all perhaps you could get away with two or three payments only. But if you agree you will pay and pay till you are tired. You will pay and you will want to run away but find nowhere to hide. You think it is easy, but I tell you it is very difficult.

Witchcraft transactions appear in such dialogue as a form of forced redistribution of wealth. Indeed it was large pools of wealth that attracted the greatest avenging activity and upon which the greatest demands were therefore made.

Nor was it only the immediate kin of the person being avenged whose wealth could be called upon. The husbands of daughters of a deceased, having married part of the deceased's wealth pool, could also be asked for payments. Wealth did change hands for other reasons, but these were often interpreted as superficial explanations for witchcraft-related exchanges. The bulk of exchanges had an underside which related them to the pattern of deaths and witchcraft revenge. It was the belief in witchcraft which put the power into the hands of those forcing the redistribution. A person claiming rights over some wealth item did not have to make the witchcraft foundation of the claim explicit in order for it to exert its force; indeed he may not have had any in mind.

Requests for things, whether made simply in the spirit of sharing valued by the culture, or made more sinisterly, were likely to be interpreted as having hidden meanings. An older man advised the young:

> A man may come and ask you for feathers or other head gear with which to decorate himself at some festival. People who do not know of these things just give them, but a man who is wise knows it is because someone has died that he is asking. If any man even a brother or a brother-in-law asks you for a razor or some tobacco you should be careful. Ask him why he is getting that from you. Later you will know why you gave it and be able to stop any rumours about it.

The danger of refusal was balanced by the danger of accusations of being involved with witchcraft transactions.

In 1975 after the death of a young man, Wad was suspected of having had dealings with witches that led directly or indirectly to that death. We saw earlier in the case of Aybap an aggressive competitor in conflict with near kin eliminated by means of a witchcraft accusation. In this much later case, a man not yet aspiring to leadership but engaged in active economic pursuits was vulnerable to witchcraft accusations. At a moot called specifically to accuse him, all his economic transactions, however benign and without internal conflict, were questioned. Rumour had linked all of them—marriage payments, compensation payments, wealth received and given—to the witchcraft underworld of Kalam economic life. He gave his defence, explaining the appropriate and innocent nature of each transaction. For example, he had made a gift to an in-law that was questioned. In answer he said:

> My in-law asked to buy a pig from me for his party. I said, 'No you take it for nothing'. When your in-law asks for something only people without thought ask for pay. An in-law is close to your heart.

He was stating a widely held Kalam principle. Yet his act led to suspicious gossip that it had been part payment for a witchcraft killing.

We have here a complex and stressful situation. Witchcraft was everywhere; the pressure by and large was to pay out, to be generous. Yet all economic activity was fraught with some danger—if not from witches then from accusers of witches. The desire to avenge dead kin, and the wish to build a reputation as a leader by the time-honoured method of distribution of wealth, maintained the witchcraft-based system of exchanges. On the other hand, people were risking being publicly called to task and vilified for their involvement in exchanges.

This was the picture for fifteen years after pacification. Gradual changes in the situation came to a head in the late 1970s.

Developments in the Ideology of Witchcraft (1975–80)

We have noted the circulation of wealth on the basis of witchcraft killings and the development of the witchcraft moot following pacification. There were other changes in this period. Roads were built and regular road work introduced. Schools were established, creating the work associated with them.[11] Similarly churches, aid posts and a gaol were set up. The economic situation changed with the recruitment of labour for plantations, and with opportunities for trade store businesses, sporadic opportunities for growing and selling coffee, and the breeding of cattle for local consumption. Later, for some Kalam, plantation labour opportunities gave way to other outside jobs. All these innovations, together with the opening of the council in 1971, led to the growth of a 'development package' in Kalam minds. A package that some, particularly younger men, identified as the road they wished to follow.

The view that witches were against 'development' was expressed in passing in a moot as early as 1965. A bigman berated an accused witch for spending his time hunting in the forest and not being available for road work on Thursdays.

This theme gathered momentum in the 1970s, and by the late 1970s there was an ideological war between the pro-development and the traditionalist factions—a war of words expressed in the idiom of witchcraft and witchcraft accusations. Councillors regularly made speeches along these lines:

> You people have lots of children whom you want to send to school but you don't help with the work of the school. Only my kin and the Pugoy councillors' kin help with the work. These young boys are being killed and there won't be enough people to help with the work. Don't you people sit down near my house making your talk of witchcraft. If anyone talks of these things near me then I will break his head. All talk of witchcraft must stop. We in the council meeting have already put an item on the agenda that when a witch kills a man for no reason and then a man asks for payment for it, we will grab that man and put him in gaol. We will gaol people for asking for money. We won't take that man to the government court at all. We will just gaol him ourselves.

In this instance he was answered by a highly respected ex-*luluai*:

> We bigmen who know of these things, we are not going to abandon them, we are going to hold strongly to them! We take this thing to our hearts. You may talk but we do not listen to you. You people work for pay and get money easily that way but we have only our old things and with these we get women and pigs and then money too. When you see a man distributing lots of pigs and shells and other wealth you say there is a bigman. But can't you understand, they did not get these things for nothing. They are witches and they get them. We are not going to abandon these ways.

Nor were the councillors and their supporters without inner conflict on the matter. In answer to a similar speech by another councillor one response was:

You talk as if you would like to fight people just for asking for pay. You wait, later when your child or your father dies then you will blame someone for that death and you will ask someone to help you avenge it. If you arrest people no one will help you. You threaten but you know this would happen and so you won't do it.

Indeed, some pro-development individuals who took the anti-witchcraft position were under great stress. A person violating traditional community values by accumulating wealth (for example, running a trade store that attempted to make a profit out of relatives) was likely to have a greater than average fear of witches at a psychological level, and yet be trying to maintain an indifference to their demands and sometimes disbelief in their existence at the same time. It is no wonder that many of them were prey to distressing omens.[12]

The change in witchcraft accusations was not only evident in what people said, but in the type of economic conflict that led to accusations. In the 1940s Maklek was accused of being a witch because he demanded stone axes; his cousins refused him because they wanted to give those axes to someone else. In a similar accusation in 1976 the underlying conflict was of a different order.

A cluster of men in one settlement had opened a small trade store. In conjunction with this one of the younger men also invested in some European bred pigs. The trade store was losing money due to the common conflict between kinship obligations and good business practices. A mother's brother of the young pig owner visited him and seeing the first litter of pigs from the imported pig indicated that two should be given to him. The uncle was a good hunter and regularly supplied his kin with game. He also suffered pain from an old injury sustained in fighting on behalf of the young man's father. On this basis, and that of having given a wife to the now dead father, the request was reasonable in traditional terms. However, the young man wished to regard these pigs as 'bisnis' and not subject to traditional demands. Not long after the request for the piglets the young man's mother died. At her wake he accused his uncle of having killed someone, thus causing his mother to be killed in revenge. He claimed that the request for the piglets had been a request for payment for whatever killing the mother's brother had undertaken. Talk of this accusation spread and led the mourners for another man to suspect that the uncle might have killed him. A large moot eventuated at which the uncle was accused and questioned lengthily. At the moot itself the visual contrast between accuser and accused was stark. The young man was in shorts and shirt and sported a wrist watch; while the accused, in traditional cordylines that barely covered him, held his hunting bow. The accused chose to sit down to talk, but the young man, helped by a councillor, bullied him into standing up as in a European court. The confrontation between the man and his uncle was a confrontation about the correct use of wealth expressed in terms of an accusation of witchcraft. It was not just a confrontation between alternative recipients within one exchange system, but between wealth for traditional exchange and wealth for 'bisnis'. The two were in direct opposition. The former maintained a flow of distribution ever designed to break down any pool of accumulated wealth (transforming it into status) and mitigated against great inequities in wealth, particularly as it interfered with father-son inheritance. The latter, in order for it to be possible at all, required accumulation of wealth that was not redistributed but 'put to work' in the interests of a few.

Fittingly, the 'developer-councillors'' public attacks against witchcraft were preoccupied with the exchange activities surrounding witchcraft, not with the occult evil powers of the witch. Two cumulative frustrations were increasing the stress felt by all and making the situation unstable.

The first factor was the increasing frequency of deaths in the late 1960s and 1970s, due, it seems, to ever more frequent influenza epidemics and greater incidence of malaria. Medical intervention had not halted those increases. The number of fatalities was horrifying all Kalam and was attributed by them to witches. As one man put it in 1977:

> Will we survive at all? Will there be anyone left to tell the children how it was in the past? Before the witches acted very secretly. Now they kill with so little care that everyone knows what they are doing. Soon they will simply slaughter us like pigs and roast our bodies along the roadside.

This sort of witch behaviour was welcomed by neither side. Many young Kalam males were not directly active in witchcraft accusations; nevertheless, the death rate among them was high. Kalam principles of culpability are very exact. A correct victim of revenge must be selected for his own action, not because his loss would pain the culprit. This was true of killing and is equally true of properly conducted witchcraft. One man died in his sleep at seventy-two and not one of his kin were killed in his stead, although attempts on his life had spanned twenty-five years. The principles of culpability are complex and I do not have space to go into them here. Because uninvolved young men were dying, it was assumed that the witches had taken to killing the sons of men who were the real targets but were too difficult to kill. This was regarded as inappropriate behaviour and was seen as evidence of social disintegration:

> We do not kill piglets and devour them. These witches have become deranged and they kill and eat young boys.

The second factor was the fringe nature of the 'bisnis' opportunities open to Kalam. The sad tale of half-baked projects, no follow-up and downright exploitation that has been their lot, at least until the late 1970s, hardly bares recounting. This increased the strain in the community and delayed the creation of a group of successful businessmen, and thus the beginnings of class distinctions between Kalam.

The present situation is not a stable one and Kalam themselves disagree as to possible solutions to the problem. Traditionalists see the answer in a return to killing and a continued embracing of traditional values. Others try to circumvent the endless litigation after a kinsperson's death, and the use of wealth for avenging that person, by destroying some of the wealth and declaring they will not avenge the death. But this to date has not been very successful. The Christian extremists advocate redemption ceremonies for witches who can be forced to confess. However, Kalam witches do not confess and any attempts to harass them to do so is seen by most Kalam as apt to produce only lies.

I see two ideological developments as crucial and permanent. In the traditional situation the accusers and the

accused were divided because one set were the mourners
and the other had some history of conflict with the deceased.
A new death split people in new ways as people clustered
on one side or the other, depending on particular personal
loyalties. Alliances shifted and changed, and although some
sequences might continue over a long period, opposition
was between like groups with shared ideology and the same
relation to the resources. Once witchcraft accusations shifted
from 'your witch versus my witch' to 'us-against-witches'
and 'you for them', the situation was very different. The
demarcation line can now be drawn deeper and deeper.
The division based on adherence to two different systems
of investing resources allows opposing forces with different
economic strategies to emerge.

The effect of this is to unglue the kinship base of society.
Some Kalam are in danger of becoming less human than
others. In the power struggle between pro-witch and anti-
witch factions the essential equality, even within enmity,
that existed is being destroyed. I see this shift as being
necessary for the development of class. Something has to
happen to people like the Kalam before they can accept
that some among them will be landless and employed by
others among them for profit. In some societies this change
occurs through warfare and conquering of another population. I am suggesting that another way the necessary
change in attitude may be brought about is through
witchcraft persecutions.

Linked to this is the idea of punishment: not just as
something that Europeans do, but as something that Kalam
would like to do to each other. It is one thing to kill a witch
who has harmed you; it is quite another to wish to punish
all witches regardless of whether they have done you any
harm. Up to the present, the issue has been of retribution
or recompense, not of crime and punishment. Foucault
(1973:47,49) says, writing of the origins of punishment,'Besides its immediate victim, the crime attacks the
sovereign [power]'; thus the violence done the criminal is
'an emphatic affirmation' of the coercive power's intrinsic
superiority. The desire on the part of the councillors to
themselves gaol people involved in witchcraft transactions
is a change in the aspirations expressed in the legal insti-

tutions of the society. In the past Kalam aspired to maintain equitable relations: in the case of compensation, with the offended; in the case of revenge killing, with the dead. Recently some Kalam have aspired to create a coercive power able to enforce conformity to its values. Placing such an item on the council agenda may be a small and ineffectual move, but it has enormous implications in terms of changes in world view.

Conclusion—the Ideology of Witchcraft

Whether or not it is possible to kill with witchcraft, an accusation of witchcraft is an encoding of events which alters the meaning of the events it purports to describe. For Kalam it is an interpretative statement with powerful social consequences, made all the more compelling by the rich psychological resonance of the character of the witch.

Once witchcraft beliefs became current, some Kalam used them to gain advantage by manipulating the wealth available for witchcraft killings and by manipulating witchcraft accusations. Witchcraft beliefs enabled them to represent their own personal vested interests as being in the interests of the whole community. Witchcraft became the idiom of resource conflicts.

A group of politically active males was able to dominate the revelation and authentication of sequences of witchcraft killings. In this way they more effectively structured future social relations to suit themselves than could women, young men and politically inactive men. However, the advantage to be gained was limited by the very nature of the ideology. The more actively involved in the revenge system someone was, the easier it was to fit him into a sequence as a potential victim, whether of witchcraft or of an accusation of witchcraft. The manipulators, rather than being invulnerable, were the key potential victims. Further, by the nature of the revenge system, advantage could not be transmitted after death. To die was to lose on all counts. Clientele groups and small land empires built up by a bigman scattered on his death, even when adult sons sought to maintain them. Thus witchcraft as an institution helped to create short-lived enclaves of dominant males, the advantage changing hands frequently even within one generation.

Later, as a struggle between traditional and fringe capitalist economies developed, manipulation of wealth on the
basis of witchcraft transactions became the weapon of the
traditionalists against the 'pro-development' faction in the
fight to control resources. The manipulation of witchcraft
accusations, however, continued to be used by both. After
the mid–1970s those espousing the modern ways began to
direct witchcraft accusations at traditionalists, both as individuals and as a group, in their attempt to free wealth from
its kinship bonds for business enterprises. Kalam since the
1960s lived under a European regime committed to creating
class distinction by favouring capitalist business enterprises
at the expense of the traditional subsistence economy. Thus
the stage was set for the persecution of one group by the
other. It is possible that the potential for capitalist development will be defeated by lack of genuine capital- based
economic opportunities; or that the traditional distributive
economy will be defeated by a wealth of such opportunities
tempting everyone to abandon the traditional system. If,
however, conflict between the two continues, with a new
wealth élite struggling to establish itself over other Kalam,
witchcraft will continue as a troublesome issue of Kalam
society. Modern conflicts over secular issues such as taxes,
land issues, the use of credit in stores and problems over
cattle have all been discussed in the idiom of witchcraft.
Unfortunately this mystifying of the situation with the
ideology of witchcraft is aided and abetted by the mystifi-
cation of the relation betwen labour and wealth in our own
society, as transmitted to Kalam, making it difficult for
them to have a clear appreciation of the new pluralistic
interest groups in their own society.

Marvin Harris (1975:239) sees witchcraft persecutions
as the 'defence' of an 'institutional structure' that 'dispersed
and fragmented all the latent energies of protest'. How
does this fit the Kalam situation? Witchcraft accusations did
not play this role until the introduced capitalist economic
system began to effect Kalam society. Since that time accusations of witchcraft have been used in defence of the
incipient new economic system against its opponents.
Moreover, these opponents have come to embrace
witchcraft as a power with which to oppose the new system.
A powerful anti-witchcraft campaign may in the future

serve to destroy opposition to the new system; to date, however, witchcraft based economic transactions, protected by a general fear of witchcraft, have given strength to the traditionalists. A strength so far corroded only by the increase in deaths deplored by all.

APPENDIX

Whether or not it is possible to kill with witchcraft and how frequently such killings occur is a question that vexes both some Kalam and some anthropologists. Without prejudice as to the answer to this question, it may be helpful if I give an outline of the sort of activities that do go on in relation to payments for witchcraft killings. After a death any one with a sense of loss at that death can attempt to have that death avenged. What is not so easily achieved is access to the shell and other wealth owned by the deceased, either to use directly to pay for the revenge killing or to reimburse oneself for one's own wealth outlayed. Such wealth goes to the person who has successfully arranged the killing of a victim accepted as appropriate by a sufficiently influential body of mourners to validate it generally as avenging that death.

Even in the time of violent killings this was no simple matter. There were disagreements as to the correct victim and competing claims between potential organizers (Riebe 1974:259–421). Any one killing usually avenged a number of deaths, so that, as well as the main co-ordinator organizer, there were among mourners for other deaths men who would conspire with the organizer as to choice of victim, and who would succeed in getting the support of their co-mourners for releasing the deceased's wealth for that killing. To succeed, the organizer had to have enough sway to mount a successful ambush party and sufficient resources, or control over the resources of the deceased, to pay killers and co-organizers handsomely. Depending on the importance of the deceased, this process could establish the leading man of a homestead, or a bigman, with considerable clientele and wide-ranging influence.

Once killing with witchcraft became the only resource of avengers, the process altered somewhat. To kill with witchcraft can be a solitary activity and a payment to one witch could theoretically succeed. Let us look at a possible sequence of events after a death.

'A' decides 'Y' is responsible for the death. He can either consult other key mourners and attempt to get their agreement, or act alone. He has a contact 'B' who is said to have access to a witch. He gives some shell wealth to 'B' telling him the deceased and the intended victim. 'B', if he accepts the shells, then passes some on to 'C' who is his contact with witches. 'C' may pass it on to 'D' and on for many more steps. Any of A, B . . . may add to or subtract from the wealth or replace it with items of their own. At this stage each passage of wealth is a sub-contract between two people, no more. Let us say that while 'D' is holding the wealth the intended victim dies. If 'D' fears the kin of the victim and thinks it likely that he will be discovered, he may return the wealth to 'C', saying he did not do it. Alternatively he may take the risk and claim a successful killing. He would then demand further wealth based on his knowledge of the shell wealth of the original deceased. If 'D' disavows the death, others along the line may still claim it as their doing and claim wealth accordingly. One way in which such shell transactions are frequently exposed is due to arguments between various people along the line of passage as to the correct distribution of the available wealth.

This becomes only a little more complicated if, rather than the originally selected victim dying, someone close to him or some other person, also a suitable victim of revenge, dies. The payments made from the deceased's wealth hinge upon pursuading the more powerful mourners to accept the substitution.

Whereas the wealth demanded for a payment of a single witch could be expected to be small, the number of middlemen rather enlarges the demand. Kalam have more and more tended to describe the physical details of witchcraft killings in terms of large-scale co-operative ventures involving numerous witches, sometimes working in collusion with non-witch humans, thus justifying the considerable outlays of wealth involved, much as for a violent killing.

At any one time there are shells travelling in relation to the avenging of a number of deaths. Shells concerned with a single avenging commonly travelled the length of the Kaironk Valley and into the Simbai and Assay valleys and back again; thus linking a series of homesteads over a large part of the Kalam-speaking area in joint transactions. Any new death raises not only the question of who killed the deceased, as asked by the mourners; but also the questions of who killed him in order to avenge whom, and in response to which shells? Gossip, intrigue and finally the public moot are the arenas in which individuals wield their influence to try to achieve the match between the paths of shells and other wealth, and the sequence of deaths that most suit them.

A Kalam wishing to acquire wealth in an illegitimate witchcraft transaction faces the same problems as organized crime in our own society. Firstly the wealth has to be acquired and secondly it has to be 'laundered', that is, made to look as if it has been acquired legitimately. It is the Kalam solution to the second problem that creates the interweaving of transactions based on witchcraft killings and legitimate transaction which further complicates the unravelling of culpability.

NOTES

[1] I began fieldwork among the Kalam in December 1965. I undertook extensive fieldwork in 1966–67 and 1975–76 and shorter field trips in 1968, 1971 and 1977. I was introduced into the field area by Professor R. N. H. Bulmer. The 1975–76 fieldwork was funded by an Australian National University Ph.D. scholarship.

[2] The most indirect transmission ever described to me was: materials affected by *kwj* were eaten by earthworms that transmitted the killing agent through their urine to growing plants; the person eating those plants was then killed by the *kwj*.

[3] There is evidence for the introduction of some disease affecting domestic fowl around this time. In the 1880s coloured fowl, probably of Indonesian origin, were plentiful in the valley, but before the turn of the century they had been wiped out by disease. Fowls were re-introduced by Europeans much later.

[4] For details of dating see Riebe 1974:546-8. For collaborative evidence as to the introduction of sweet potato and spread of pigs in fringe highland areas see Riebe 1976.

[5] All verbatim quotes from Kalam informants in this paper are taken from translations of transcriptions of tapes recorded between 1965 and 1977. These tapes include interviews and recordings of both small discussions and major moots.

[6] I can recall only two in the 1960s and 1970s. One of a woman who inadvertently ate at the fire of the close kin of a man her husband had helped kill; the other of a man who having performed war sorcery continued to eat fish, the two being hot and cold respectively and incompatible.

[7] In Melanesian societies cults and elaborated witchcraft systems do not seem to occur together. Both emerge in response to the need to correct or maintain relations with ancestors once these have been disturbed by pacification. Often cults are anti-individualistic, encouraging collective ownership and group activities. Among Kalam, at least, witchcraft exchanges similarly maintain traditional group initiative against individualization. Both are set against the inroads of 'development' as dictated by the colonial and neo-colonial governments.

[8] Although women were as active as men in those smaller moots within a parish concerning conflicts over gardens, marriage or pigs, they took only a minimal part in witchcraft moots. I myself think this is the result of wider prohibitions to protect women from contact with potentially hostile outsiders. Women were involved in pre-moot discussions, but even where a woman was

a key informant she did not often speak at a moot. Kalam said that the reason women at moots sit at a distance just within earshot was the fear that if a fight broke out women could be arrested along with the men. This effectively bars women from developing a wider reputation as masters of rhetoric.

9 See Appendix for details of this process.

10 Kalam recognize shells individually. The movement history of particular shells and their whereabouts at any time is an important area of study by Kalam adults.

11 The long-term effects of schoois are only beginning to create major changes in the 1980s.

12 In 1976 the councillor and the health worker in the hamlet complained continuously of noises and winds around their houses which they attributed to witches.

REFERENCES

Foucault, M.
    1977   *Discipline and Punish: the Birth of the Prison*. New York, Pantheon Books.

Freud, S.
    1957   'Mourning and Melancholia'. In *The Standard Edition of the Complete Psychological Works of Sigmund Freud*. Vol. 14. London: Hogarth Press:243-58.

Harris, M.
    1975   *Cows, Pigs, Wars and Witches: the Riddles of Culture*. London: Hutchinson & Co.

Mauss, M.
    1966   *The Gift: Forms and Functions of Exchange in Archaic Societies*. London: Cohen & West.

Needham, R.
    1978   *Primordial Characters*. Charlottesville: University of Virginia Press.

Riebe, I.
    1974   '. . . and then we killed': An Attempt to Understand the Fighting History of Upper Kaironk Valley Kalam from 1914-1962. M.A. thesis, University of Sydney.

    1976   'Introduction of Witchcraft in the Upper Kaironk Valley'. Unpublished paper, Oral History Seminars, University of Papua New Guinea.

Sack, P. and Clark, D.
    1979   (eds) *German New Guinea: The Annual Reports*. Canberra: Australian National University Press.

PART FIVE

Sorcery and Witchcraft in Melanesia: an Overview

8

Contrasting Images of Power

MICHELE STEPHEN

Despite much lively theoretical debate among anthropologists over the last several years on witchcraft and sorcery, Melanesianists have shown comparatively little interest in the topic. Earlier ethnographers, like Malinowski, Fortune and F. E. Williams, provided valuable data. In the postwar era, with the opening of the New Guinea Highlands to fieldworkers, attention focused on problems of group structure and exchange; information on witchcraft and sorcery was collected incidentally to these concerns or only as it related to them. The beginnings of a renewed interest are marked by Patterson's (1974–75) survey. Further indications of a new theoretical interest are Lindenbaum's recent monograph on Fore sorcery (1979) and the 1981 special edition of *Social Analysis* devoted to 'Sorcery and Social Change in Melanesia'. Perhaps because it is an area that has been subjected to little scrutiny until recently, a number of generalizations about Melanesian sorcery and witchcraft have become widely—and too easily—accepted.

The contributors to this book contest many of these commonly held views, and provide case studies that challenge existing theoretical frameworks. My task in this final chapter is to relate their arguments and evidence to the broader ethnographic picture for Papua New Guinea, and thus offer an overview of the problems of categorizing and interpreting the diversity of phenomena to be found here.[1] I begin not by asking 'What are sorcery and witchcraft?' but rather by asking 'What have scholars described as sorcery and witchcraft in Melanesia?' Discussion is divided under four headings. The first section, on the basis of descriptions of social action and beliefs, identifies two contrasting social roles represented by the sorcerer and the witch respectively. The second section examines the nature of this polarity in more detail. The third section deals with the effects of social change and the blurring of the two roles over time and under external pressures. The final section traces the psychological underpinnings of the opposed images of sorcerer and witch. In moving through these several layers of analysis, the discussion attempts to resolve the contradictions of the Melanesian material into two contrasting concepts of cosmic power. My aim is not to impose an explanatory theory on the data but rather to allow a pattern to emerge from it.

The Diversity of Melanesian Sorcery and Witchcraft

Postwar interpretations of Melanesian sorcery and witchcraft clearly reflect the sociological emphasis on accusations that has dominated the theoretical literature in general (see Crick 1976:109–27 for a trenchant criticism of the prevailing sociological mode). This approach reverses the indigenous perception of sorcery and witchcraft as the means of mystical attack on innocent or defenceless victims, asserting that the real victim is the accused witch or sorcerer (see Glick 1973:182–3 for a succinct statement of this approach in relation to Melanesia). It treats sorcery and witchcraft as culturally standardized fantasies about the capacity of some people to injure others by occult powers.[2] Assuming (a) that such practices are socially condemned and (b) that in fact no such powers exist and no one actually engages in such nefarious activities, this approach reasons that accusations of plying the black arts can best be understood as indirect attacks on the person accused, who is thereby branded as a despicable, anti-social being. Accusations thus reflect the tensions and conflicts existing between individuals and groups; and it is this context of social action that is the real concern of the social anthropologist, not the 'academic' differences in beliefs (Glick 1973:182). It further follows that there is little point in attempting to distinguish between sorcery and witchcraft; once their ideological frills are removed they are essentially the same social phenomenon (Glick 1973:182; Patterson 1974–75:140–1; Zelenietz 1981:13–14; Lindenbaum 1981:127, n.1).

Up to this point Melanesianists have followed the Africanists' guidelines, but whereas in Africa and elsewhere sorcery and witchcraft accusations usually operate between members of the same community, a different situation is said to prevail in Melanesia. Here accusations are directed outside the local group (Marwick 1964; Patterson 1974–75:139; Hayano 1973:180); witchcraft is rare, being confined mainly to a few societies in south-eastern Papua, and sorcery predominates (Patterson 1974–75:144–5). Though scholars have been inconsistent in their terminology and there is much confusion in the Melanesian literature, where distinctions are drawn between sorcery and witchcraft they usually follow Evans-Pritchard's (1937) definitions—'sorcery' refers to the deliberate use of magical rituals to injure and kill, and 'witchcraft' to an unconscious capacity to harm others (e.g. Glick 1973; Patterson 1974–75; Zelenietz 1981).

The widely accepted assumptions and generalizations just outlined—that sorcery and witchcraft are socially condemned; that no one actually engages in such practices; that sorcery and witchcraft beliefs are primarily reflections of social conflict; that accusations are usually directed outside the local group; that witchcraft is confined to a few societies in south-eastern Papua; that sorcery and witchcraft, regardless of the differences in belief, have the same social consequences—gloss over the great diversity of phenomena to be found in Papua New Guinea alone, and are now inadequate to cope with the growing contradictions in the data. Since so much discussion has centred on patterns of accusations, let us use this as a framework for our survey of the data. Discussion will be confined mainly to Papua New Guinea, with only occasional reference to other parts of Melanesia.

Patterns of Fears and Accusations

The contributions to this volume highlight the inadequacy of a simple schema of out-group accusations; indeed in all the societies described there are fears of sorcerers or witches within the community or among close relatives and associates, though the nature of these fears and their social consequences vary greatly. Nor does one need to look far in the existing literature to find similar evidence.

Despite the general disclaimer that it is impossible or pointless to separate sorcery and witchcraft, in practice scholars do categorize their data as one or the other when writing of specific societies. Throughout this section I will follow the authors' labelling of their data. Having reviewed the kinds of practices described as 'sorcery' and as 'witchcraft', I will then attempt to formulate a basic distinction between the social roles of sorcerer and witch.

(i) Sorcery from within

Fears and accusations of sorcery within the local group are characteristic of three societies described in this volume—the Kwoma, the Kove and the Mekeo. Among the Kwoma (Bowden, this volume) of the Sepik and the Kove (Chowning, this volume) of New Britain sorcery accusations following deaths concentrate within the local group, usually on persons related to the victim and belonging to the same sub-clan or lineage. Most deaths are attributed to sorcery but violence against the reputed sorcerer is rare. Both societies tend to accept illness and death resulting from sorcery as the expected result of defying social norms and neglecting obligations to others. When revenge is sought for a death it is attempted through counter-sorcery and social relationships remain smooth on the surface. Kove sorcery is the prerogative of the village leaders who openly threaten its use against subordinates. In contrast, no Kwoma openly admits to practising sorcery, but it is believed to be available to all by commission and the senior ritual experts and bigmen are thought to practise it.

Publicly acknowledged and rewarded sorcerers are regarded as the henchmen of hereditary village leaders among the Mekeo (Stephen, this volume) of the central Papuan coast. Sorcerers may also be hired by ordinary persons. It is generally accepted that sorcery is the result of breaking social norms and there is little emphasis on revenge for sorcery deaths. No public accusations are made against sorcerers or those believed to be hiring them; but privately people suspect members of the same local group, in particular members of the same clan and sub-clan (Hau'ofa 1981:269–78). My data (Stephen 1974:358–62) indicates that fears are strongest among close agnates and affines.

A similar situation in which hereditary leaders are said to employ 'official' sorcerers to threaten subordinates is well known from Malinowski's (1926) Trobriand study, though he provides little specific information on directions of accusations or fears. Sorcerers acting as the henchmen of hereditary leaders are also reported for the Roro (Seligman 1910; Monsell-Davis 1981), a coastal people neighbouring the Mekeo, and among the south-eastern Ambrymese of Vanuatu (Tonkinson 1981).

According to F. E. Williams's (1940:88) prewar study of the Elema of the Papuan Gulf, the elders of the community constituted a sort of ruling clique which used sorcery to maintain its privileges and to punish breaches of custom. The *Heheve* ritual cycle, the centre of Elema culture, was heavily protected by sorcery sanctions and deaths within the *eravo* group were often thought to be retribution for deliberate or even inadvertent trespassing on its secrets (ibid.:423). Such deaths were accepted by the victims' kin as appropriate punishment. In other cases, where revenge was sought, it was attempted through counter-sorcery and not open violence; though feuding might result when members of different communities were involved (ibid.:108). Williams stresses that sorcery was a 'two-edged' sword which contributed to social order but might also result in tension and feud.

Tuzin's (1980) recent study of a Sepik people, the Ilahita Arapesh, reveals certain parallels with the Elema use of sorcery. The Ilahita attribute most deaths to sorcery and every fatality implicates an insider, for only an insider can obtain the personal leavings necessary for the sorcerer's use. The elders, who are the most influential members of the community, not only possess sorcery powers themselves, but are responsible for divining the cause of a sorcery death. In most cases their rituals indicate that the death was a punishment required by the Tambaran, the dominant spirit of the men's cult. The human sorcerer responsible thus becomes merely the agent of the Tambaran and no revenge is sought. Fortune's (1939:31) prewar study of the Arapesh also notes the belief that no warrior died in battle unless insiders had supplied enemy sorcerers with his leavings.

Another Sepik group, the Abelam, implicate insiders in all sorcery deaths, though open accusations are made only against foreign sorcerers. Forge (1970) emphasizes that every death is believed to involve an insider who supplied the victim's personal leavings to the sorcerer. Moreover, sorcery is controlled by the village bigmen, and it is they who have the contacts in other communities and thus access to foreign sorcerers. Though the whole matter is shrouded in secrecy, the community at large is well aware of the complicity of the bigmen in all sorcery deaths (ibid.:271).

The Kalauna of Goodenough Island, south-eastern Papua, fear sorcery from within the local group and a high proportion of accusations involve close agnates (Young 1971:130–3). Here, too, sorcery is firmly in the hands of the village leaders. A leader's prowess in sorcery is as important to his reputation as is his success in the competitive food exchanges (ibid.:89–90). The threat of sorcery enables leaders to bend others to their will and to extract services and credit. As in the other examples we have looked at, revenge for deaths is limited to counter-sorcery; and most ordinary men do not dare to challenge the superior occult powers of the leaders. Young (1971:127) observes a similarity with Dobuan sorcery, suggesting that the Kalauna are even more plagued by fear since at least Dobuans feel safe within the matrilineage, whereas the Kalauna are nowhere free from fear of sorcery attacks.

Fortune's (1963) account of Dobuan sorcery emphasizes its importance as a means of asserting oneself in a society which allows one individual little opportunity to dominate another. Sorcery is used '. . . for collecting bad debts and enforcing economic obligation, in vendetta to avenge one's own sickness or one's kinsman's death, to wipe out any serious insult . . .' (Fortune 1963:175). Sorcery prowess is also essential for leadership, though leadership seems less clearly defined than among the Kalauna, and sorcery is more widely available.

Moving from the Southern Massim to the Southern Highlands, we find that among the Foi sorcery becomes the means whereby senior men control their juniors (Weiner 1982). Foi men regard sorcery as an appropriate strategy to be used in revenging themselves against rivals, particularly rivals in courtship. In a system where protracted bridewealth payments result in most men marrying late, older men suspect that the unmarried men of the community are liable to indulge in adulterous liaisons with the married women. The most common and important Foi sorcery technique, *irika'o* (a poison concocted from menstrual blood) is the elders' legitimate defence against this infringement of their privileged access to women.

Fears of sorcery attacks from insiders are also reported for Hanuabada village, Port Moresby (Belshaw 1957); for the Hula of the central Papuan coast (Oram 1982); and Lindenbaum's (1979) study of Fore sorcery reveals similar fears. Both the Fore and the Hanuabada data relate particularly to situations of social change and will be discussed in the third section of the chapter.

Before proceeding further with our survey, two general points should be raised. The first is the difficulty of attempting to correlate insider fears with particular forms of social structure. Berndt (1972:1060) has suggested that in-group fears are characteristic of matrilineal societies, but of the several examples discussed so far only the Trobriands and Dobu are matrilineal. Patterson (1974–75:149) argues that accusations following sorcery deaths are usually directed outside the local group. Exceptions to this should presumably fit her 'type A' society in which the rules of descent, inheritance and residence result in the local group having a varying male membership. Again, of the examples just discussed, only the Trobriands and Dobu support her argument.

Another issue we can no longer avoid is the appropriateness of the term 'accusation'. While the term is applicable in situations where public forums are held to identify and confront the sorcerer, such is by no means always the case. Often we are dealing not with the public identifying of a culprit but with privately expressed fears and suspicions. Few people are ever rash enough to openly accuse a Mekeo sorcerer—such a foolhardy action could only be expected to lead to further trouble; but suspicions of sorcery are endlessly discussed in private. Different individuals, depending on their relationship to the victim, are likely to take different views of the matter; over time a group consensus seems to emerge but the matter is never settled in any final way. A similar situation exists among the Kwoma, the Kalauna and possibly many other groups. The evidence is often not clear on this point, as Patterson (1974–75:226) notes. But it is important to recognize that in some societies with acute fears of insiders, like Kwoma and Mekeo, no public accusations are made; whereas in others, like Abelam, fears of insiders are masked by public accusations of foreigners. Certainly more precision is needed in indicating whether public accusations or private fears are involved.

(ii) Sorcery from without but also from within
In addition to the societies just discussed in which fears of insiders predominate, we find in other societies that the use of in-group sorcery is recognized, and even condoned in certain circumstances, though fears of foreign sorcerers appear more prevalent.

The Siuai of Bougainville regarded sorcery used against enemy groups, or to avenge a death attributed to sorcery, as legitimate; and in the past nearly every political unit had its own 'professional' sorcerer (Oliver 1967:304). But attacks from within the local group were also expected (ibid.:241); and though condemned, sorcery might be used against any associate 'for whom the sorcerer bears personal grudges' (ibid.:304). The double-edged nature of sorcery is very apparent here: it is a powerful weapon which may be used for the good of the group, or perversely to serve the selfish interests of the individual.

In Busama, a coastal village of the Morobe Province, sorcery powers were possessed by the headmen and were used to punish offenders against the social norms (Hogbin 1951:144). Sorcery was also regarded as an important weapon to combat the enemy in warfare. Though it was used generally against people living in different communities, sometimes a sorcerer would attack a fellow villager (ibid.:142).

The Koaka of the Solomons attributed a knowledge of sorcery to most village headmen and many elders, to the extent that a man's identification as a sorcerer was 'a measure of his social distinction' (Hogbin 1965:57). Disease sorcery was used without compunction on members of the same community (ibid.:51). Most deaths were attributed to outsiders but in the case of a habitual trouble-maker, the community might assume that the headmen had disposed of him. Revenge for sorcery was usually by counter-sorcery, except in the case of a headman (ibid.:58–9).

Inter-group sorcery suspicions were so endemic among the Keraki of the Morehead River region that Williams (1936:359) believed the scattered settlement pattern was the result of such fears. Though the Keraki were less concerned with sorcery within the local group, Williams (ibid.:252) noted, 'this is not to say that a comparatively close neighbour, or even a member of the local group itself, cannot supposedly procure a professional sorcerer at a distance to do what he cannot do himself'. Though the Keraki observed a strict secrecy concerning sorcery and all to do with it, Williams (ibid.:338–9) found that influential men might have covert reputations for it and that men who professed such powers did so to their advantage.

The Orokaiva usually suspected sorcery from other communities, nevertheless Williams (1928:218) observed, 'It is not always an enemy who receives the blame. Any piece of circumstantial evidence may be sufficient to implicate the innocent, and especially so if he be an old man; for there is apparently a kind of *mana* about old age which argues a special fitness for sorcery'. Though sorcery used within the local group was 'frowned upon' (ibid.:223), anyone might be accused, particularly respected elders.

Berndt (1962:217–18) reports that sorcery fears among the North Fore, Usarufa, Kamano and Jate of the Eastern Highlands were primarily between groups; but he also describes a particular technique which was thought to be undertaken by insiders being bribed to sorcerize their fellows. Lindenbaum's (1979) more recent study of Southern Fore sorcery which reveals chronic in-group fears will be discussed later. On South Pentecost, Vanuatu, in-group sorcery, though condemned, occurred. In theory, sorcery was used only outside the local group but, in fact, 'actual personal relationships were more of a force in determining victims than formal relationships . . . attacks both within the sib and within the village were known' (Lane 1965:262). The ambivalent nature of sorcery—as a force for public good and as an instrument in the hands of the malicious individual—was clearly recognized here, as in a number of other societies.

In all these societies fears of insiders are present and, in the hands of the headmen, the use of in-group sorcery may even be condoned.

(iii) Sickness from within, sorcery deaths from without
Many societies attribute non-fatal maladies to insiders but accuse foreign sorcerers when death occurs. In noting this, Patterson (1974–75:148–9) focuses attention on accusations following deaths. While admitting the paucity of data, I would argue that the attribution of disease sorcery is important in understanding the nature of the sorcerer's role, and should be considered more carefully than it has been. I will return to this point in the second part of the chapter.

(iv) Sorcery from outside but within the horizon of social interaction
The Garia (Lawrence, this volume) of the Madang Province regard sorcery as a weapon to be used against those they fight with physical violence; but the context is one of personal feuding rather than group warfare. The problem here is of defining 'groups' where social action takes place within ego-centered networks rather than bounded local groups. In such situations, the use of sorcery itself may become one criterion defining the 'in-group'. The Garia do not employ sorcery against unknown individuals representing the enemy; they use it for personal reasons to worst

rivals and competitors interacting within the same social horizon. Moreover, the use of non-lethal sorcery is permitted against members of one's security circle, thus even close kinsmen might be suspected in certain circumstances. This further illustrates the difficulty of drawing sharp distinctions between 'in-group' and 'out-group' patterns of accusations.

A similar situation prevails among the Tauna Awa of the Eastern Highlands, but here the 'in-group' can be more easily correlated with the local group. Most deaths are attributed to individuals living in other villages; the majority of accusations, however, are not against distant communities but neighbouring villages with whom the Tauna most frequently interact (Hayano 1973:187–8). As Forge (1970:258–9) reminds us, Melanesian local groups cannot be regarded as moral universes in themselves; their small size compels them to interact with neighbours, even when these are regarded as enemies. The directing of hostility against 'outsiders' must be seen in the broader context of inter-group relations and how they relate back to internal politics.

(v) Sorcery from without, witchcraft from within
A strikingly different pattern emerges among the Kuma of the Western Highlands (Reay, this volume), where some deaths are attributed to enemy sorcery but other fatalities are thought to be brought about only with the connivance of insider witches—beings quite different from sorcerers. Kuma war sorcery is of two types, that directed at the enemy in general and that aimed at specific individuals, particularly bigmen. In order to kill specific individuals the enemy sorcerer must obtain personal leavings of the intended victim. Since enemy groups come into contact with each other only during combat, there is no opportunity for an enemy to acquire the necessary material, it must be supplied by an insider—but no ordinary man or woman would engage in such a betrayal. Witches—harbouring within themselves an evil supernatural entity that provokes their despicable actions—are believed to collaborate with the enemy. On the death of a bigman the hunt is on for the insider witches responsible for passing his leavings to enemy

sorcerers. Reay observes that any functionalist interpretation is hard pressed to explain why, at a time when group
solidarity is essential, the group should kill or drive off as
many as ten members of the community.

Fears of foreign sorcerers and insider witches also occur
among the Gururumba (Newman 1965) and the Chimbu
(Brown 1977), both of the Eastern Highlands. The
Gururumba, however, only occasionally accuse witches
(Newman 1965:100). While witch killings are now rare
among the Chimbu, ostracism is not uncommon and
witchcraft accusations are an element in changing patterns
of residence and mobility (Brown 1977:27-9).

The Wola of the Southern Highlands (Sillitoe, this
volume) combine external sorcery accusations with vague
fears of insider witches. Sorcery is an adjunct to warfare,
as it is for the Kuma, the Chimbu and the Gururumba;
though in the case of the Wola definitions of 'insider' and
'outsider' become more difficult, owing to the fluidity of
group composition. Nevertheless, sorcery is conceptualized
as a mystical weapon used only against those whom one
deals with by physical violence. Within the circle of kin and
neighbours one does not suspect sorcery, but there are
indeterminate fears of harm emanating from envious
witches; no public accusations are made, however, and the
phenomenon is said to be a recent one, a sort of infection
spreading with the extension of outside contact into the
region.

The Kyaka of the Western Highlands also use sorcery
against those they fight but believe in a 'mild form of
witchcraft' which arises mainly from envy over food. The
witch may attack anyone, including close kin (Bulmer
1965:156). The Huli of the Southern Highlands believe in
exclusively female witches who attack only men. An identified witch is killed by the victim's kin and no compensation
is paid for her death 'for she is a public menace' (Glasse
1965:36).

Female 'witches' and male 'sorcerers' are also reported
for the Trobriands, Dobu, parts of the Southern Massim
and the Abelam of the Sepik but I will return to these
examples later, arguing that they represent a different case.

(vi) Witchcraft from within and from without

The Kalam of the Western Highlands (Riebe, this volume) provide yet another variation. Like the Kuma, the Kalam believe that a witch harbours within his body an evil entity, something like a spirit familiar, which generates inhuman appetites in the host. The belief has been gradually modified to allow the witch some conscious control over his evil potentiality to the extent that he is able to kill deliberately. Accusations may be directed against close kin and associates competing for scarce resources, or used to discredit political rivals. No simple correlation can be made between local group and the 'in-group', but it is clear that witchcraft operates between individuals who interact within the same social horizon.

Following pacification in the late 1950s and the out-lawing of physical violence, the Kalam revenge system, which was the nub of complex economic exchanges, began to operate clandestinely through the hiring of witches to perform revenge killings. At this point, Kalam witchcraft begins to look little different from revenge sorcery. I think, however, that Riebe is correct in distinguishing it from such because of the important differences in the social conse-quences. To accuse another Kalam of witchcraft is to brand him as something less than human; it is sufficient excuse to kill a close associate or to discredit and bring down a political rival. Witchcraft is an abomination to all and those who harbour it must be exterminated. In total contrast, the Kove or Mekeo or Elema sorcerer is open to counter-attacks but his social reputation suffers not a jot from imputations of sorcery—in fact it is quite the opposite, for such are proof of his powers.

(vii) Witchcraft from within

Accusations and witch killings within the local group are reported for the Etoro (Kelly 1977) of the Great Papuan Plateau and the Bimin-Kuskusmin (Poole 1981) of the West Sepik hinterland. Etoro usually accuse members of the same longhouse community (Kelly 1977:135). Following three accusations, the witch is executed or driven out; if a person is accused once, he or she is likely to be accused again (ibid.:257). The intensity of witch fears keeps groups small,

though this conflicts with the advantage of larger numbers
in warfare and raiding (ibid.:134–6). This reflects the Kuma
situation on the death of a bigman, with the important difference that among the Etoro all deaths lead to the
accusation of witches.

Bimin-Kuskusmin witchcraft also operates within the
smallest local grouping, the hamlet. Fear of witches is rife
and frequently leads to the execution of the witch (Poole
1981). Both Etoro and Kuskusmin witches are mainly
women. Here also, as among the Kaluli and the Hewa discussed below, we encounter the 'classic' image of the witch—
a creature of inhuman appetites and of sheer evil.

(viii) Witchcraft from without
The Kaluli (Schieffelin 1977), neighbours of the Etoro,
attribute all deaths to witches but those accused are usually
men and are of different, though related, longhouse communities. Raiding parties set out to kill the witch; and if the
condition of the executed witch's heart bears evidence of
witchcraft, his kin will not seek revenge (ibid.:79).

The Hewa (Steadman 1975), located in a far corner of
the Western Highlands near the West Sepik hinterland,
regularly engage in raiding other groups to kill witches,
who are usually women or unimportant old men.

(ix) Sorcery or witch beliefs not acted upon
A final mention should be made of societies like the Grand
Valley Dani (Heider 1979:119–20) of West Irian and the
Mae Enga (Meggitt 1965:128–9) of the Western Highlands
who admit the existence of sorcery and witchcraft among
other peoples but take no interest themselves in such
matters. Once again, it is difficult to make any correlation
with social structure. The highly mobile Dani society, with
its emphasis on residence and territorial alliances, totally
contrasts with the closely-knit agnatic groups of the Mae
Enga.

A Plethora of Sorcerers and Witches
The listing of patterns of accusations just offered is not
intended as an exhaustive categorization of types, but merely
as an illustration of the variety found in Papua New Guinea.
It is sufficient, however, to demonstrate the inaccuracy of

the generalizations with which we started. In the first place, these societies display a complex mixture of fears about sorcery and witchcraft within and without the community. Far from a simple directing of accusations outside the local group, we find some societies concerned primarily with in-group fears; others fear insiders, while espousing ideologies which deny the use of mystical powers within the group; others totally reject the possibility of inside sorcery but kill insider witches; some show little concern with either sorcerers or witches.

It is apparent that witchcraft is reported more widely than has been generally recognized: in addition to the well known Trobriand and Southern Massim examples, witchcraft beliefs are found among the Kuma, the Kalam, the Wola, the Gururumba, the Chimu, the Kyaka, the Huli, the Abelam, the Hewa, the Bimin-Kuskusmin, the Kaluli and the Etoro. It is also clear that in many societies individuals openly acknowledge and boast of their occult powers. Even in societies where sorcery is not openly admitted, like the Kwoma, this is not to say its use is socially condemned. Indeed, sorcery commonly features as an instrument of personal power, either of the individual who uses it to dominate others and extract debts and credit, or of the leaders of the community who use its threat to intimidate subordinates. Where sorcery is used by leaders, it operates to help maintain social order, even though in other contexts it is the means of expressing social conflict.

Finally, it becomes obvious that we are not dealing with a unitary phenomenon, 'sorcery and witchcraft': we face a whole range of holders of mystical, destructive powers who play very different social roles. Sorcerers may be bigmen or socially respected ritual experts, as among the Kove and Mekeo; leaders who collaborate with foreign sorcerers, like the Abelam bigmen; solid citizens, like the Kuma war sorcerers who use their powers to placate the ancestral ghosts; secretive, shadowy figures like the Keraki sorcerers who nevertheless gain social rewards for their skills. Witches emerge from the social landscape in varying guises and provoke very different reactions, ranging from the vague suspicions of the Wola and Kyaka, the occasional witch killing of the Gururumba, the eruption of accusations on the death of a Kuma bigman, to the continuous extermination campaigns of the Hewa, Kaluli and Etoro. Even among groups with a high level of witch killing, the patterns of accusations are different: the Etoro accuse insiders, the Hewa and Kaluli outsiders, yet the Etoro and Hewa suspect mainly women, while the Kaluli fear male witches.

Despite these variations, the material reviewed in this section reveals a basic division between those individuals described as 'sorcerers' and those described as 'witches'. We have seen that 'sorcery' is the attribute of powerful men, or its attribution brings power and social rewards; its use is socially approved in particular contexts; revenge for sorcery deaths is usually carried out by counter-magic rather than open violence, even in sorcery feuding. When physical violence is involved, the local group and the kin of the sorcerer are implicated in his attack and serve as appropriate targets for revenge. In contrast, we have seen that 'witchcraft' is imputed to the vulnerable or the weak, or its imputation brings social ruin; it is abhorred not only as an immoral but as an inhuman act; witchcraft deaths are usually acted upon publicly with physical violence. The insider witch is ostracized or killed; foreign witches are hunted down by raiding parties aiming to kill the offending witch alone, and kin are implicated only if they defend the culprit.

Two opposite effects are operating here. The witch—despised, driven out or slain—is indeed the victim of accusation. The sorcerer, on the other hand, uses the threat of his powers to gain social influence and to impose his will on others. As Chowning and Bowden (this volume) point out, current theories are inadequate to interpret situations where sorcery is socially approved; most scholars do not seem even to consider the possibility of in-group sorcery being condoned.[3] The current emphasis on the accused as victim tends to obscure the potential for power in the sorcerer's role.

Another circumstance which has clouded the distinction between the social roles of sorcerer and witch in Melanesia is the fact that sorcery and witchcraft are usually separated on the basis of a difference in beliefs about the nature of the occult powers involved—sorcery being the deliberate manipulation of ritual, witchcraft being an unconscious capacity. This difference is suggestive of, but not easily correlated with, a division in social practice. Since sorcery represents controlled, intentional use of mystical power, it seems symbolically appropriate that it should be employed to uphold the status quo, while witchcraft, as an uncontrolled, unconscious force would operate against it (cf. Douglas 1978:107). But we do not have to look far for Melanesian examples to refute this, such as the Tangu (Burridge 1969) and Fore (Lindenbaum 1979) sorcerer who seem closer to the despised witch than the socially influential sorcerer. We also have to deal with the paradox of Kalam witches who are believed to have a degree of deliberate control over their inherent capacity for evil. While among the Trobrianders, the Dobuans and in parts of the Southern Massim we find the highly incongruous figures of 'witches' who display the classic symbolism of witchcraft—night flying, coloured lights, cannibalism—yet are paid for their services and gain social influence as a result of their powers. Since these apparent anomalies cannot be dealt with satisfactorily until later in the discussion, I will put them aside until then.

For the time being, let us return to the basic polarity just identified in the data. In the following section I will examine in more detail the nature of the two opposite social roles I have referred to as 'sorcerer' and 'witch'.

Sorcerer and Witch

Sorcery, Status and Personal Power

As we have seen, sorcery skills in Melanesia are consistently associated with high status. Forge (1970) has drawn attention to the association between sorcery and political power, as more recently has Zelenietz (1981); and Patterson (1974–75:150) observes,

> In those societies where political power is held by a limited number of men . . . those who exercise it . . . are believed to monopolise the techniques of sorcery or access to such techniques.

The fact that sorcery is the prerogative of those in power is hard to explain if accusations of it are an indirect attack on those accused. It is not, however, difficult to see why Melanesian leaders actively encourage reputations for sorcery. Where leaders (including those whose positions are ascribed) must rely on persuasion and work through group consensus, sorcery provides a valuable weapon in the battle of wills underlying any social situation. Moreover, in the uncertainties of a gift exchange economy, where there is no assurance that a gift will be returned, the threat of sorcery is a useful stratagem to assert one's claims over the competing interests of others or to press reluctant debtors (cf. Riebe, this volume, on witchcraft and gift exchange). As Fortune's study of Dobu so clearly reveals, sorcery gives the possessor a means of imposing his will on others—in societies which provide few structural means of doing so.

In this context, the notion of 'accusation' seems misleading; rather we might speak of 'attribution'. Sorcery deaths of ordinary people are attributed to powerful men, who gain respect for their prowess. Where the use of sorcery is confined to warfare, the sorcerers of the opposing sides can openly glory in the losses suffered by their opponents. The situation is rather more delicate where in-group sorcery is condoned. Open boasting of responsibility or attributions of it immediately following a death might, in the heat of the moment, lead to a violent confrontation. Matters are thus better not voiced publicly, but left to private suspicion and rumour until some general consensus concerning the reasons for the death is reached. In this climate of rumour and innuendo, powerful men may covertly vie for responsibility which will increase their reputations.

A further element in the complex process of attribution, competing for responsibility, or establishing blame, is the part played by divination rituals. This has been virtually overlooked in the Melanesian literature (but see Chowning and Sillitoe, this volume).

Sorcery and Cosmic Power
If the sorcerer's role as a manipulator of men has received little attention, his role as a mediator of supernatural, or cosmic, power has attracted even less. Peter Lawrence (this volume) draws attention to the very narrow focus imposed on interpretations of Melanesian sorcery by the prevailing sociological models. He urges that it is high time we stopped

treating sorcery as merely an aspect of indigenous political systems—as a substitute for outlawed violence or as a means of conflict management; rather it should be understood as part of a magico-religious worldview in which illness, misfortune and death are made culturally meaningful. For the Garia—as for many other Melanesians—sorcery is an integral part of their most basic assumptions about the operation of the cosmos, man's place in it, and his capacity to control it through ritual.

Lawrence, Stephen and Reay all (this volume) emphasize the role of the sorcerer as a ritual expert, often the most important in his community, who mediates between men and the spirit realm. In addition to destructive powers, he usually possesses other important ritual knowledge.

Commonly allied with sorcery powers are powers to heal. (Arapesh, Tuzin 1980:197; Elema, Williams 1940:103; Garia, Lawrence, this volume; Kalauna, Young 1971:92,98; Keraki, Williams 1936:338; Koaka, Hogbin 1965:51; Mekeo, Stephen, this volume; Orokaiva, Williams 1928:56–7; Trobriands, Malinowski 1961:75). It should also be recognized that in all instances where sorcerers are paid to remove their influence, they are in effect being credited with healing powers. This double aspect of the sorcerer's role has hardly been considered in the recent literature (though see Mitchell 1977). Older ethnographies, however, note the close association of healing and harming. Malinowski (1961:75) observes that '. . . the art of killing and curing is always in the same hand'.

The sorcerer's importance as a healer will, of course, vary according to the availability and capacities of other healers, whether sorcery is thought to be used within the group or only outside it, and the extent to which it is in the hands of many or an élite few. Even in societies which draw clear distinctions between beneficent magic and harmful practices, the two may be found in the hands of one individual, who is regarded as healer in one context, sorcerer in another. But while healing may be performed publicly and be easily observable, sorcery is usually hidden from view—and thus may escape the ethnographer's notice.

Emphasis on accusations and social conflict has resulted in disease sorcery being almost entirely overlooked. Yet this is to ignore what is probably one of the most significant aspects of the sorcerer's role in the daily life of the community. People are always sick and minor ailments may presage serious maladies; relatives look for means to allay their anxieties and to bring relief to the sufferer. It is within the context of these everyday concerns that the sorcerer as healer operates. The sorcerer cannot be dismissed as a shadowy, or entirely imaginary, mystical assailant; in another guise he may also be the 'wise man' or 'doctor' whom one seeks out in the hope of curing one's ills. In this dual role, he is seen to control the destructive forces of illness and death that plague men. He becomes a veritable master of life and death.

It is not surprising, Tuzin (1980:197) points out, that the Ilahita master artists, the highest ritual experts, are also healers and sorcerers,

> . . . since the mystic powers of artistic creation, as perceived in this society, are not dissimilar from those which magically confer life and death.

Nor is it surprising that—as master of life and death—the sorcerer's mantle is claimed by bigmen and the highest ritual experts elsewhere: that the Elema sorcerer was 'the elite of the magical profession' (Williams 1940:109); that the Orokaiva Taro man was doctor, weatherman and sorcerer, all in one (Williams 1928:56–7); that the Kalauna headman's knowledge of sorcery is one of his most prestigious attributes (Young 1971:89); that Busama headmen controlled disease sorcery within their village (Hogbin 1951:144). Even among a group like the Kwoma, where no open admission is ever made, it is the most senior and respected ritual experts who are thought to possess sorcery (Bowden, this volume).

Protecting the community from foreign sorcerers and combating enemy groups with mystical attacks are other important functions carried out by the sorcerer. In some societies—for example, the Mekeo and Roro—war sorcery is a separate area of specialization; in many Highland societies only war sorcery is tolerated. Reay (this volume) emphasizes the religious significance of warfare to the Kuma. Beyond the physical violence between men is a struggle of cosmic forces—the spirits and ancestors of the opposing sides. The war sorcerer directs the supra-human powers of the clan spirits against the enemy; he is also guardian of clan relics and sacra, and his rituals invoke the spirits' protection of the clan territory. Sillitoe's (this volume) description of Wola sorcery divination reveals a similar cosmic view. Wola sorcery is part of warfare; the *komay* divination ritual brings together enemies to appeal to the spirits of both sides to punish the culprits in a sorcery death, thus removing the need for human retribution and bringing to a halt the revenge cycle. The placing of responsibility for the decision on a cosmic level is the explicit aim of the ritual. A reassessment of the importance of war sorcery in Melanesia is needed in the context of this sacred or cosmic aspect of warfare.

For the Western observer, whose cultural traditions have been moulded by a religion which predicates the godhead as the source of all good, and thus of human morality, the notion of the sorcerer as a channel of sacred power seems almost a contradiction in terms. The Melanesian world view, however, defines morality in human, social contexts, and places 'divine' or cosmic power beyond such judgements. Within the total cosmic order—divided into the empirical realm of the natural environment and human society, and the non-empirical realm of spirit beings and forces (Lawrence and Meggitt 1965a:9)—order, predictability and morality are the characteristics of *human* society. It is these characteristics which men, through ritual, attempt to impose on the unpredictable, non-reciprocal and thus amoral forces of the non-empirical realm.

Burridge's (1969) description of the Tangu concept of *imbatekas*, which he translates as the 'divine', clearly reveals the contrast between human moral order and 'divine' chaos. The moral world is the world of reciprocal relationships between human beings. The 'divine' is beyond reciprocity,

> 'While *imbatekas* connotes the anomalous, the unconstrainable and unobliged, it also evokes the generative and originating impulse' (Burridge 1969:157).

Spirits and the legendary heroes of the myths are *imbatekas*, so is the *ranguma*, the sorcerer/witch.

Nachman's (1981) analysis of Nissan sorcery provides a striking instance of the sorcerer as a 'master of terrible power', beyond the constraints of the moral order, yet mediator of powers both destructive and creative,

> People were unable to resist his power. None even dared to touch the *tansa's* person, eat food he had held, or walk behind him. The *tansa* claimed close ties to the spirit world and, because he neither shaved, cut his hair, nor washed, somewhat resembled a 'wild spirit' himself. (Nachman 1981:49).

Nachman captures well the play of cosmic forces behind present-day Nissan dance performances, the spectacle of the dance being on one level a competitive display, on another level a battle of supernatural forces.

My account of the Mekeo sorcerer (this volume) compares him with the shaman—for like the shaman, he communicates with the spirits in visions, trance and dreams, and his soul journeys (in controlled dreams) are the means of ensnaring the souls of others or of restoring them. Unlike the shaman, however, it is the punitive aspect of his role that is stressed by his community. In common with the Nissan *tansa*, he is a mediator of 'terrible power'; his command of many areas of esoteric knowledge—in particular healing, love and hunting magic—are but confirmation of this in the eyes of the community for all major forms of the esoteric rituals (for whatever purpose) involve a dangerous interaction with the powers of the spirits and the dead.

The double-sided nature of the sorcerer's role revealed in the examples just described is closely paralleled—as is my comparison with the shaman—by Mitchell's (1977) description of the Lujere (Upper Sepik) *nakworu*, whom he designates a 'shaman-witch'. The *nakworu* combines in the one person the murderous powers of *sangguma* (assault sorcery)—which he does not hesitate to use against members of his own community if need be—with healing powers, the ability to protect the community against foreign *sangguma* sorcerers, and hunting magic vital to the group's subsistence. His positive powers of healing, protection and hunting magic are dependent upon his destructive capacities, and these are openly recognized and acknowledged. Mitchell rightly points out the contrast with the African image of the witch, who possesses only evil capacities; but his identification of the *nakworu* as a figure combining aspects of both witch and shaman tends to confuse the issue. Rather, I would suggest, his richly detailed account of the *nakworu* provides us with a clear instance of the sorcerer who commands powers of both life and death.

The problem of determining the legitimacy of sorcery—its 'contextual' nature (Zelenietz 1981:4)—is often commented on in the literature. I would suggest that in Melanesia 'morality' in general is defined in specific situations and is regarded as a product of human society and action, not a universal principle. In this respect the use of sorcery is judged no differently from any other human action. Divine power is sheer power: it becomes creative or destructive, 'good', or 'bad', only in a specific human context. He who mediates between the world of men and the divine is necessarily a master of 'terrible power'.

In identifying the sorcerer as a mediator of sacred power, and thus as an important ritual expert, I am not implying that the role is everywhere the same in Melanesia. I am merely pointing to certain general similarities in several societies. The overall significance of the sorcerer as a ritual expert, the variations in the role, and its relationship to other ritual specializations (or divisions of ritual power into different social roles), are important questions which I can do no more than raise here.

Sorcery and Responsibility

Though the sorcerer trafficks with powers beyond society and human morality, he nevertheless uses them *within* the moral order. The sorcerer himself may be the ultimately non-reciprocal man, yet it is apparent that the Nissan 'master of terrible power', the Ilahita master artist and sorcerer, the Mekeo 'man of knowledge' are all seen to exercise their powers ultimately in accord with the common good. Individuals may suffer and seek revenge as a consequence of their actions, but overall social harmony and order are thought to benefit.

Control is a crucial aspect of the sorcerer's role. He deliberately exercises and controls the powers he invokes.

His learned knowledge of ritual provides him with the means of directing to human purposes sheer cosmic power. His mastery of this power is demonstrated in his ability not merely to wreak destruction but to reverse destructive influences in his capacity as healer: powers to heal are thus symbolically integral to his role. The importance of control is further symbolized in the strict ritual prohibitions he undergoes before he can exercise his powers: these include isolation, fasting, purging, all kinds of dietary restrictions, taboos against washing and sexual intercourse (Patterson 1974–75:148). These restrictions, aimed at eliminating all that is weak and 'cold', and intensifying 'heat', reveal that the sorcerer must first of all develop a rigorous self-control.

His role as a mediator between men and the realm of cosmic power incurs an ultimate responsibility for human fate—*he* must take that responsibility once the work of creation has been completed by supra-human beings. Upon him rest the decisions of life or death.

In this ultimate responsibility and power lies an inherent weakness in the role. As long as the community survives, prospers and feels secure in its relationship with cosmic powers, all is well for the sorcerer. Individual deaths and misfortunes can be fitted into the existing moral framework and he gains power and respectability from each event that validates the existing scheme of things. If, however, the continuing pattern of life and death is disrupted, the sorcerer cannot appeal to the actions of angry gods, for he himself is directly responsible and therefore directly held to blame. This inherent ambivalence in the role, as we shall see, makes it vulnerable in times of change.

Controlling the Sorcerer

In attributing powers of life and death to the sorcerer, the community must find some way to ensure he uses his awesome capacity for the common good. Some of the important variations we observe in sorcery practices can be explained in terms of this need.

In the first place, we can see that the widespread monopolization of sorcery by leaders of the community helps to serve this end. Powers of life and death are properly controlled by those entrusted with the directing of the community, and not allowed into the hands of unscrupulous individuals.

In societies like Nissan and Mekeo, sorcerers are attributed with great powers but their social and political role is sharply delimited by the rigours of their ritual observances. They become so charged with 'divine' power that they must virtually isolate themselves from ordinary human beings.

In other societies the sorcerer's field of action is confined to war sorcery. This, I suggest, is not simply a matter of directing aggressiveness outside the group. Patterson (1974–5:156), for example, has argued that in small, closely knit groups of male agnates accusations of sorcery within the group cannot be risked for fear of tearing it apart. My emphasis on sorcery as a potential for personal power suggests rather that it is a question of dominance within the group—a dominance totally in conflict with the egalitarian ethic of a small, closely related community. Thus in societies with marked structural inequalities—as between senior and junior, wife-givers and wife-takers—sorcery within the community may (though not necessarily) be deemed appropriate to maintain the relationship of dominance or privilege. Where the only important structural differentiation is between insiders and outsiders, then sorcery will be deemed proper only against the enemy or its use may be eschewed altogether—as among the Mae Enga, who prefer to attack their enemies by purely physical means.[4]

Regarding sorcery as a potential for personal power which needs to be controlled also leads me to approach Fortune's Dobu material rather differently from Patterson. Dobuans expect that every individual asserts himself as best he is able, at the expense of his fellows (Fortune 1963:78–9). Life is conducted as a covert battle between individuals in which sorcery plays a crucial and accepted part, and is widely available to all, both men and women having destructive powers. Patterson (1974–5:156, 214) argues that the structure of the local group, based on alternating residence rules so that the group composition is constantly changing, creates a situation where conflict is multiple but so are the ways to avoid it. Thus sorcery accusations flourish, whereas in more stable groups they must be avoided. Fortune's account, however, reveals that Dobuan 'accusations' are far from being attacks on the sorcerer held responsible. In fact, the sorcerer or 'witch' is identified and then 'publicly appeased and placated' (Fortune 1963:157); if the victim dies it is assumed that some other sorcerer not identified and placated must be involved. Revenge, when it is sought, is attempted through counter-sorcery. For Dobuans there is nothing offensive in the idea that one individual might use sorcery to intimidate another; but the fact that sorcery powers are so widely available prevents any one individual or a small élite from dominating the rest of the community.

Limiting the sorcerer's range of action also serves to protect his position since it limits the extent of his responsibility. For example, Trobriand sorcerers do not claim responsibility for epidemics, which are attributed to malignant spirits (Malinowski 1974:131), and with good reason as we shall see later. In societies where disease, but never death, is attributed to insiders, the sorcerer's position is probably strongest of all, as he can take credit for appropriate punishments but he never has to justify taking a life.

Sorcery and Secrecy
Secrecy is integral to the whole nature and purpose of sorcery, a circumstance which makes it very difficult to investigate in depth. As dangerous knowledge which cannot be safely allowed into the hands of many access to it is controlled by secrecy. All members of a community know something about sorcery and how it is supposed to operate; but it should be remembered that only the practitioner himself is privy to its real secrets.[5] Barth (1975) has drawn attention to the importance of deception and secrecy in the handling of sacred knowledge in Melanesia. His arguments apply as well to sorcery (of which there are even fewer adepts) as to male cults. Secrecy protects the exclusive rights of those who possess sorcery, and confirms its importance in the eyes of all. To reveal sorcery knowledge—except to an initiate—is to devalue it and risk it in the hands of the irresponsible.

Witchcraft and Status

Whereas the powerful are credited with sorcery, those accused of witchcraft are deviants (Kuma), women (Etoro, Hewa, Gururumba), unimportant old men (Hewa)—that is, the vulnerable and socially unimportant in these societies—or else the fact of accusation brings social ruin. (Those apparent exceptions where socially influential women have been described as 'witches' will be discussed later.)

Witchcraft Accusation as Attack

Whereas sorcery can be seen as a direct medium of personal power used to influence others, witchcraft operates in reverse. In the examples described so far as 'witchcraft', accusation is clearly a means of attacking the accused. Public 'moots' or 'trials' become forums in which those accused of witchcraft meet death, ostracism or, at the very least, social discrediting. This public denouncing, exposure and punishment of the witch is in direct contrast to the secrecy which commonly screens the sorcerer's activities.

Where witches from other groups are accused, retaliation is not left to counter-magic, as is usually the case with sorcery. Raiding parties set out to execute the witch and the aim is not generalized revenge against the witch's group but to dispatch an inhuman creature that represents a threat to all (Steadman, 1975:116). Even the kin of an executed witch are said not to seek revenge or compensation for the death if there is clear post-mortem evidence that the deceased was indeed a witch.

Witchcraft and Cosmic Power

The witch, though apparently human, is the vehicle of inhuman, destructive power. As Riebe (this volume) observes, the accusation of witchcraft is a way of dehumanizing a member of the community. The witch is characteristically possessed by some witch creature or substance, or supernatural being (e.g. Huli, Glasse, 1965:36); thus beneath the apparently harmless exterior of some ordinary member of the community is a fiend of sheer destructive malice. The symbolism of witchcraft—canni-

balism, inversion and so on—points to the inhuman nature
of the witch. In those cases surveyed here, the witch is not
merely the opposite of a moral person but the very antithesis
of a *human* being—an evil of cosmic proportions. The Kuma
witch, according to Reay (this volume) 'gathers all the
varieties of what is considered unnatural into a single
concept'. Poole's vivid account of the Bimin-Kuskusmin
witch conveys the nightmarish grotesqueness of the image:

> . . . the *tamam* . . . becomes a hideous caricature of uncon-
> trolled female substances. She menstruates constantly, even
> during pregnancy and lactation and beyond the normal age
> of menopause . . . she is sluggish, fat, insensitive, unbalanced
> in gait and in emotional character, dull, and nasty. She is
> always dirty, and her hair is tangled and matted. She is
> covered with the grease of male foods and the sweat of the
> heat of menstruation. Her genitalia may be massive and
> deformed. She exudes pollution and 'black blood' illnesses
> from all the orifices of her grotesque body (Poole 1981:64).

The sorcerer, though he may sometimes become more
spirit than man, is not *less* than human. He acts from understandable human motives, and those who suffer injury from
him seek revenge as they would against any person. The
witch is an entirely different creature. Witches kill for no
predictable human reason; they may attack anyone. Reay
(this volume) stresses that the Kuma witch is thought to be
'jealous of all ordinary men and not necessarily of anybody
in particular'. There is no point in seeking revenge against
a witch; the witch itself must be destroyed to remove the
source of danger to all. And while the actions of a sorcerer
reflect on his group, the actions of a witch cannot be held
against anyone, except those who attempt to shield the
culprit. The sorcerer's use of destructive power is active,
controlled and deliberate, guided by reasonable motives.
The witch is the passive vehicle of destructive power
unleashed indiscriminately on the community, for no reason
but inhuman malice.

Both sorcerer and witch represent channels of cosmic
power, but their mediation of that power is in opposite
directions. The sorcerer accepts responsibility for life and
death and thus gains social influence; the witch is forced to
take the blame for misfortune and death and thus faces

social ruin.[6] One is a role of cosmic responsibility, the other a role of cosmic blame, as summarized below.

Cosmic Power

The Witch	mediated by	The Sorcerer
witchcraft/cosmic blame		sorcery/cosmic responsibility
uncontrolled/passive		controlled/active
only destructive		creative and destructive
used against the social order		used in support of the moral order
harboured by the weak and anti-social		used by the socially influential
exposed in public		protected by secrecy
punished		socially rewarded

I now wish to turn to the effects external changes have had on these two sharply contrasting roles.

Social Change, Sorcery and Witchcraft

Much discussion of sorcery and witchcraft in Melanesia, and elsewhere, has assumed that we are dealing with fixed structures and institutions—or static beliefs predicated on fixed social structures. In the broader perspective of change over time, it becomes clear that sorcery and witchcraft represent flexible ideologies and roles responding to external pressures and change, as well as to internal needs.

Loss of Legitimacy and the Sorcerer

Lindenbaum's (1979) recent study of Fore sorcery reveals the effects of demographic disasters on indigenous perceptions of cosmic power. In the late 1950s and early 1960s the Southern Fore experienced the ravages of a disease called *kuru*. *Kuru* was known to the Fore and was recognized as part of the repertoire of the Fore sorcerer, but it had not previously occurred in epidemic proportions. As deaths rapidly increased in the late 1950s, people frantically sought cures and when these failed, suspicion grew that the culprits were not foreign sorcerers but members of the same community. Public meetings began to be held in each community at which sorcerers were urged to confess and to cease attacks on their fellows. Lindenbaum provides an impressive analysis of the processes whereby a community exposed to a severe epidemic becomes consumed by fears of internal mystical aggression; but in using the Fore as a general model to explain Melanesian sorcery, she appears to underestimate the changes the epidemic had caused in the role of the sorcerer.

Fore sorcery was a complex art (Lindenbaum 1979:59–65) and used against the enemy it was entirely legitimate (105). In the past, when deaths from it were few, Fore sorcerers had claimed responsibility for *kuru*; when deaths began to increase at an alarming rate, responsibility turned to blame. The sorcerers who had formerly been regarded as the defenders of their communities against enemy groups, now emerged as the destroyers of their own people. The Fore sorcerer is thus, I suggest, a classic example of the emergence of the witch-like sorcerer—one who is seen to lose control of his dangerous powers, unleashing them indiscriminately on his own community. He is, however, a product of change.

The witch-like sorcerer is also identifiable in Burridge's (1969) account of Tangu sorcery. The Tangu *ranguma* appears in guises now witch-like, now powerful. Though Burridge tends to emphasize the witch-like characteristics of the *ranguma*, he notes that 'Some men readily confess to being *ranguova*: it makes them feared, may be profitable' (ibid.:149). Moreover, Tangu leaders are those thought most likely to be *ranguova* (ibid.:150). The region's chequered history of migration and depopulation, followed by the disruptive effects of colonial rule (ibid.:3–36), suggest that the witch-like *ranguma* may well be the product of processes similar to those observed by Lindenbaum among the Fore. Burridge estimates that the total population has been reduced from roughly four thousand to half that in the last four or five generations. The Tangu themselves attribute this to epidemics caused by sorcery; Burridge (1969:143–4) surmizes that the escalating death rate could no longer be attributed solely to enemy sorcery, and suspicions thus began to turn inwards on the community. In seeing themselves as the victims of threatening, uncontrollable external forces, the Tangu reflect their present worldview. The inadequacy of the old order to deal with the new seems to be embodied in the ambivalent figure of the *ranguma*, who asserts a weak and perilous control over the dangerous forces he invokes—he is both a creation of, and a reflection of, change.

Evidence of the loss of legitimacy of sorcery powers in several societies is provided in the special issue of *Social Analysis* (1981) on 'Sorcery and Social Change in Melanesia'. Zelenietz (1981:4) notes in the introduction:

> Clear, locally-defined notions of the propriety of the use of sorcery are noted for several societies. Furthermore, the authors demonstrate that those notions of propriety have changed in the period following contact.

Two basic trends can be seen. Firstly, in societies like South Ambrym (Tonkinson 1981), where sorcery was formerly controlled by the chiefs, it has now become available to many, mainly through returned labourers claiming to have purchased foreign sorcery. Secondly, in societies like the Mendi (Lederman 1981), where sorcery was used legitimately only against enemy groups, it is now thought to be used against members of the same community. What we see, then, is a weakening or dissolution of the traditional cultural means of constraining the sorcerer's actions within the moral framework of society.

The influence of Christianity has been important in this process in some communities, as Belshaw's (1957: 193–210) study of Hanuabada, Port Moresby, reveals. Accepting Christian teaching that sorcery was evil, Hanuabadans forswore the use of it. As a result, they began to feel exposed to the sorcerers of less sophisticated neighbouring groups who continued to ply their black arts. Suspicion grew that others in the community were hiring foreign sorcerers to do their dirty work for them. Fears increased as people accused relatives and neighbours of using hired sorcerers to harm them. Making no headway against the belief in sorcery, Christianity has succeeded only in damaging its legitimacy and the cultural controls that formerly guided its use.

With the restraints on its acquisition and use gone, sorcery becomes an instrument of naked personal power for those who claim it—at least for as long as belief in its efficacy persists. Lawrence (this volume) draws attention to the enduring nature of these beliefs, observing that up to the present day sorcery continues to be 'a dominant socio-political and intellectual force'. He argues that such beliefs will lose credibility only when the whole magico-religious worldview is replaced; and this, he emphasizes, will require an intellectual, not a social, revolution.

An inherent weakness in the sorcerer's role was pointed out in the previous section. Here we have seen the sorcerer's cosmic responsibility turn to cosmic blame as communities are exposed to the ravages of epidemics.[7] We have also seen that the sorcerer, as a mediator of destructive powers, finds the legitimacy—though not the efficacy—of his powers easily discredited under conquerors and colonizers, who assert the superiority of different ideologies and rituals. Nevertheless, a potential for power remains for those daring or unscrupulous enough to claim the sorcerer's mantle anew.

Insecurity and an Increase in Witches

If witches, as Douglas (1978:102) argues, are created by ambiguity and contradiction, creatures emerging from the interstices of social structure, then they are obviously likely to appear in times of social change. She (1970:xx-xxi) rejects the idea that witchcraft is the product of social and moral collapse—but social change does not necessarily involve total collapse, either of order or of morals. Rather, it is the redefining of roles and boundaries that characterizes situations of change, and as Douglas (1970:xxv) observes, witchcraft beliefs are 'essentially a means of clarifying and affirming social definitions'.

This is not to deny that witch fears may grow out of existing structural ambiguities. A Kuma community erupts into a fury of self-recrimination and witch fears on the death of a bigman, whereas at other times occasional accusations fall on obvious deviants. This suggests a structural gap on the death of a bigman—an ambiguity in succession which necessitates a purging of loyalties. Yet it is also associated with change—in this case a cyclical change in leadership.

Competition, Individual Insecurity and Witch Fears
Riebe's (this volume) account of the variations in Kalam witch beliefs over the last century underlines the flexibility of witchcraft as an ideology and, in particular, its importance in redefining moral boundaries in times of change. Witch beliefs first gained currency among the Kalam in the late nineteenth century, at a time when epidemics of newly introduced diseases were sweeping the area. These reverses were followed by a period of prosperity and an increase in population. The economy began to increase in scale and the Kalam soon began to feel the pressures of competition for scarce resources. As competitiveness increased, overly demanding kin or rivals for the same resources came to be seen as threats to the individual's economic survival. At the same time, witchcraft began to operate in a humanly pre-dictable manner, and the witch was believed to have acquired a degree of control over his destructive capacities. As a result, the revenge killing sequence, which underlay the exchange economy, began to incorporate deaths caused by witchcraft; thus men were paid to kill by physical violence but witches might also be commissioned to kill by witchcraft. Following pacification of the area in the late 1950s, hiring witches became the only means left to perpetuate the revenge cycle.

At this point, far from undermining the social order, witches had become an essential part of it. Yet no one publicly claimed to be a witch. Witchcraft was still despised—grounded in a tension between the generosity and rec-iprocity that were integral to Kalam values, and the growing competitiveness of the economic system. In the late 1960s new pressures in the form of government programmes for development heightened the existing conflict in values; soon exponents of 'development' were turning accusations of witchcraft against representatives of the old order.

Witchcraft beliefs can be seen to reflect the Kalam's changing perception of their world and the dangers threatening them. As a group they have increased and prospered over the last century, but individually they have been subjected to a struggle to exist and assert themselves in a situation of increasing competitiveness and conflicting values. Riebe shows how witch beliefs and accusations have

provided both a means of expressing the individual's insecurities and the means of resolving them in specific
circumstances.

Epidemics, Group Insecurity and Witch Fears

Since witchcraft (and sorcery) provides an explanation for
disease and death, it is logical to expect some correlation
between such beliefs and sudden changes in mortality rates.
Riebe associates the introduction of Kalam witch beliefs
with epidemics; and we have seen the effects of epidemics
on the position of the Fore sorcerer. A close correlation
between epidemics and witch beliefs is also revealed in the
case of the Etoro and Kaluli, both of the Great Papuan
Plateau. Here we are dealing with what is clearly witchcraft:
a belief in the existence of inhuman creatures of totally
malicious evil who must be exterminated by physical
violence. Both the Etoro and the Kaluli are small, scattered
and diminishing populations, who believe themselves to
be—and are in fact—dying out, a circumstance which they
both attribute to witchcraft (Kelly 1977:30–1; Schieffelin
1977:14–15). In the late 1940s a wave of measles and
influenza epidemics swept the region. The Etoro and the
Onabasulu were hardest hit, with 30 per cent and in some
places 70 per cent of the population dying. The Kaluli
suffered less, but Schieffelin estimates that approximately
25 per cent of the population was wiped out. The devastating effect of these epidemics was still apparent in the late
1960s.

The Kaluli and the Etoro remain gripped by a 'sense
of fatality' (Schieffelin 1977:15). Their feelings of help-
lessness in the face of radical depopulation due to epidemics
are reflected in their fears of witches. I would further
suggest that the apparent paradox of these already diminishing groups hastening their demise by continuous witch
killing can be understood as an attempt to prolong their
survival. The witch is seen as the channel whereby
destructive cosmic power enters society bringing disease
and death; the only means of dealing with the situation is
to cut off each point of entry as it is identified. Witch killing
thus becomes a desperate attempt to stop up the cracks in

the cosmos; though, as the Kaluli and Etoro themselves are aware, it is no more than a stopgap.

The Hewa, located in a remote region of the East Sepik, suggest a similar insecure cosmic view. An estimated one per cent of the total population per year is killed in witch extermination campaigns (Steadman 1975:115). This high level of killing is combined with a small, scattered population which may give evidence of recent epidemics, or severe military reverses, but in any case is in itself sufficient cause for feelings of insecurity.

Insecure Dominance and Fears of Witches

Lindenbaum has argued convincingly on the basis of her Fore material that insecurity in dominance relationships is an important cause of fears of mystical aggression. She suggests that those in power fear the retaliation of those they dominate and thus attempt to control subordinates through accusations of mystical aggression. Chowning (this volume) points out that this argument is inapplicable where in-group sorcery is condoned and is thus invalid as a general explanation of Melanesian sorcery. Nevertheless, the notion of insecure dominance is illuminating in situations where fears of witchcraft, or of sorcery that has lost its legitimacy, prevail—though it needs certain qualification.

The Hewa, for instance, accuse as cannibal witches those who are consistently deprived of meat, mainly women. The link here between insecure, or guilty, dominance is persuasive; but one wonders why, when in many Melanesian societies men assert rights to prestige foods, particularly animal protein, witch beliefs of this nature are not more widespread. Why do Hewa men feel so insecure and not others? Similarly, we can see that Etoro accusations of women and adolescent boys as witches are elucidated by the belief that men, by virtue of their 'gifts' of semen to females and boys, are responsible for the growth and perpetuation of the group (Kelly 1976). Witches are thus those beings who place excessive demands on male strength and semen. Yet would Etoro men feel so drained by witches if the survival of the group was not in doubt, if men were not beset by fears that their communities are dying out? Poole's

(1981) analysis of Bimin-Kuskusmin witchcraft reveals a connection between accusations and an imbalance in exchange and power relationships with neighbouring Oksapmin peoples—an imbalance brought about under colonial rule.

In short, I suggest that those in power—in these cases the adult men—are likely to be troubled by fears of those they dominate when their attempts to sustain the group (by ritual or other means) seem in doubt. Lindenbaum's dominance theory needs to be allied with the existence of external pressures acting to discredit the status quo—as, indeed, is the case with Fore sorcery and the *kuru* epidemic. Chronic witch fears and campaigns of extermination are thus not indications of a collapse of moral or social order; rather they reflect the fears of those in power that their control over the cosmic forces on which the community's survival depends is slipping—a fear they project on to those they dominate, who are felt to be sapping their strength and their capacity to exert control.

It was argued in the previous section that witchcraft is a belief in uncontrollable, destructive cosmic power unleashed on human society through the passive vehicle of the witch—a statement of cosmic insecurity. In this section we have traced in several societies the correlation between witch fears and insecurities caused by external forces of change: epidemics, demographic fluctuations, and the conflicts in values and other changes brought about under colonial rule.

Evidence of the importation of witch beliefs from outside—as in the case of the Kalam; and probably in the case of the Kuma, since Reay suspects the belief may have been adopted from the Chimbu; and the Wola, who associate witches with the arrival of the white men and the beginning of contacts with the outside world—is also indicative of the connection between witch beliefs and external change.

Change and the Blurring of Opposites
In tracing the effects of change on the roles of sorcerer and witch, we have seen the distinctions between the two begin to blur as the sorcerer loses his legitimacy and fears of

mystical aggression within the community increase. The Fore sorcerer assumes a social role which seems closer to the despised witch; while the Kalam witch of the post-pacification era begins to look more like the sorcerer who is paid for his indispensable skills.

Nevertheless, the one never finally merges into the other. When pacification forced the revenge system to operate clandestinely on the basis of witchcraft, Kalam witches might well have reached the point where they could publicly declare themselves and claim responsibility for their services to society. Yet this did not happen. Bigmen were prepared to admit that their activities relied upon the use of witches as agents, but would not themselves confess to being witches. Nor was it long before others were to use the accusation of 'witch' to bring down rivals. 'Witch' continued to be an image of all that was abhorrent. Though Lindenbaum describes Fore sorcery very much as if it were witchcraft, she recognizes that the Fore sorcerer and the witch are not identical figures (1979:132–3). Fore sorcery still holds a potential for power: some identified sorcerers may 'gain in reputation and wealth (through bribes) as a result' (ibid.:125), and the sorcerer represents an 'image of power with one of denigration' (ibid.:126). For the Kalam, to admit to being a witch is to deny one's humanity. With the Fore, admitting to socially condemned sorcery is admitting only to using it in the wrong context. There was, Lindenbaum notes, never any suggestion that the use of sorcery against enemies should be forgone (ibid.:105).

In other words, I am arguing that the nature of the beliefs themselves ultimately give a different meaning to the two roles, even when sorcery is condemned—for what is condemned is its improper use. The situation is somewhat different in Hanuabada and other communities where Christianity has had a deep influence. But even if sorcery is here regarded as evil, it remains a human sin which can be forsworn, not an innate capacity for evil; and its threat may still be used by the bold and manipulative to influence others.

In contrast, witchcraft becomes a means of direct power only if some external agency like the colonial or national government prevents physical action being taken against the witch. Reay (1968:199–200) provides a vivid example of an accused witch manipulating such a situation to terrorize her community; but this success depended on the presence of an external agency to protect her. In the case of the Tangu or Fore sorcerers, those who achieved power did so without having to appeal to agencies outside the system. Both sorcerer and witch are roles that individuals may be forced into or choose to play, but it is evident that the role of sorcerer holds a potential for power or for ruin, while the role of the witch leads only to ruin. In this respect the two are distinct, even when sorcery loses its legitimacy.

Witchcraft and Female Sorcery

While the effects of social change can be seen to result in a blurring of roles in several societies, this argument does not apply in situations where exclusively male 'sorcerers' and female 'witches' are reported, as among the Trobrianders, Dobuans and in other parts of the Southern Massim. Dobuan and Trobriand 'witches', while endowed with the classical symbolism of witchcraft—cannibalistic appetites, night flying, lights, familiars, etc.—are socially respected and rewarded. Since the powers attributed to these women bring them social influence and respect, I contend that we are dealing here with *female sorcery*. The Hewa cannibal witch is summarily murdered: the Dobuan cannibal witch is placated and paid to remove her influence. The contrast in roles here is too extreme to ignore. On the basis of this contrast, I suggest that in the Hewa case we are dealing with witchcraft, but in the Dobuan case with female sorcery.

The fact that Dobuan and Trobriand sorceresses are designated by a different term from that used for male sorcerers, and that their capacities are thought to be different, does not provide any serious difficulty. Melanesian societies usually draw sharp distinctions between male and female roles and spheres of action; it is thus only to be expected that female sorcery will differ from male sorcery. Given the general association in Melanesia of masculinity with order and control, it is appropriate that female sorcery should be less deliberate and less fully controlled than male powers, and that it will be symbolized by the destructive aspects of femininity. The powers of the Dobuan witch are inherited from her mother—that is, are intrinsic to her femaleness—yet their execution requires the deliberate use of learned spells; and she controls her powers to the extent that she can cure as well as harm (Fortune 1963:150–7; cf. Malinowski 1961:240–1). Though she, together with the Hewa witch, is associated with the devouring mother and other images of destructive female power, the Dobuan sorceress deliberately conjures such images, using them to intimidate and control others. In total contrast, the Hewa woman accused of witchcraft makes no claim to such powers; male fears of destructive femininity are focused on her and she becomes their victim. Dobuan and Trobriand female sorcery can be seen as a reflection of the high status women have in these societies, since women are able to turn fears of their powers into a means of intimidating others.

Forge's (1970:267–8) brief description of Abelam 'witchcraft' is also suggestive of female sorcery rather than witchcraft. He notes that some old women were credited with special abilities to heal spear wounds. Moreover, the fact that 'witchcraft' here operates in a strictly feminine, domestic context further suggests that it has a legitimate context—that is, between women. Thus in addition to sorcery exercised by men, we need to recognize the existence of female sorcery—a similar but by no means identical practice.

Yet another variation on female sorcery is provided by the Bokondini Dani of the highlands of West Irian (Ploeg 1979:170–1, 176–7). An unusual division of powers operates here. Men assert themselves through the use of physical violence in the form of warfare waged against other parishes; women assert themselves through the use of sorcery, usually against members of the same parish. The employment of sorcery by women to exercise social influence parallels the Trobriand and Southern Massim situation; what appears unusual, if not unique, for Melanesia is the female monopoly of mystical destructive powers.

Sorcery or Witchcraft—a Distinction on the Basis of Social Roles

In distinguishing between witchcraft and sorcery, the symbolism of the beliefs involved is not an accurate guide taken in isolation. Witches may gain some control over their powers, and sorceresses can be expected to have less control than male sorcerers and to act differently; the degree of control, deliberate manipulation and unconscious capacity can be expected to vary over time and in different situations. In the Melanesian context, Evans-Pritchard's classic distinction between controlled and unconscious powers is a valuable guide to the basic divergence in roles, but may be confusing in specific circumstances. I have indicated here that a clear dividing line separating the two is to be found in the *social roles* created by the beliefs. Where the imputation of destructive mystical power is used as a means to gain social influence (at least by some), we are dealing with sorcery; where it unavoidably leads to social ruin, we are dealing with witchcraft.

Psychological Processes and Experiential Reality

Underlying the intellectual justification which a magico-religious worldview provides for beliefs in sorcerers and witches are powerful psychological processes adding emotional force to the logic of investing certain human individuals with cosmic responsibility and cosmic blame.

Witchcraft, Guilt and Projection

The psychological underpinnings of witch beliefs are familiar from the literature (e.g. LeVine 1973; Mitchell 1977) and are well explained by Riebe (this volume) in relation to the Kalam. By projecting repressed fears or feelings of inferiority on to others, the individual and the group are able to rid themselves, at least consciously, of such feelings. The witch becomes the focus of all such negative emotions for the group. This helps to explain the at times devastating emotional force aroused in witch trials and the intense anxiety attached to the image of the witch. My point here is that underlying conscious intellectual assumptions about the nature of witchcraft, which are in themselves sufficient to create anxiety, are unconscious processes intensifying that anxiety.

The general notion of projection can be made more specific: what is projected is blame for misfortune and death.

It has already been argued in relation to Lindenbaum's theory of insecure dominance that those accusing the witch are attempting to avoid fears that they, themselves, are to blame. Moreover, disaster and death are widely, if not universally, associated with punishment and thus with guilt. Suffering provokes the same question in all of us: what have I done to deserve this?

In Melanesian societies death is specifically linked with punishment. The agents and reasons vary. They may be neglected spirits of the dead, angry ancestors, vindictive nature spirits whose sites have been disturbed, or human magicians. Not all deaths are related to transgression against other people but all are connected with some breach of the proper ordering of relationships between human beings or with cosmic forces. When death and misfortune strike, people examine their consciences and confess their sins. Inevitably, illness and death arouse intense feelings of guilt in the community which are handled in different ways. I suggest that the psychological significance of witchcraft as an explanation for death is that it provides a means of dissipating these guilt feelings—particularly in circumstances where the usual explanations for death as punishment become inadequate or intolerable. Witchcraft is thus an assertion that the misfortunes suffered by the group are unmerited, being the result of totally malicious evil. It is, therefore, particularly likely to emerge during serious epidemics or among groups that are fragmented and diminishing.

The witch can be seen, in Jungian terms, as a cultural formulation of one of the basic structures of the human psyche—the 'shadow'. Jung's theory of archetypal structures, it is true, provides a notoriously slippery analytical tool. As Jung (1978:58) himself stressed, 'The archetype is a tendency to form ... representations of a motif—representations that can vary a great deal in detail without losing their basic pattern'. Thus it becomes extremely difficult to define precisely the characteristics of any archetype, which may take numerous forms and transformations across different cultures. Whether or not such structures or patterns can be shown to be 'universal', the Melanesian witch, as defined here, seems a classic exemplification of what Jungians refer to as the 'shadow'. The shadow represents all the inferior and base aspects of the individual personality, and of human nature in general (Jung 1968a:8–10). Existing below the threshold of consciousness, it is not part of the conscious ego or recognized by it and thus is easily projected on to others, who are then invested with all its vileness. Existing in all of us, this image, or 'complex' of emotions, is not necessarily projected on to other people but may also find expression in individual fantasies, dreams and nightmares, and cultural productions such as folktales and myths, and even the fictional narratives of modern literature, plays and films. For Jung, witches emerge from the very structure of the human imagination and need no specific features of social structure to provoke them. But where the identification and destruction of human witches become a key concern, then social and other external factors are clearly at work.[8]

The Sorcerer, Responsibility and Dependency

If in the role of the witch we see the readiness of the group to project its guilt and the dark side of its nature, we see a projection of a different kind in the role of the sorcerer. The sorcerer is the focus of a projection of power—specifically, of punitive authority. He is both given and claims responsibility for life and death. He is the father figure writ large, the symbolic representative of controlled, male power. His image is conjured by conscious guilt and the fear of punishment. The community's willingness to accept the claims of certain individuals for responsibility over life and death can, of course, be at least partly explained in terms of the belief in the effectiveness of magic; but this belief finds psychological support in feelings of dependency triggered off by conscious guilt and the aura cast by the parental image, the father who takes responsibility. Psychological and psychoanalytic studies of dependency and transference reveal the sorts of projections of power which modern patients, with no magical or even religious convictions, focus on healers, i.e. doctors and psychotherapists (Frank 1961).

As a projection of the punitive father, the sorcerer is a focus for the strong ambivalence attached to the father, who is envied, hated and loved all at once. The individual's ability to manipulate this ambivalence will vary, and if the positive is to prevail he must be careful of what he claims or accepts responsibility for. In situations of change—for example, where new sorcery is brought back by returning labourers—some individuals by luck, intelligence or intuition will be able to use the projection to increase their power; while others, with less judgement, will provoke only fear and eventually become the victim of their own machinations.

What then of the sorceress? While I would argue that sorcery is particularly equated with male power and the father image, the sorceress can also be seen as representative of parental authority. But as a reflection of the mother image, she is associated with instinctive, autochthonous powers, both creative and destructive. The psychological associative links with *social* authority and responsibility—primarily the domain of the father, and the sorcerer—are weaker in her case. In matrilineal societies, however, where membership of the social group is traced through the mother, it is understandable that she becomes more closely linked ideologically with concepts of social responsibility.

Spiro's (1982) reworking of Malinowski's data has thrown new light on the psychodynamics underlying Trobrianders' fears of female occult powers. He identifies the origins of such fears in the severe Oedipal conflict provoked by the Trobriand mother's seductive treatment of her child—a conflict explicitly denied by Malinowski but which, Spiro argues, is revealed by his ethnographic evidence. Growing out of the painful ambivalence provoked by the seductive yet sexually forbidden mother, is, according to Spiro, an unconscious identification of female sexuality with dangerous, destructive powers. Spiro is not, however, concerned with the question of why Trobriand women are able to turn this negative identification to their advantage, gaining social respect and rewards for their assumed occult powers, whereas in other societies, as among the Hewa or the Bimin-Kuskusmin, a similar negative identification with the bad/destructive mother leads to the victimization and execution of women. We must await further studies to clarify whether psychodynamic or sociological processes determine these differences. My point here is merely to emphasize that the destructive mother image is found in association with high social status for females and in association with female social vulnerability.

Having identified the sorcerer with the father image, it is tempting to equate the witch with the mother. Roheim (1948:279) notes that on Normanby Island (Dobu), sorcery is said to be 'the father's way', and witchcraft 'the mother's' (I have, of course, already argued that Dobu 'witchcraft' is female sorcery). But it is evident that the negative mother image attaches to both the socially respected sorceress and the victimized female 'witch'. A further point should be made. It is true that witchcraft in Melanesia, and in general, is often attributed to women and associated with female imagery even when men are accused (see Reay and Riebe, this volume). In the sense that sorcery is related to strength, the status quo, and controlled masculine power, while witchcraft is linked with the weak, the peripheral, and unconscious power, witchcraft will logically be associated with the female pole of opposition. But while the negative mother image is often a component of the witch projection, it is not exclusively female characteristics that attach to the witch. The Kaluli, for one, associate the witch with male creative power gone wrong (Schieffelin 1977:127n). Rather than simply a projection of negative femaleness, the witch is an image of all that is abhorrent and that the community wishes to rid itself of, including male aggression and destructiveness.

Thus, I would argue that in the very nature of their psychological origins, the image of the sorcerer and the image of the witch are quite distinct. The witch can be seen as a projection of repressed guilt—or, in Jungian terms, a projection of all that is inferior in the human psyche. In contrast, the sorcerer is a projection of the father image and thus more akin to the shaman and priest, a representative of 'divine' power, but one in which the ambivalence adhering to the father image has not been resolved. Tuzin's (1980) study of the Ilahita Arapesh Tambaran cult suggests that this ambivalence may be overcome when community and sorcerer give final responsibility to an entirely supernatural entity, in this case the Tambaran spirit. When the sorcerer is seen to be only carrying out the will of the Tambaran, social solidarity and the role of the sorcerer is thereby enhanced. The sorcerer then has relinquished the father's mantle and becomes only his agent; but in disclaiming ultimate responsibility he is also spared blame. While in general psychoanalytic usage, the potency of the father image is explained in terms of infantile dependency, Jungian psychology attaches a more positive value to it, identifying it as an aspect of the deeper structures of the unconscious containing a special potential for self-knowledge and an ability to integrate the total personality (Jung 1968:187;60–5). Since, like the shadow, this is an unconscious capacity, it is experienced as outside the conscious ego and thus is easily projected on to others, investing that person with esoteric knowledge or spiritual power. The psychopomp, the wise old man, the wizard, the sorcerer are all, according to Jung (1968:35–8), cultural refractions of the archetype of the self—representing the highest goals and potentiality of the individual.

Indeed, a Jungian perspective suggests that the unconscious processes underlying the symbolic prototypes of sorcerer and witch display as marked a polarity as that to be found in the *social* roles played by witch and sorcerer in Melanesia. It is clear enough, however, in general psycho-dynamic terms that the two images are related to very different psychological roots.

The Experiential Reality of Magic
As Reay (this volume) observes, much writing on the topic has assumed that witches and sorcerers are purely imaginary figures, that is to say no one actually believes themselves to possess the destructive powers attributed to them. The arguments presented here have progressed on the basis that real people are, in fact, forced into, or themselves elect, these roles. The individual's image of himself is in large part created by others' perceptions of and response to him. People who are treated like witches may well end up convinced that they are. Sorcerers who are acclaimed for their cures, like Lévi-Strauss's (1972:175–8) sceptical shaman, may come to believe in them, despite themselves. Deviants among the Kuma seem to gain certain

satisfactions in playing on the community's fears. The standardized cultural belief may well give the emotionally disturbed a recognized idiom in which to express their neuroses. Moreover, since normal individuals harbour some repressed feelings of inferiority and guilt, it is not surprising that, under the stress of accusation, they come to identify consciously with the group projection of guilt.

The fact that empirically impossible activities—flying, changing into animal familiars, resuscitating dismembered corpses—are attributed to witches and sorcerers is taken by some literal-minded scholars to prove that such persons cannot exist. Assumptions of this kind ignore the high epistemological value many cultures, including those of Melanesia (Stephen 1979), place on experiences such as dreams, trance, and drug-induced states of non-ordinary reality (Price-Williams 1975:81–94). These states, especially when ritually induced, are widely regarded as the means of access to the potency of the spirit realm (Peters and Price-Williams 1980; 1983). My description of Mekeo sorcery (this volume) attempts to show that the rituals of sorcery and magic are specifically intended to create states of non-ordinary reality in the practitioner; I further suggest that at least some of the techniques employed succeed in influencing subliminal levels of consciousness in both the magician and his subject.

That is to say, the sorcerer deliberately induces and controls dream and trance states, in which he performs—as an experiential reality—the magical act. Roheim's (1948) interviews with Normanby witches vividly attest to the experiential reality of the witches' participation in eating corpses, in bizarre initiations and in visiting the underworld. But the witch herself, like the Mekeo 'man of knowledge', is well aware that these are not the experiences of the body: it is her *yaruyarua* (soul) that 'goes out at night, her body stays at home' (ibid.:300, also 298). Likewise, the Trobrianders distinguish clearly between the witch as a physical woman and the soul of the witch that leaves the body at night to perform its nefarious tasks:

> the *yoyova* . . . . . means a woman endowed with such powers, whereas *mulukuwausi* describes the second self of the woman, as it flies disembodied through the air. (Malinowski 1961:236).[9]

I consider that *sangguma*, or assault sorcery, and projectile sorcery, in which stones, spears and the like are 'shot' into the victim's body, should be understood in similar terms. The assault or dismemberment of the victim's body is more likely to be a magical operation performed on the victim's soul, similar to those ritual dismemberments familiar in Aboriginal initiations of medicine men, or the magical insertion of quartz crystals into the neophyte's body (Elkin, 1977). After being stunned by his assailants, or collapsing from fright when encountering them, the *sangguma* victim regains consciousness and returns home, physically little harmed but already in a severe state of shock. Indeed the victim may not even encounter his mystical attacker, as we see in Lawrence's (this volume) account of Garia *ämale* shooting, or projectile sorcery. In this case again, the sorcerer is evidently aware of the non-physical nature of the assault, since he waits for 'the god to send *na'oa*, a whistling sound, up from his stomach and out of his mouth' which then propels the arrow head to the victim. Describing the sorcery beliefs of the Kaoka of Guadalcanal, Hogbin (1965:57) observes that the sincerity of individuals' belief in their own powers need not be doubted, and he suggests that they 'must seek out their victims *in controlled dreams*' (my emphasis). In evaluating reports of *sangguma* and similar practices it should be kept in mind that informants explaining the techniques may well not be aware, unless they themselves are adepts, of the non-physical nature of the exercise.[10]

My point is not that the adept mistakes dream for reality, but that dreams and similar states represent to him a different reality underlying mere surface appearances; in this respect his view, and his attempts to manipulate this other level of experience, are not dissimilar to many current psychoanalytic and psychotherapeutic practices (Lévi-Strauss 1972:181–4; Frank 1961; Peters and Price-Williams 1980:406). Magic is perhaps best regarded as a means of manipulating reality; altering one's perception of reality changes one's experience of it. The ability of the sorcerer to effect such changes in his own and others' perceptions should not be overlooked or underestimated.

It is in these deep experiential and psychological roots that we can see further reason for the tenacity of beliefs in sorcery and witchcraft.

Conclusion

Emphasis on accusation as indirect attack, the notion that witches and sorcerers are purely imaginary figures, and the difficulty of getting detailed information due to the secrecy integral to the role, have all combined to obscure the importance and the nature of the role of sorcerer in Melanesia. Melanesian sorcery represents a potential for power growing out of an attribution of cosmic responsibility—a potential which is used by different societies, and even different individuals in the same society, in different ways. Though the role is open to corruption, and the sorcerer who begins by being attributed with cosmic responsibility may end by being blamed for all the community's misfortunes, it still remains distinct from that of the witch. The sorcerer's role retains a potential for power; when circumstances improve, the epidemic has run its course, when the community again feels secure in its relationship with cosmic powers, the sorcerer may reassert his position, or new claimants to power may emerge. The witch, on the other hand, is associated only with blame, and is a projection of the unconscious guilt of the group activated in times of stress and insecurity. Individuals are more likely to be forced into the role of the witch than accept it by choice, but once condemned to it, some will use it for what it is worth and may get psychological gratification from it. Whereas the sorcerer is able always to hold to some last vestige of the father's magic, the witch is ever hard pressed to slough off the group projection of inferiority and guilt. But as the cultural traditions surrounding sorcery wither, the legitimate role of the sorcerer as a mediator of divine power fades into the opportunism of new claimants manipulating the role for personal gain.[11]

Interpretations of sorcery and witchcraft as the correlates of particular forms of social structure are inadequate to explain the variety of social practice we encounter in Melanesia. Sorcery and witchcraft are not a single, or even two, institutions, but numerous cultural variations on two themes, variations which are moulded by external pressures as well as internal structures, which vary over time, and which may serve many different social and cultural ends.

In restricting attention to the specific functions performed by sorcery and witchcraft in society, we have tended to reify flexible ideologies as 'institutions' which must serve a specific functional end, and then become confused because we find they serve different ends in different societies.

Crick (1976) is right to draw our attention to the meanings expressed in the image of the witch. As yet we hardly begin to have the data necessary to provide a study of Melanesian sorcery and witchcraft along the lines Crick suggests. My attempt here to draw out what is common to the roles relies largely on descriptions of social action and related beliefs, not on analyses of indigenous symbolic categories. On this basis it identifies two contrasting images of power, the origins of which can be traced through common epistemological assumptions to underlying psychic structures. Though my argument has progressed in a very different manner from Needham's (1978), the conclusion I reach supports the view that these images are cultural variations on universal themes. The images of witch and sorcerer reflect the propensity of the human psyche to project on to the external world its own unconscious contents. The infinitely varied beliefs and practices associated with them reflect the ways in which specific cultures translate and transform what is unconscious into the actuality of social behaviour.

NOTES

[1] This is not to suggest, of course, that the other contributors to the volume necessarily support the arguments presented here. I am, however, indebted to all the contributors, both for the stimulation of the arguments presented in their case studies and for the ideas that have grown out of conversations and correspondence with them all over the many months preparing this volume. In particular I would like to express my gratitude to Professor Peter Lawrence for his comments on the draft of this chapter, and for his constant support throughout the project. A special thanks is due to Dr Dawn Ryan; her meticulous reading and comments on the draft have greatly assisted me in clarifying and refining the arguments presented here. I am also deeply grateful to Dr Gilbert Herdt, University of Chicago, for his constructive criticisms and suggestions concerning this chapter.

[2] Though I agree with Lawrence (1973:201) and others that terms such as 'supernatural', 'mystical' and 'occult' do not accurately convey Melanesian concepts, I have found them necessary in this introduction to indicate unambiguously the distinctions which we, as outside observers, make between the empirical and 'non-empirical' realms.

[3] Though Douglas (1978:107) considers the possibility of sorcery as a legitimate use of mystical power, she specifically rejects it on the basis of African data. She is concerned with sorcery accusations as a covert form of attack on the accused sorcerer, not with sorcery as an instrument of personal power.

[4] This argument would apply to both the Dani and the Mae Enga, whereas Patterson's thesis leaves the Dani an inexplicable anomaly.

[5] The Abelam belief, described by Forge (1970:260-1), that sorcery 'paint' is prepared by a large party of men, in a dramatic performance involving a huge bonfire and an exploding container of activated 'paint' skyrocketing into the air, strikes me as deliberately intended to produce the conclusion that Forge draws from it—i.e. that no one in fact performs sorcery (in their village). Protected by this general assumption, the sorcerer may well go about his task in a quite different manner that attracts no attention or suspicion. Certainly the 'openness' of these supposed techniques contrasts suspiciously with the secrecy surrounding sorcery payments (ibid.:265).

[6] As we have seen, the extent of the sorcerer's responsibility and the weight of blame loaded on to the witch vary a great deal in different societies, and in changing circumstances over time, in the same society.

[7] Epidemics are not necessarily to be equated with a loss in the legitimacy of the sorcerer's powers. As we have seen, epidemics are interpreted as *confirmation of the efficacy* of these powers—a circumstance that might be turned to his advantage. Hau'ofa (1981:46), for example, argues that Mekeo sorcerers took advantage of epidemics following European contact to increase their power in society. See also Stephen (1977:3-4) for an instance in recent contact history when sorcerers were able to reassert their challenged powers by claiming responsibility for an influenza epidemic. In the case of diseases with the catastrophic demographic effects of *kuru*, however, the sorcerer was unlikely to avoid blame. Claiming responsibility for epidemic diseases was a risky ploy, suitable perhaps for the parvenu, but it is understandable that those whose position in society was well established, such as the Trobriand sorcerer, explicitly denied responsibility for such misfortunes.

[8] This is not to suggest, of course, that Jung was unaware or uninterested in the historical circumstances which activated the group 'shadow'.

⁹ This crucial distinction between actions performed in the body and actions performed by the 'soul' is one which is often overlooked. Patterson (1974-75:213), for example, complains that Malinowski does not make clear the difference between the *mulukuwausi* and the *yoyova*.

¹⁰ Also, in attempting to impress upon the sceptical European what they see to be the real dangers of sorcery, informants tend to stress those features which they have learnt from experience that he is likely to accept. Thus it is often maintained that sorcery depends on the use of poison, since the European *kiap* or magistrate is prepared to take seriously the possibility of death from poisoning.

¹¹ The conclusions drawn here are based solely on Melanesian data and are intended to apply only to Melanesia. It is worth noting, however, that if the image of the sorcerer emerges more clearly from this than from the African material, it is not surprising in view of the much more complicated historical patterns of contact, change, indigenous military conquests and state formation in Africa, where more complex political and religious structures developed from or were imposed on simpler forms.

REFERENCES

Barth, F.
> 1975   *Ritual and Knowledge among the Baktaman of New Guinea.* New Haven: Yale University Press.

Belshaw, C. S.
> 1957   *The Great Village; the Economic and Social Welfare of Hanuabada, an Urban Community in Papua.* London: Routledge and Kegan Paul.

Berndt, R. M.
> 1962   *Excess and Restraint: Social Control among a New Guinea Mountain People.* Chicago: University of Chicago Press.

> 1972   'Social Control'. In *The Encyclopaedia of Papua New Guinea.* Carlton: Melbourne University Press:1050-65.

Brown, P.
> 1977   '*Kumo* Witchcraft at Mintima, Chimbu Province, Papua New Guinea'. *Oceania* 48:26-9.

Bulmer, R. N. H.
> 1965   'The Kyaka of the Western Highlands'. In Lawrence and Meggitt (1965:132-61).

Burridge, K. O. L.
  1969   *Tangu Traditions: A Study of the Way of Life, Mythology and Developing Experience of a New Guinea People.* Oxford: Clarendon Press.

Crick, M.
  1976   *Explorations in Language and Meaning: Towards a Semantic Anthropology.* London: Malaby Press.

Douglas, M.
  1970   (ed.) *Witchcraft Confessions and Accusations.* London: Tavistock.

  1978   *Purity and Danger: An Analysis of the Concepts of Pollution and Taboo.* London: Routledge and Kegan Paul.

Elkin, A. P.
  1977   *Aboriginal Men of High Degree.* St Lucia: University of Queensland Press.

Evans-Pritchard, E. E.
  1937   *Witchcraft, Oracles and Magic among the Azande.* Oxford: Clarendon Press.

Forge, A.
  1970   'Prestige, Influence, and Sorcery: a New Guinea Example'. In Douglas (1970:257-75).

Fortune, R. F.
  1939   'Arapesh Warfare'. *American Anthropologist* 40:22-41.

  1963   *Sorcerers of Dobu: the Social Anthropology of the Dobu Islanders of the Western Pacific.* New York: Dutton.

Frank, J. D.
  1961   *Persuasion and Healing: A Comparative Study of Psychotherapy.* London: Oxford University Press.

Glasse, R. M.
  1965   'The Huli of the Southern Highlands'. In Lawrence and Meggitt (1965:27-49).

Glick, L. B.
  1973   'Sorcery and Witchcraft'. In Hogbin (1973:182-6).

Hau'ofa, E.
  1981   *Mekeo: Inequality and Ambivalence in a Village Society.* Canberra: Australian National University Press.

Hayano, D. M.
  1973   'Sorcery Death, Proximity, and the Perception of Out-Groups: the Tauna Awa of New Guinea'. *Ethnology* 12: 179-91.

Heider, K. G.
  1979   *Grand Valley Dani: Peaceful Warriors.* New York: Holt, Rinehart and Winston.

Hogbin, H. I.
  1951   *Transformation Scene: the Changing Culture of a New Guinea Village.* London: Routledge and Kegan Paul.

1965 *A Guadalcanal Society: The Kaoka Speakers*. New York: Holt, Rinehart and Winston.

1973 (ed.) *Anthropology in Papua New Guinea: Readings from the Encyclopaedia of Papua New Guinea*. Carlton: Melbourne University Press.

Jung, C. G.
1968 *The Archetypes and the Collective Unconscious*. Vol. 9, Pt 1, *Collected Works of C. G. Jung*. Princeton: Princeton University Press.

1968a *Aion: Researches into the Phenomenology of the Self*. Vol. 9, Pt 2, *Collected Works of C. G. Jung*. Princeton: Princeton University Press.

1978 *Man and His Symbols*. London: Picador.

Kelly, R.
1976 'Witchcraft and Sexual Relations: An Exploration in the Social and Semantic Implications of the Structure of Belief'. In P. Brown and G. Buchbinder (eds): *Man and Woman in the New Guinea Highlands*. Washington: American Anthropological Association: Special Publication No. 8.

1977 *Etoro Social Structure: A Study in Structural Contradiction*. Ann Arbor: University of Michigan Press.

Lane, R. B.
1965 'The Melanesians of South Pentecost, New Hebrides'. In Lawrence and Meggitt (1965:250-79).

Lawrence, P.
1973 'Religion and Magic'. In Hogbin (1973:201–26).

Lawrence, P. and Meggitt, M. J.
1965 (eds) *Gods, Ghosts and Men in Melanesia: Some Religions of Australian New Guinea and the New Hebrides*. Melbourne: Oxford University Press.

1965a 'Introduction'. In Lawrence and Meggitt (1965:1-26).

Lederman, R.
1981 'Sorcery and Social Change in Mendi'. *Social Analysis* 8:15-27.

LeVine, R. A.
1973 *Culture, Behaviour and Personality*. Chicago: Aldine Publishing Company.

Lévi-Strauss, C.
1972 'The Sorcerer and His Magic'. In C. Lévi-Strauss: *Structural Anthropology*. Harmondsworth: Penguin: 167-85.

Lindenbaum, S.
1979 *Kuru Sorcery: Disease and Danger in the New Guinea Highlands*. California: Mayfield Publishing Company.

1981 'Images of the Sorcerer in Papua New Guinea'. *Social Analysis* 8:119-28.

Malinowski, B.
1926   *Crime and Custom in Savage Society.* London: Routledge and Kegan Paul.
1961   *Argonauts of the Western Pacific: An Account of Native Enterprise and Adventure in the Archipelagoes of Melanesian New Guinea.* New York: Dutton.
1974   'Myth in Primitive Psychology'. In B. Malinowski: *Magic Science and Religion: and Other Essays.* London: Souvenir Press: 93-148.

Marwick, M.
1964   'Witchcraft as a Social Strain-Gauge'. *Australian Journal of Science* 26:263-8.

Meggitt, M. J.
1965   'The Mae Enga of the Western Highlands'. In Lawrence and Meggitt (1965:105-31).

Mitchell, W. E.
1977   'Sorcellerie Chamanique: "Sanguma" chez les Lujere du Cours Supérieur de Sépik'. *Journal de la Société des Océanistes* 33:179-89.

Monsell-Davis, M. D.
1981   Nabuapaka: Social change in a Roro Community. Ph.D. thesis, Macquarie University, Sydney.

Nachman, S.
1981   '*Buai*: Expressions of Sorcery in the Dance'. *Social Analysis* 8:42-57.

Needham, R.
1978   *Primordial Characters.* Charlottesville: University of Virginia Press.

Newman, P. L.
1965   *Knowing the Gururumba.* New York: Holt, Rinehart and Winston.

Oliver, D. L.
1967   *A Solomon Island Society: Kinship and Leadership Among the Siuai of Bougainville.* Boston: Beacon Press.

Oram, N.
1982   Personal communication.

Patterson, M.
1974-75 'Sorcery and Witchcraft in Melanesia'. *Oceania* 45:132-60, 212-34.

Peters, L. G. and Price-Williams, D.
1980   'Towards an Experiential Analysis of Shamanism'. *American Ethnologist* 7:397-418.
1983   'A Phenomenological Overview of Trance'. *Transcultural Psychiatric Research Review* 20:5-39.

Ploeg, A.
1979   'The Establishment of the Pax Neerlandica in the Bokondini Area'. In M. Rodman and M. Cooper (eds):

The Pacification of Melanesia. Ann Arbor: University of Michigan Press: 161-77.

Poole, F. J. P.
1981   '*Tamam*: Ideological and Sociological Configurations of "Witchcraft" among Bimin-Kuskusmin'. *Social Analysis* 8:58-76.

Price-Williams, D. R.
1975   *Explorations in Cross-Cultural Psychology*. Los Angeles: University of California.

Reay, M.
1968   Review of M. Marwick, *Sorcery in its Social Setting*. *Journal of the Polynesian Society* 77:198-201.

Róheim, G.
1948   'Witches of Normanby Island'. *Oceania* 18:279-308.

Schieffelin, E. L.
1977   *The Sorrow of the Lonely and the Burning of the Dancers*. St Lucia: University of Queensland Press.

Seligman, C. G.
1910   *The Melanesians of British New Guinea*. Cambridge: Cambridge University Press.

Spiro, M. E.
1982   *Oedipus in the Trobriands*. Chicago: University of Chicago Press.

Steadman, L.
1975   'Cannibal Witches in the Hewa'. *Oceania* 46:114-21.

Stephen, M.
1974   Continuity and Change in Mekeo Society, 1890-1971. Ph.D. thesis, Australian National University.

1977   'Cargo Cult Hysteria: Symptom of Despair or Technique of Ecstasy?' *Occasional Paper No. 1, Research Centre for Southwest Pacific Studies*, La Trobe University: 1-16.

1979   'Dreams of Change: The Innovative Role of Altered States of Consciousness in Traditional Melanesian Religion'. *Oceania* 50:3-22.

Tonkinson, R.
1981   'Sorcery and Social Change in Southeast Ambrym, Vanuatu'. *Social Analysis* 8:77-88.

Tuzin, D.
1980   *The Voice of the Tambaran: Truth and Illusion in Ilahita Religion*. Berkeley: University of California Press.

Young, M. W.
1971   *Fighting With Food: Leadership, Values and Social Control in a Massim Society*. Cambridge: Cambridge University Press.

Weiner, J.
1982   'Blood and Skin: The Structural Implications of

Sorcery and Procreation Beliefs among the Foi'. Paper presented at the conference 'Sorcery, Healing and Magic in Melanesia', La Trobe University, 1982. To be published in *Ethnos*.

Williams, F. E.
1928   *Orokaiva Magic*. Oxford: Clarendon Press.
1936   *Papuans of the Trans-Fly*. Oxford: Clarendon Press.
1940   *Drama of Orokolo: The Social and Ceremonial Life of the Elema*. Oxford: Clarendon Press.

Zelenietz, M.
1981   'Sorcery and Social Change: An Introduction'. *Social Analysis* 8:3-14.

CONTRIBUTORS

Dr Ross Bowden, Senior Lecturer, Sociology, La Trobe University

Professor Ann Chowning, Professor of Anthropology, Victoria University, Wellington, N.Z.

Professor Peter Lawrence, Professor of Anthropology, University of Sydney

Dr Marie Reay, Senior Research Fellow, Anthropology, Research School of Pacific Studies, ANU

Ms Inge Riebe, Anthropologist

Dr Paul Sillitoe, Lecturer, Anthropology, University of Durham

Dr Michele Stephen, Senior Lecturer, History, La Trobe University

Index